W9-ABR-580

The Idea of Loyalty in Upper Canada, 1784–1850

The Idea of Loyalty in Upper Canada, 1784-1850

DAVID MILLS

McGill-Queen's University Press
Kingston and Montreal

©McGill-Queen's University Press 1988
ISBN 0-7735-0660-8

Legal deposit second quarter 1988
Bibliothèque nationale du Québec

Printed in Canada on acid-free paper

This book has been published with the help of a grant
from the Social Science Federation of Canada, using
funds provided by the Social Sciences and Humanities
Research Council of Canada.

Canadian Cataloguing in Publication Data

Mills, David, 1952-
    The idea of loyalty in Upper Canada, 1784-1850
    Includes index.
    Bibliography: p.
    ISBN 0-7735-0660-8
    1. Ontario – Politics and government – 1791-1841
    2. Ontario – Politics and government – 1841-1867
    3. Allegiance – Ontario – History.   I. Title.
    FC454.M44 1988   971.3'02   C88-090148-9
    F1058.M44 1988

For Jeffrey

Contents

Acknowledgments

The research, writing, and publication of this work have led to the accumulation of numerous debts. Much of the original research was funded by the Social Sciences and Humanities Research Council and the Government of Ontario in the form of doctoral fellowships; the University of Alberta supported much of the final preparation of the manuscript. This book has been published with the help of a grant from the Social Science Federation of Canada, using funds provided by the Social Sciences and Humanities Research Council of Canada.

The assistance of the many archivists (notably Paulette Dozois) and librarians at the National Archives of Canada, the National Library, the Provincial Archives of Ontario, the Toronto Public Library, the United Church Archives, and the University of Toronto Archives was essential to the completion of this book.

Several people offered assistance and support in the process of reworking the manuscript. These include John Foster, David Hall, Rod Macleod, Paul Voisey, and especially Doug Owram at the University of Alberta. I am indebted to the readers for the Social Science Federation of Canada for their valuable suggestions for change and to Donald Akenson, of McGill-Queen's University Press, for prodding me to clarify several points. I would also like to thank Jane Errington for permission to use the proofs of her book, *The Lion, the Eagle and Upper Canada*.

My thanks go as well to Pat McDonald, Sharon Mackenzie, Lydia Dugbazah, Patricia Bokenfohr, and Eli Brooks, who helped prepare the manuscript, and to Jean Wilson who copy-edited it.

Finally, special debts are owed to the late W.G. Ormsby and S.F. Wise, who sparked my interest in the history of Upper Canada, and to S.R. Mealing, who supervised the doctoral dissertation upon which this work is based.

To my wife Janice I am especially grateful. Her confidence and support were more important to me than she may know.

John Strachan, Anglican archdeacon of York and member of the executive council. *Courtesy National Archives / Archives Nationales*

Robert Gourlay, Scottish radical banished from Upper Canada in 1819. *Courtesy Metropolitan Toronto Library Board*

John Beverley Robinson, High Tory spokesman as Attorney General and later Chief Justice of Upper Canada. *Courtesy Ontario Archives*

John Rolph, a spokesman for the Reform movement in the 1820s and 1830s.
Courtesy National Archives / Archives Nationales

Egerton Ryerson, leading spokesman for the Episcopal Methodists and editor of the *Christian Guardian. Courtesy National Archives / Archives Nationales*

Robert Baldwin, leader of the Moderate Reformers and advocate of responsible government. *Courtesy National Archives / Archives Nationales*

Francis Hincks, political strategist for the Moderate Reformers. *Courtesy National Archives / Archives Nationales*

W.H. Draper, spokesman for the Moderate Tories in the late 1830s and 1840s.
Courtesy National Archives / Archives Nationales

The Idea of Loyalty in Upper Canada, 1784–1850

The Idea of Loyalty in Upper Canada

In an article written almost fifty years ago, the Canadian historian George W. Brown wrote: "The history of the concept of loyalty would form one of the most important contributions to the story of the development of Canadian attitudes ... and when that history comes to be written one important chapter at least will be given to Upper Canada ..."[1] While Brown may not have been able to predict the propensity of modern historians to transform chapters into monographs, he did recognize that the study of the idea of loyalty was basic to an understanding of the political culture[2] of Old Ontario. But since that time there has been little comprehensive analysis of the concept of loyalty in Upper Canada.

David Bell, a political scientist, has suggested that the idea of loyalty embraced two themes: one was patriotism, which was attachment to place, and the other was loyalism, or attachment to the parent.[3] In the United States, the first theme was central to an understanding of the idea of loyalty. An American historian, Merle Curti, believed that loyalty was a fundamental component of American nationalism which evolved through attachment to, and pride in, a distinct geographical place and ultimately produced a sense of mission. Curti wrote: "the growth of loyalty was slow and unconscious. In the colonial period one can discern the same broad patterns in the growth of loyalty that appear in the later stages of [American] history ..." He argued that the imperial connection was weakened both because of the American colonies' remoteness from the mother country and of the impact of the North American environment upon the development of a new society; loyalty was gradually transferred from Great Britain to North America. The foundations of American loyalty were thus predicated upon "not only pride in the vastness, the distinctive landscape, and the resources of America but also the conviction that nature had intended a separate and united nation to rise off the shores of the Atlantic." Loyalty to place was reinforced by the emphasis placed upon the traditions which shaped American society. The consciousness of the past stimulated a belief that the development of the United States was divinely ordained; Americans looked to "the glorious deeds of the fathers, the inspiration of their record, the obligation to remain steadfast to their ideals, admiration of the achievements for which they suffered and sacrificed themselves, [and by] ... the conviction that the hand of God had guided American patriotism from the very start." This sense of mission was to be inculcated through a reverence for national symbols; it required continuous nurture through a national system of education; and it was tested in the crucible of war. Loyalty was fundamental to American nationalism; Curti equated it with patriotism and concluded that loyalty was "love of country, pride in it, and readiness to make sacrifices for what is considered its best interest."[4]

Upper Canadian attitudes about loyalty differed fundamentally from those of the Americans because, of course, there was no rejection of Great Britain, the parent. Yet when loyalty was first examined by historians focusing on constitutional forms, loyalty was discussed as one aspect of the conflict between the executive and its opponents which resulted in the triumph of responsible government. Chester Martin, for example, stressed the importance of both the loyalist tradition and the imperial connection in shaping Tory attitudes towards Reformers: "For many years the officials of the province, most of whom had no personal connection with the loyalist migration, appropriated the loyalist tradition and labelled every movement of reform which assailed their privileges as 'treason and republicanism!' In the motto of the province 'fidelis' was interpreted as fidelity to the old colonial system ... The fact that loyalism coalesced in the end almost everywhere with the prevailing temper of the British provinces was proof not only of its own vitality but of a congenial environment."[5]

The Whig interpretation of Canadian history, with its focus upon the victory of Reform views, provoked a response in the 1960s that emphasized the conservatism of Upper Canadian political development. S.F. Wise, the most perceptive analyst of the Tory mind, suggested that loyalty was "the crux of conservative attitudes" in the province. "Loyalty did not simply mean adherence to the Crown and Empire, although it started there. It meant as well adherence to those beliefs and institutions ... considered essential in the preservation of a form of life different from, and superior to, the manners, politics and social arrangements of the United States." The Tories envisioned the development of a provincial society, strengthened by the imperial connection, which was distinct from, and hostile to, the American republic. Wise likened them to "men living on the slopes of a volcano" who "tried to anticipate every rumble from their revolutionary neighbor through the use of state, church, and school to control immigration, check loyalty, ferret out treason, and inculcate the right values." Those groups who appeared "soft" on the American question, such as the Reformers, were labelled disloyal; therefore, the concept of loyalty was debated on Tory terms. Upper Canadian Toryism produced an "accommodative" political culture which provided, perhaps, the only means to unify the scattered and diverse population; as Wise has concluded: "It made no assimilative demands beyond its insistence upon adherence to vital survival values – loyalty, order, stability – values that coincided with the interests and outlooks of many of the groups and collectivities that made up colonial society."[6] A straightforward emphasis on Tory attitudes does not fully explain the nature of Upper Canada's political culture. This is a study of the evolution of the concept of loyalty, the central political idea in Upper Canada during the first half of the nineteenth century. Across nearly the whole of the political spectrum loyalty was the basis not only of political legitimacy but also of acceptance into the provincial society. It also represented a complex of ideas; Tories and Reformers attached different intellectual and moral qualities to loyalty and these qualities themselves evolved over time. The result of that evolution produced, by the 1850s, an ideological consensus in which loyalty remained as important as ever but in which its definition was at last the common property of moderates of both groups.

In the period before 1830 the Tory oligarchy framed the political debate. Its members drew upon the Loyalist tradition to argue that loyalty required unquestioning adherence to the imperial connection to ensure the continued existence of the province faced with the ever-present danger of the United States. This threat was political because as a republic America was seen as radical and subversive; it also represented a social and cultural threat because the United States was expansionist and aggressive. The external threat was compounded by the massive migration into the province of American settlers whose perceived republicanism challenged the idea that Upper Canada was a special Loyalist bastion – the homeland of persons whose loyalty had been tested and found to be pure during the American Revolution and the War of 1812. Tory consciousness of the past strengthened the exclusiveness attached to loyalty.

The Loyalist tradition was reinforced by the importation of English Tory values and predisposed many Upper Canadians to seek to imitate idealized versions of the forms and institutions of the mother country. English Toryism, for instance, required adherence to a stable, hierarchical society and a balanced constitution, both dominated by a Tory elite. The development of any opposition to the administration posed a threat to social harmony and political tranquility; consequently dissent was not tolerated and was believed to be disloyal. Thus the Tories used loyalty as both the means to distinguish those of Loyalist origin from the American late-comers and as the means to differentiate those who supported the political status quo from those who did not.

In response, an opposition conception of loyalty began to develop. Although critics of the government were as committed to the imperial connection and a belief in the necessity of a stable, hierarchical society as any Tory, they introduced new ingredients to the idea of loyalty. The oppositionists accepted the British constitutional model and looked to the Crown as the symbol of English rights and liberties; but they permitted individual dissent based on the concept of constitutional rights and the necessary independence of legislators. Drawing upon late seventeenth-century Whig views of politics, they stressed the dangers to the Constitution posed by the arbitrary use of prerogative power and the corruption of the executive. They stood for the maintenance of the old loyalty to British constitutional models, as they understood them, against the misguided policies of colonial ministers – actions which would upset the delicate balance of authority versus liberty and truly threaten the colonial relationship.

Before the War of 1812, the critics of the government remained a collection of individuals rather than a formed opposition. By the 1820s, a new group of oppositionists labelling themselves Reformers began to appear. The Reformers did not challenge the importance of loyalty but they did wish to broaden its definition in ways that would legitimize their own political goals. They shared the Tory belief that loyalty could be earned, as the Loyalists had done, or that it could be inculcated through such institutions as the church or the school; yet unlike the Tories they also believed that it could be acquired by assimilation. Loyalty would develop naturally through proper social values and good citizenship shaped by settlement in the community; the farmer who contributed to the building of society would become a loyal subject. The Reformers placed less emphasis upon the spiritual or emotional component of loyalty than the Tories and more upon material well-being. Reform loyalty was not exclusive; rather it became a broad, accommodating concept.

The focus of the debate over loyalty began to change in the 1830s. Upper Canadians became less concerned with the values relating to the nature of loyalty and concentrated more closely upon the future development of the province: whether it would remain as a British colony or drift into the American orbit. Politics seemed to offer only two choices – loyalty or disloyalty. Explanation of attitudes was no longer necessary because rhetoric had replaced analysis; labels and symbols became the staples of debate. Although there were bitter conflicts between the supporters of the provincial administration and its opponents which polarized Upper Canadian politics, the period was transitional. It was characterized by two significant developments. The first was the emergence of moderate Toryism as a response to the exclusive policies of the provincial oligarchy, known as the Family Compact, and the political success of its opponents. The second was that the moderate Reformers, who were briefly squeezed out of the political process by the radicals, re-emerged after the rebellion with a clearer emphasis on reform within the imperial context through the introduction of responsible government.

While the High Tories continued to frame the official definition of loyalty during the 1830s, the moderates contributed new ingredients which reflected an increasing acceptance of some moderate Reform assumptions. Loyalty became less exclusive and more accommodative, accepting that settlement in Upper Canada could produce a loyal feeling for the land. This, in turn, stimulated the growth of provincial sentiment; there was less willingness to accept uncritically imperial interference in local affairs. More and more, loyalty was expressed in nationalist rather than Loyalist terms.[7]

Moderate Toryism developed because other groups who were not prepared to acquiesce in their political and social exclusion had been drawn into the debate over loyalty and made their own contributions to it. The Methodists, for example, were attacked by High Tory spokesmen, such as John Strachan, the Anglican archdeacon of York, as ignorant religious enthusiasts; they were dissenters whose loyalty was suspect because of their connections with American conferences and their association with the Reformers. Egerton Ryerson, the most forceful defender of the sect, embraced the traditions of his own Loyalist background and the conservatism of English Wesleyan Methodism and therefore feared the growth of radicalism in Upper Canada. But Ryerson's conservatism was tempered by his opposition to church establishment and Anglican exclusiveness; he brought to Toryism the concepts of the legitimacy of individual if not of organized dissent and the assimilative nature of the provincial society. The Methodist definition of loyalty contributed to the development of a conservative consensus in Upper Canada.

Spokesmen for the Orange Order, which became the institutional means of organizing the Irish Protestant immigrants into a potent political bloc, also exploited the loyalty issue in their attempts to attain social legitimacy. As a group outside the social and political mainstream in 1830, the Orange Irish adopted Tory definitions to emphasize distinctions between settlers of North American origin and loyal British subjects; they reinforced the political polarization taking place. They also believed that only through the imperial connection could Upper Canada remain British, and as a result they were drawn into the Tory coalition developing by the mid-1830s.

The emergence of a broad conservative consensus of loyal groups was a major factor producing the Tory victory in the "loyalty election" of 1836. But the polarization of politics also contributed to the second major development of the period. The moderate Reformers, such as Robert Baldwin and Francis Hincks, were gradually pushed out of the political process in favour of radicals, like William Lyon Mackenzie, who favoured the establishment of a social democracy modelled on the United States and sought fundamental changes in both the Constitution and the imperial relationship. By 1837, the radicals provided the focus for a small disloyal grouping supported, as the Tories had always argued, by some American settlers from north of Toronto and around London. The failure of the rebellion eliminated the radicals from the political spectrum and led to the re-emergence of the moderates. But the moderate Reformers had been influenced by the Tories during the political debates of the period; they were loyal and therefore they placed limits upon the extent of their dissent. With their goal of responsible government they sought reform within the imperial context. The moderates rejected the republicanism and independence offered by the rebellion. Their reforms, shaped by British Whig traditions, permitted the legitimacy of political dissent, the idea of a formed opposition, and, finally, political parties. The acceptance of party government provided the means in practical politics and a justification in political theory for the expansion of local autonomy.

The failure of the rebellion did not signify the end of the debate over loyalty. During the 1840s the emphasis on loyalty was as central as ever; but the definition of it had significantly changed. The moderate Reformers not only survived but soon entered the administration of Sir Charles Bagot. The moderate Tories also prospered, at the expense of the old Compact, by the adoption of what had been a moderate Reform position. The substance of the change consisted of three steps: the acceptance of formed opposition as legitimate in politics, the further acceptance of parties as necessary without being necessarily evil, and the consequent acceptance of party goals. These were tremendous changes for the Tories because they provided the practical means and a conservative justification for the expansion of self-government and for the pursuit of what became nationalist goals. In addition, the exclusiveness of the High Tory definition had been supplanted by an accommodative concept of loyalty which enabled the growing urban commercial and professional class, represented by men such as John A. Macdonald, to enter the provincial elite. The result was the formation by the 1850s of a broad conservative consensus which dominated Old Ontario. The basis for this conservatism lay in a changed definition of loyalty which had evolved, not as a result of the strength of Upper Canadian Toryism, but rather through the initiative of the moderate Reformers.

The idea of loyalty was central to Upper Canadian politics and was revealed by a variety of political actions. In the period before 1850 the provincial society was characterized by growth and change; these produced rivalries which occasioned public and private pressures to make choices and defend particular points of view. The intellectual and moral qualities attached to the idea of loyalty which developed from these rivalries helped to shape the political culture of Upper Canada. This work continues what S.F. Wise has noted as the task of the intellectual historian, "to analyse the manner in which externally-derived ideas have been adapted to a variety of local and regional environments, in such a way that a body of assumptions uniquely Canadian has been built up ..."[8] It also reflects John Higham's definition of the external approach to the history of ideas: it stresses the significance of popular beliefs and the reactions to perceived developments in terms of concrete political actions.[9] Loyalty was not part of a logical system of belief; the attitudes being examined did not represent a "coherent body of abstract thought" which was the result of general theorizing upon the state of society by political philosophers. Neither were they "rationalizations of socio-economic interests." Loyalty was simply part of the political culture; like many attitudes, it reflected "the intellectual commonplaces of an age, its root notions, assumptions and images ..."[10] It was based, for example, upon the constitutional rights of British subjects and the idea of a balanced constitution. Upper Canadians appealed to Burke and not to Paine, to British and not to American models, to moderate and not to radical objectives. In addition, attitudes about loyalty often remained latent; they were ascertained through their relationship to the dominant values within the society. When the anonymous "Cato" addressed the electorate in York during the election of 1800, neither he, nor most Upper Canadians, believed it necessary to provide further elaboration upon the statement: "I pause to admire, and gratefully contemplate that noblest fabric of human wisdom, the *British Constitution*."[11] His statement represented a whole set of conservative attitudes.

Accordingly, while an examination of attitudes poses certain difficulties, the behaviours and statements of literate Upper Canadians are sufficiently direct evidence to illustrate contemporary public values. This is especially true of loyalty because of the belief so widely held in Upper Canada that loyalty was central to politics and was revealed by a variety of political actions. Also, Herbert Bloch, a sociologist, has claimed that: "We are not always conscious of our loyalties: to an extent, we are content to take them at their face values. But a loyalty must always be crystallized and defined to some point of view by our attitudes. It can never in itself be inchoate and aimless. It is the necessary locus in our social definition as individuals ..."

In order to study the idea of loyalty, a variety of primary sources, both published and unpublished, was utilized; these include personal correspondence, government documents, petitions, and pamphlets. Newspapers provide the major primary source for the work because the debate over loyalty was, by and large, a public debate; as Bloch has suggested, the articulation of attitudes about loyalty "arises ... when the need for prerogative and choice presents itself."[12] Newspapers provided the public forum through which attitudes and ideas could be presented – through editorials, letters, or electoral addresses. Newspapers also published the debates in the Legislative Assembly and therefore were the means by which many Upper Canadians were made aware of differing opinions.

The result does not, and cannot, provide the complete picture of Upper Canadian values and attitudes. Beliefs about loyalty contributed to the development of a political ideology, but they only reveal the responses of the articulate elite of Upper Canada. And, as this book shows, even the views of these leaders differed sharply over the first half of the nineteenth century because they were speaking for a variety of groups in the community. Moreover, while it is assumed that the views outlined were held by many Upper Canadians, the attitudes of the majority of settlers remain largely unknown. The complete study of the political culture of Old Ontario remains to be written.

CHAPTER TWO

The Ideological
Foundations of Loyalty

In the period before 1820 the concept of loyalty reflected the two streams of thought which shaped the conservative tradition in Upper Canada. "One was that brought by the Loyalist founders of the colony: an emotional compound of loyalty to King and Empire, antagonism to the United States, and an acute, if partisan sense of recent history. To the conservatism of the émigré was joined another, more sophisticated viewpoint, first brought by Simcoe and his entourage, and crystallized in the Constitutional Act of 1791: the Toryism of late eighteenth-century England."[1] Both sets of attitudes were clearly defined in the colony by the War of 1812. The local oligarchy envisioned the development within an imperial structure of a provincial society loyal to the Crown and deeply committed to fundamental British values and institutions.

Among the Upper Canadian Tory elite there was unquestioning acceptance of these broad loyalties and any challenge to their traditional values met an immediate, almost reflexive, response. The perceived vulnerability of the province in the face of the external threat posed by the United States and the internal menace of republicanism embodied by the massive influx of American settlers was one legacy of the Loyalist experience. English Toryism, expressed by colonial officials and pre-war British immigrants like John Strachan, reinforced the belief that any opposition to the administration was to be crushed because it created political turbulence and thus disrupted social harmony. The conservative mentality, which became more inflexible as a result of the War of 1812, equated political dissent with disloyalty and so reacted sharply to the activities of a Scottish radical, Robert Gourlay, who was ultimately expelled from Upper Canada. The pervasiveness of these values imposed a large measure of ideological conformity upon the provincial mind before

1820. The contribution of Loyalist spokemen to the development of loyalty in Upper Canada was quite significant and the motivations of this group provide the basis for an understanding of the ideological perceptions which they brought to the province. It is difficult to analyze these attitudes though, because the Loyalists did not leave a substantial body of literature which reflected their views about the nature of the society in which they lived.[2] Most were farmers concerned with carving homesteads out of the Upper Canadian forests rather than leaving records. Moreover, few Loyalist leaders articulated their fundamental beliefs because they were not concerned with analyzing the reasons for their loyalty; instead they sought to capitalize on that loyalty by linking it with such tangible rewards as land grants, government offices, and political and social influence.[3]

The Loyalists have been the subject of a wide-ranging body of literature in both the United States and Canada. The primary concern of historians focusing upon the American Tories is to explain why this group remained loyal during the Revolution; in a recent study of their ideology Janice Potter has argued that Loyalists from New York and Massachusetts shared "the vision of an Anglo-American empire: Britain and America ... were united by history, trade and a common attachment to the empire and to British institutions."[4] There has also been general acceptance that Loyalism was a conservative movement and that the nature of that conservatism was shaped by the desire to balance liberty with authority. An American Tory, Jonathan Sewell, a Massachusetts lawyer and later Attorney-General, supported the rational liberty embodied in the British Constitution because it was "best adapted to procure to individuals the blessings and advantages of society, and at the same time, to secure them that Liberty, the loss of which only, can overbalance these advantages." Yet the Constitution was threatened by the activities of demagogues seeking an unrestrained liberty, "consisting in freedom of speech, freedom of the press, uncontrol'd by the ... tyes [sic] of duty and decency, a liberty to rail at Kings and those in authority, and boldly bid defiance to good government, good breeding, and common sense ..." The fears that such liberty would lead to the dissolution of society were confirmed by the American Revolution.[5]

In his study of the ideological origins of the American Revolution, Bernard Bailyn has argued that Americans "found in the defiance of traditional order the firmest of all grounds for their hope for a freer life ... [F]aith ran high that a better world than any that had ever been known could be built where authority was distrusted and held in constant scrutiny." The lesson of the American Revolution was that checks must be put on the growth of tyranny. To the Loyalists the lesson was different; they believed that checks must be put on the growth of anarchy. The Loyalists feared the absence of authority and the threat posed by the unchecked passions of man more than imperial attempts to restrict colonial liberty.[6] Therefore they looked to Britain for support and refused to break with their past. This refusal could be regarded as a matter of high principle; Anthony Stokes, a Loyalist who migrated to England, stated: "My Conduct, in America, was not influenced by Events, but by Duty to his Majesty – an attachment to my native Country – and a Sense of mine own Honor; nothing therefore can annihilate my Attachment to my King & Country."[7] Because they would neither accept the legitimacy of the American Revolution nor break the imperial connection, the Loyalists were forced outside the mainstream of American politics and finally into exile.

It has been suggested that the Loyalists also remained outside the mainstream of American colonial society. William H. Nelson analyzed the areas of Loyalist strength and has argued that cultural influences, particularly ethnic and religious differences, were significant factors shaping the Loyalist outlook. Groups that had not been assimilated – groups which, in fact, feared the assimilative threat posed by American society – required protection to maintain their cultural identity. This was especially true of the "patchwork societies" of New York and Pennsylvania; for example, the Dutch and German communities which had not been anglicized and the Scottish Catholics in the New York back-country remained loyal. In addition, "adherents of religious groups that were in the local minority were everywhere inclined to Loyalism, while adherents of the dominant local denomination were most often Patriots." Thus Nelson concluded that the Tories were a socially heterogeneous group who represented a cross-section of American society. They were linked by one common bond: "Almost all the Loyalists were, in one way or another, more afraid of America than they were of Britain. Almost all of them had interests they felt needed protection from an American majority."[8]

When the culturally diverse communities of Loyalists scattered across what was to become Upper Canada they retained the intellectual baggage accumulated in revolutionary America;[9] consequently, several fundamental assumptions shaped their beliefs about the nature of loyalty. Many Loyalist leaders remained hostile towards their old homeland because, as S.F. Wise has noted, it "was essential for [Upper] Canadians not to believe in the United States and to assume that the country they lived in was not a kind of sub-arctic, second-best America, but rather a genuine alternative to this revolution-born democracy and organized upon principles and for purposes quite different from it."[10] They also believed that the American Revolution had been unnecessary and unjust; it was the result of the efforts of a minority of disaffected demagogues seeking their own selfish ends. There had been no grievances serious enough in the Thirteen Colonies to justify rebellion, and, thus, the sense of loss among the Loyalists was intense. Richard Cartwright, one of the wealthiest merchants in the pioneer society and a prominent political figure as well, had left America in 1777 because he could not reconcile his loyalty with demands for independence; he was "Displeased with the selfish views of the disaffected, feeling no oppression from Parliament, nor greater restrictions than appeared necessary for the unity of all parts of the empire, and convinced that if any grievance existed rebellion was not the remedy." Cartwright also believed that the Revolution was socially disruptive; he wrote of the "disturbed Condition of my native Country, where all Government was subverted, where Caprice was the only Rule and measure of usurped Authority ..." He became a Loyalist because he wanted to be "secure from these petty Tyrants who had involved my once happy country in every Species of Distress and made all the Misery that Cruelty joined with Power can cause."[11] The new homeland in Upper Canada was to provide a marked contrast to the United States because of its loyal beginnings and its development as a model British society in North America.

The strong attachment to the Crown remained. Loyalty was a duty for men like Cartwright; he had been "Brought up in habitual reverence to the King and Parliament by his loyal parents ...," and had always been "a supporter of the liberty and independence of the subject, and a steady asserter of all these privileges which every Briton enjoys by our happy constitution ... [He] knew how easily they were reconciled to the finest loyalty and patriotism."[12] Their justifications of their actions emphasized that they were not motivated by "Pay and Plunder," but rather "they contended for the constitutional Rights of the Crown, which they had been taught to revere ..." Cartwright "fondly cherished" the opinion that "the donation of lands to them in this county was intended as a mark of peculiar favour and a reward for their attachment to their Sovereign."[13]

The Loyalists benefitted from the imperial connection. Certainly the introduction of the British constitutional system and its political traditions would allow a loyal society to flourish. In addition, there were tangible economic rewards for loyalty; farmers received free land grants and merchants, like Cartwright and his partner, Robert Hamilton, prospered as a consequence of their ability to supply the British military during the American Revolution.[14] The Loyalists also envisioned the emergence of an integrated economic empire in which the mother country would supply the support necessary for Upper Canada to exploit her natural resources and provide the commercial channels and markets to stimulate provincial development. Upper Canadian potential could only be realized through the economic, political, and cultural stability imposed by the imperial structure. A letter to the Kingston *Gazette* from "Falkland" articulated this vision most fully just before the outbreak of war in 1812. He suggested that loyalty did not develop simply "from the dignified sentiments excited by these honorable and splendid displays of the National character; nor from the general feelings which naturally attach the subjects of every Government to their country ... The very soil on which we reside is the gift of her [England's] bounty ... and she has moreover liberally assisted us in our exertions to cultivate and improve it ... We enjoy the most perfect security for our persons and property under her own admirable system of Law, administered by a most respectable judicial establishment ... She has given us a Constitution as near to that envied one to which she owes her greatness as is consistent with the situation of a Colonial establishment, and we are called upon for no taxes to defray the expence [sic] of the Government by which it is kept in operation. And in matters of religion we are left free from restrictions ..."[15] The Loyalist leaders expected that they would comprise the governing elite of this model society.

Proven loyalty during the Revolution was not the only claim they made in support of that expectation. Cartwright, for example, described the Loyalists as "the most valuable Class of his Majesty's Subjects in this Province" because of both their proven commitment to pure loyalty and their former social status. "The truth is," he wrote, "that the generality of those gallant men, so little known, and so much undervalued by their pretended advocates, were men of Property; and some of them the greatest handholders in America."[16] Moreover, they came to believe that they personified the conception of loyalty in Upper Canada; an editorial in the York *Observer* contributed to Loyalist myth-making after the War of 1812: "Rather than submit to a successful rebellion, they foresook the land of their forefathers, – their homes, – their families, – in many instances, their friends, and all they hitherto held dear upon earth; and plunged unhesitatingly into the depths of difficulties of a boundless forest, there to teach their children, amidst every species of privation those lessons of patriotism and faithfulness, they had so nobly illustrated in action. – It is impossible not to entertain a profound respect for such men ..."[17]

It has been pointed out that although Upper Canada "was a British colony and many of its residents were firmly committed to their King and the British connection, it was, during its formative stage, also very much an American community."[18] In an important contribution to our understanding of the conservative tradition, Jane Errington has pointed out that not all Upper Canadians were anti-American; many "argued that only by acknowledging the Americanness of the colony and, indeed, by carefully adopting certain economic, social and political ideas from south of the border could Upper Canadians be expected to remain loyal members of the British Empire." These leaders were "consciously Anglo-American," embracing both heritages.[19] Thus, Loyalist spokesmen like Richard Cartwright and Robert Hamilton often found themselves in opposition to the views of British officials who administered the province in the 1790s.

The late eighteenth-century Tory attitudes imported from England often reinforced the conservatism of the Loyalists. The "aristocratic resurgence" in England after the American Revolution resulted in the passage of the Constitutional Act, which crystallized these sentiments; and John Graves Simcoe was sent out as the first Lieutenant Governor of Upper Canada to carry out the intentions of the imperial authorities.[20] The British government was attempting to re-establish the old and flexible colonial system in which social and political institutions approximating those of the mother country were to be transplanted in the provinces, as far as colonial conditions would permit. Accordingly, British politicians attempted to strengthen the monarchical and aristocratical branches of the constitution to restore the balance which they believed had been upset in the American colonies before the Revolution. Simcoe, for example, sought to appoint Aeneas Shaw, a captain in his former militia unit, the Queen's Rangers, and "a character of approved loyalty" to his executive in an effort to strengthen his council before the disaffection of Robert Hamilton, who was critical of the administration's policies, disrupted the colony.[21] Simcoe wrote to the Colonial Office: "Upon the whole tho' there be no systematic opposition to Government, it is apparent, that on the other hand there is no direct support of its measures; and in particular it seems at the present season to avoid making use of the negative of the Crown, I am sorry to observe there is too great reason and probability that the Legislative Council are much more likely to promote than to suppress any attempt that may demand the exertion of that prerogative." In addition to his power of appointment to the Executive and Legislative Councils, Simcoe sought to strengthen his colonial executive through such social supports as titles of honour and land grants.

Yet these attempts to restore balance in the colonial constitution were to be accomplished without departing from representative government; elected assemblies were necessary for taxation purposes. As a result, Simcoe was prepared to make some compromises to the popular branch in order to avoid political problems; for instance, the government persistently denied the demands of the settlers for township meetings. But in 1793, a bill was accepted which would provide for the annual election of township officers (although the authority to call elections was placed in the hands of the justices of the peace who had real power).[22] It was Simcoe's intention to provide Upper Canada "with a Constitution which ... is the very image and transcript of that of Great Britain, by which she has long established and secured to her subjects as much freedom and happiness as it is possible to be enjoyed under the subordination necessary to civilized Society."[23]

The attitudes of colonial officials were shared by pre-war British immigrants like John Strachan, an Anglican clergyman and school teacher. He believed in the Blackstonian concept of a balanced constitution which provided true liberty and inspired loyalty; it was founded "upon the most equitable, rational and excellent principles: a constitution of free and equal laws, secured on the one hand against the arbitrary will of the sovereign, and the licentiousness of the people on the other ..."[24] Of course, not all Upper Canadians were as clear about the constitution as Strachan; in a confused appeal to the electorate in 1808, one Robert Henderson said: "I am a British born subject, I have lived under the Government, I have *read* that great and wonderful *production*, the Constitution, and admire it."[25]

Even in the harsh environment of pioneer Upper Canada, the benefits of the Constitution could make British subjects "happy and free ...," as Strachan noted: "behold comfort, wealth and grandeur flowing upon us, and our liberty giving our country the most solid charms, notwithstanding its freezing sky and procrastinated snows. To the freed man, labour loses its pain, he may be poor, but he feels himself independent ..." The situation in the province was a marked contrast to that of the revolution-born United States. Strachan wrote: "In point of real happiness the British are far superior to the inhabitants of this celebrated republic ... The frequency of their elections keeps them in a constant broil."[26] In return for the benefits provided under the British Constitution, the subject was expected to be animated by a sense of loyalty: "Surely ... you will return that affection and love for our august Sovereign which he has manifested to you ... [Y]ou will teach your children the value of the benefits which you have received, and inspire them with gratitude and loyalty." Therefore, in Strachan's view, admiration of, and commitment to, the British Constitution were closely linked with loyalty; this idea was central to the Tory mind. Strachan also believed that loyalty implied the recognition of a hierarchical social structure; it involved "proper resignation and obedience to the laws, a due deference and homage for superiors, and for those who are publicly entrusted with the administration of the province." True loyalty, then, demanded support of the government. The Tory elite required social harmony and sought to avoid any disaffection; as Strachan said: "let not this sacred attachment to our king be cankered with the spirit of discontent ..."[27] Political dissent and opposition were equated with disloyalty.

Political opposition before the War of 1812 was highly personal and of a limited nature; it reflected the primitive state of politics in Upper Canada.[28] But opposition of any kind was viewed as a threat to order and stability and, thus, was interpreted as being disloyal. During the administration of John Graves Simcoe, for example, Richard Cartwright and Robert Hamilton, who were important merchants and members of the Legislative Council, were labelled republicans because they criticized the Lieutenant Governor's programs.[29] Consequently Cartwright, who believed that the Loyalists were the natural leaders of the provincial society, wrote: "It seems, then, that every man who will not be a mere tool, and pay implicit respect to the caprice and extravagance of a Colonial Governor, must be the object of jealousy and malevolence, not only here but at home."[30]

Perhaps the best example of the intensely personal nature of politics in Upper Canada before 1812 was the official response to the activities of Robert Thorpe.[31] Thorpe, an Irishman who was a friend of Lord Castlereagh, the Colonial Secretary, arrived in Upper Canada in September 1805 to serve as a puisne judge of the Court of King's Bench. Within months of his appointment Thorpe was sending letters back to the Colonial Office which were highly critical of the administration and especially of the Lieutenant Governor, Peter Hunter. Thorpe exploited his position as a judge to attack the government; in the fall of 1806 he went on circuit in the western part of Upper Canada and encouraged juries to consider the "fifteen years of disgraceful administration in this province."[32]As a result of his activities Thorpe faced the ever-increasing hostility of the administration and the colonial elite drew upon traditional Tory perceptions of opposition to set out their case against the judge.

There were grounds for the charge that Thorpe associated the redress of grievances with his own personal advancement; he believed that he should be appointed Chief Justice to cure the ills of the province. Thorpe wrote to the Colonial Office that "in twelve months I will be ready to carry any measure you may desire through the Legislature ..."[33] In a letter to the York *Gazette*, "Spy" (who was probably S.P. Jarvis, a member of the provincial administration) expressed the Tory fear of faction based upon the selfishness and personal ambition of one man: "You [Thorpe] have endeavoured, while preaching and pratting upon harmony and union to fill one class of subjects with enmities against another, to fill them with foul suspicions of every man in office but yourself and to destroy the original confidence so necessary to the existence of civil society. You endeavoured to violate the peace of the public ... upon the altar of your indistinguishing malice and ... ambition."[34]

There was also a strong belief among the elite that Thorpe's charges were unfounded and that no grievances existed in the province. The new Lieutenant Governor, Sir Francis Gore, resented Thorpe's activities and wrote to the Colonial Office: "What grievances he alludes to, I do not know, the most respectable persons, with whom I have conversed do not complain ... and have called upon me for the sake of public tranquility to oppose and discountenance those principles and their supporters which at this moment agitate the Lower classes of the community ..."[35] Thorpe and Gore finally met at York on 31 October 1806 and the meeting was recorded by the Governor's secretary, William Halton. Thorpe argued that land in Upper Canada was seen as the reward for men of proven loyalty and yet it was granted away to the favourites of a corrupt administration. Therefore the economic and political development of the province was retarded. The meeting served to convince Gore that Thorpe's claims of popular grievance were imaginary and that his industry in sowing "the seeds of Ingratitude and Disloyalty" made him a threat to the continued existence of Upper Canada as a British province. Gore further interpreted Thorpe's election to the Assembly in December 1806 as a victory for republicanism: "he was proposed by the Democratic Party as a proper person to succeed Mr. Weekes ... The solemn mockery of his invoking at the opening of the Poll, the shade of his departed friend, 'as looking down from Heaven with pleasure' on their 'exertions in the cause of Liberty'; The seditious emblem of his Party [a Harp without the Crown]; Thorpe and the Constitution inscribed on badges, which he distributed to his partisans, and his almost Treasonable allusion to the American Revolution at the close of the Election, are indeed ample proof, that he was not an unworthy successor to Mr. Weekes." As a result, Thorpe's opposition was perceived to be disloyal. The effect of his criticism would be disruptive; to Gore, Thorpe was simply a "factious Demagogue" bent on destroying social stability and political harmony.[36]

Dissent was not to be tolerated in Upper Canada because of the dubious loyalty of its inhabitants. By the 1790s the total population of the province was about 20,000, a majority of them Loyalists.[37] Lieutenant Governor Simcoe, who believed that many Americans still remained at least passively loyal to the Crown, issued a proclamation in 1792 which invited settlers into the province and promised them free grants of land upon their taking an oath of allegiance, freedom of religion, and free political institutions.[38] The attraction of free and accessible land drew great numbers of Americans into the province and by 1812 there were about 100,000 inhabitants, of whom 80 per cent had recently migrated from the United States.[39] As early as 1799 Richard Cartwright had warned the Lieutenant Governor, Peter Hunter, about the dangers inherent in the massive migration of American settlers into Upper Canada. He did not believe that the Americans came into the province because of "any preference they entertain for our government. They came probably with no other interest than to better their circumstances, by acquiring land upon easy terms. Now, it is not to be expected that a man will change his political principles or prejudices by crossing a river, or that an oath of allegiance is at once to check the bias of the mind ..." Major William Graham, of the York garrison, feared that American settlers would infect the population with republican views: "[T]he Schoolmasters use all their efforts to poison the minds of the youths, by teaching them in republican books ... Youths educated in such books, by and by will have the privilege of voting members for our Assembly, and filling the House with their own kind, and when that is the Case, what may the Governor and the council of the Province expect – trouble too much ..." Lieutenant Governor Gore also believed the loyalty of the American settlers to be suspect because they retained "those ideas of equality and insubordination, much to the prejudice of this Government, so prevalent in that Country."[40]

Not all Upper Canadians feared the Americans. Robert Hamilton and William Dickson looked to farmers from the United States as the settlers who would fill up their lands in the Niagara region.[41] Yet many articulate members of the populace did share official perceptions. A letter from "Sancho," for example, described Upper Canada as "an asylum to *exiles* and *aliens*, to *atheists* and to *prawling democrats*." Thomas Welch noted that nine out of every ten inhabitants of Oxford County, in the southwestern part of the province, celebrated the Fourth of July and he remarked that these settlers "may ... be well enough[,] provided we have no war with the United States, but Should we unfortunately be plunged into a War ... the people above alluded to ... under the cloak of Subjects would ... be much to be dreaded."[42]

Thorpe's opposition to the administration intensified Tory fears about the growth of disloyalty in Upper Canada and as a result Gore sought the judge's dismissal. In the fall of 1807, Thorpe was suspended for "exceeding his duties as a Judge ... mixing in the political parties of the Province and encouraging opposition to the Administration."[43] The activities of Thorpe and his supporters, who included David McGregor Rogers and Benajah Mallory in the Assembly, plus Joseph Willcocks and John Mills Jackson, were based primarily upon personality conflicts and the ambitions of the men involved. Ethnicity was also a factor because many of the oppositionists were of Irish or Loyalist origin and they distrusted the clique of Scottish merchants surrounding the Lieutenant Governor. As early as 1806 Thorpe had written to the Colonial Office about the economic and political domination of Robert Hamilton and Richard Cartwright: "I found [Gore] ... surrounded by the same Scotch Pedlars that had insinuated themselves into favour with General Hunter and that have so long irritated and oppressed the people; there is a chain of them linked from Halifax to Quebec, Montreal, Kingston, York, Niagara and so on to Detroit – this Shopkeeper Aristocracy has stunted the prosperity of the Province and goaded the people until they have turned from the greatest Loyalty to the utmost disaffection."[44] There were also ideological underpinnings to this opposition; these men did articulate a different conception of loyalty from the Tories. Their definition challenged the supporters of the administration on three main questions: who was loyal? what was the proper object of loyalty? and did it allow dissent?

After Thorpe's dismissal an opposition newspaper, the *Upper Canadian Guardian or Freeman's Journal*, began publication at Niagara. It was published by Joseph Willcocks, an Irishman who arrived at

York in 1800 and had been dismissed as Sheriff of the Home District in March 1807 because of his attacks on the administration. It was reported that Willcocks "expressed his admiration of a Republic system of Government and hoped that system would prevail thro' the world."[45] Willcocks was later elected to the Assembly and imprisoned by the other members for libelling them in his newspaper; he was re-elected the next year, in 1809. (He remained in opposition throughout his political career and in 1813 joined the American forces invading Upper Canada. Willcocks was killed in action in 1814.) The *Upper Canadian Guardian* became the published voice for the opposition in the province. Willcocks printed a letter from "A Loyalist" (whom Lieutenant Governor Gore believed to be Thorpe)[46] which described a more accommodative conception of loyalty than that embraced by the colonial elite: Upper Canada was not the exclusive domain of the Loyalists because loyalty could develop naturally through settlement in the province. Governor Simcoe had first articulated this idea in the 1790s because he believed that American settlers could be assimilated to the dominant British political culture: "[Even] those who may not see the necessity and immense advantage of experience in the form of Government ... may be attached to it by the undisturbed benefits and the prospect of future advantages for their families." "A Loyalist" also believed that the American farmers could earn their loyalty through the "sufferings and perseverances" experienced in settling the "Wilderness." He asked: "Are these ... not sufficient to insure us the character of Loyalists, and the rights and privileges of subjects ...?"[47]

The oppositionists did not fear that the American settlers would retain their republican values because the process of assimilation would transform them into loyal Upper Canadians. Therefore they rejected the exclusiveness of Tory loyalty because the long-term consequences of such a belief would be disastrous for Upper Canada. David McGregor Rogers, a Loyalist who represented the counties of Hastings and Northumberland in the Assembly, attacked the exclusion of American settlers from the administration. He wrote that "all appointments of consequence are made and given to persons favourites of those in power in Europe ... Viewing an appointment in a distant country, unacquainted with the Capacity and genius of the people they are sent amongst, they [the appointees] find themselves in a new world naturally prejudiced in favour of the Inhabitants & Country they have left. They despise those they come amongst ..." The exclusion of the American settlers from the administration of the province would only weaken the loyalty of the inhabitants and increase discontent. Rogers believed that the American Revolution had similar causes: "Americans I suppose have as tender feelings as Europeans and no doubt thought themselves equally entitled to all the privileges of British subjects[;] but when to the neglect of their Persons was added their taxing them and disposing of the revenues arising from such taxes without their consent ... [No] wonder they thought themselves ill used, being completely deprived of the Privileges of the rest of the subjects of the empire."[48] "A Loyalist" also stressed the falseness of the claims of government officials to share the Loyalist tradition; their loyalty was not proven, they were simply office-seekers. The people, it was argued, should be protected "from the insults of these pedling [sic], upstart office-hunting hypocrites whose loyalty has never been tried." Tory loyalty was seen as simply the commitment to patronage and the monopoly of office; they "arrogate to themselves the right of deciding upon the policy and justice of every public measure, and who with as little effrontery continually assert, that the people are stupid[,] ignorant and rebellious, not competent to judge between right and wrong and that they are utterly incapable of knowing what is calculated for their good, or the extent of their rights and privileges."[49]

Thorpe's supporters resented the misrepresentations which labelled them as disloyal. The "Independent Freeholders of the East Riding of the County of York, and the Counties of Durham and Simcoe" resolved in January 1807: "That we know no discontented Demagogues nor if we did could not be deluded by them, many of us have fought, bled & sacrificed our families & properties for the British Government, we have exerted & ever will exert ourselves to preserve the freedom of Election from all undue influence to the last moment of our lives shall we be ready to support our King, & Constitution."[50] The oppositionists, accordingly, rejected Tory loyalty, which they argued was too exclusive; neither national origin nor possession of office were sufficient reasons to allow the colonial elite a monopoly on loyalty.

In addition to this assimilative idea of loyalty the opposition group challenged the Tories on the proper objects of loyalty. Their fundamental assumptions were still conservative because they drew upon late seventeenth-century Whig political traditions. Thorpe, for example, defined loyalty as "a faithful ... attachment to our king and government ... a proper observance of the laws combined with a determination to support the Constitutional rights and immunities of the people ..." Joseph Willcocks developed this idea in more depth when he wrote: "True loyalty is to be faithful to your King, to guard his prerogative, to support him in his dominions, to protect inviolably the constitution of which he is the head, and to obey and uphold the law which he has sworn to administer and maintain ... [But] surely it would not be loyal ... to assist a monarch in rendering himself absolute, [for] who would overturn the constitution and subvert the law?"[51] Oppositionists like Thorpe and Willcocks appealed to a conservative historical tradition which gave them a clearer and narrower definition of the nature of loyalty than the Tories could show – it was attachment to a set of constitutional principles rather than to the administration. It followed that political dissent was not only compatible with true loyalty but might actually be required by it; the oppositionists were concerned with defending the legitimacy rather than defining the limits of dissent. They also sought to protect the constitutional rights of the inhabitants of the province against the encroachments of the administration; and the defence of those rights was as sacred, as loyal, and as distinctively British, as the defence of the empire against rebellion or of the province against invasion. By 1812, therefore, a distinctive opposition idea of loyalty had developed.

The outbreak of the War of 1812 had important repercussions for attitudes about loyalty in the province because the views of the Tory elite were strengthened at the expense of those of their opponents.[52] The war confirmed the worst fears of the Tories about the threat posed by the United States; they believed that Upper Canada was invaded by "an Army of Banditti whose sole object was cowardly Plunder." According to John Strachan, the province was "environed almost with our enemies, and mixed with doubtful characters and secret Traitors."[53] Hence it was essential that the inhabitants affirm the loyal character of the society. John Powell, a son of the Chief Justice, William Dummer Powell, stressed the social obligation of every Upper Canadian to prove his loyalty: "Every Canadian freeholder is, by deliberate Choice, bound by the most solemn oaths to defend the Province as well as his own property; to shrink from that Engagement is a Treason not to be forgiven ..." The continued existence of Upper Canada as a British province was at stake, according to Powell: "It is no longer the time for Indulgence or private feelings & private virtues at the Expense of public duty ..." While Powell emphasized the idea of social duty, John Strachan linked loyalty with Christian duty, in a sermon delivered on 2 August 1812: "The Christian soldier loves his country. Were patriotism a determination to support our country when in the wrong, were it an inclanation [sic] to do evil to promote her advantage, then might we admit to be a narrow and illiberal prejudice; but the patriotism for which we plead, is an ardent and fixed disposition to promote our country's good ... It is that warm affection which a good man feels for the happiness of his kindred and friends, extended to the society of which he is a member."[54]

As a result of their own activities during the War of 1812, the Tories immediately adopted a myth that Upper Canadians had proven their loyalty. The accuracy of the myth is beside the point; the Tories believed that loyalty was earned in 1812 as it had been by the original Loyalists in 1776, except that this time it was earned by staying rather than by leaving. John Powell argued that: "In this moment who is not an active friend, is, and must be considered as an Enemy ... If there be, as doubtless there are, amongst us ... those who cannot conquer their repugnance to meet their kindred in Arms, Honor ... and Honesty require that they should withdraw and abandon the property which they will not undertake to defend."[55] The number of people who could claim to have demonstrated loyalty was increased and yet the exclusiveness of the Tory definition did not have to be relaxed to admit them.

The War also reinforced the anti-American sentiment exhibited by the Tories. In 1812 Sir Isaac Brock, the Administrator appointed a year earlier, believed that much of the population in western Upper Canada was disloyal; he wrote: "There can be no doubt that a large portion of the population in this neighbourhood [Fort George] are sincere in their professions to defend the country, but it appears likewise evident to me that the greater part are either indifferent to what is passing, or so completely American as to rejoice in the prospects of a change of Government."[56] It was believed that many American settlers had supported or even joined the armies invading Upper Canada from the United States; the Adjutant General, Edward Baynes, contrasted the role of the inhabitants of Loyalist background with the activities of the American settlers: "The high value and estimation in which the Loyal settler is deservedly held has been placed in the most conspicuous point of view by the contrast it has formed with the American interloper, industriously undermining the fidelity of his neighbors by disseminating Democracy, affording intelligence to the enemy and frequently concluding his career by going over to him."[57] John Strachan also felt that the American settlers were disloyal: "In several Districts, where they were the majority, or supposed themselves to be so, rebellion was organized."[58]

The survival of the province after the War seemed miraculous and men like Strachan firmly believed that Upper Canadians were truly "God's chosen people." The province was the homeland of those whose loyalty had once again been tested and found to be pure: "Upper Canada is the asylum of those brave men who risked their lives to maintain the unity of the British empire – men ... who proved, in the late war, that they retained the same love for the king and our happy constitution, which conducted them through an unnatural rebellion."[59] Members of the elite also assumed that their vision of Upper Canada was confirmed by the results of the War and, consequently, Upper Canadian conservatism was crystallized.

The Tory belief in the importance of the imperial connection to the continued political existence and material development of Upper Canada intensified. John Powell, for example, emphasized the social benefits of the imperial connection and questioned any attempt to end the colonial relationship because grievances simply did not exist under British rule: "Where is the Canadian Subject, who can truely [sic] affirm to himself that he has been injured by the Government in his person, his Property or his Liberty?" The Tories also became more insistent upon maintaining the British Constitution unaltered. In his electoral address in 1817, Henry John Boulton, a member of the York elite, stressed the importance of constitutional balance as the guarantee of social harmony: "With respect to my political opinions, I should glory in the name of an independent supporter of the Rights of the People, and the Loyal defender of the Prerogatives of the Crown; each should assimilate and be in unison with the other. – But must remain inviolable and untouched; as the too great increase of the one, would prevent and destroy the free exercise of the other ..."[60]

There was increased emphasis upon the necessity for internal unity in the province in the face of the persistent American threat. Upper Canadians had to support the government, and the administration must be given the authority to maintain social control; John Powell declared that "The Law should enable the Government to discriminate and control the few, for the benefit of the whole ..." The desire for internal unity precluded any conception of legitimate opposition, as "A Traveller" noted in a letter to the Kingston *Gazette*: "The possibility of disaffection is so great, that the slightest murmur against government would almost be considered as a breach of allegiance."[61] The War had confirmed the belief that dissent was equated with disloyalty because of the defection to the American cause of the most conspicuous pre-war opponents of the government – Joseph Willcocks, Abraham Markle, and Benajah Mallory. Therefore Tory spokesmen condemned the appearance of opposition in a fragile society like that of Upper Canada; it was factious and hence disloyal. John Strachan stated: "In a free country like this, where differences of opinion concerning public affairs may be sincerely maintained, great danger arises lest a few designing men should take advantage of any party spirit that may exist and induce by specious pretences the adoption of the most pernicious measures, under the cloak of securing their liberties, and maintaining their independence."[62]

In spite of Tory condemnations of dissent, opposition to the administration began to resurface in the immediate post-war period. Although this opposition was still largely personal, it did harken back to the pre-war notion that dissent could be loyal if that loyalty was to constitutional principles rather than to the administration. Discontent was fuelled by economic factors, including the end of wartime prosperity, the failure to pay compensation to those who had suffered losses as a result of the American invasions, and the failure to make the land grants promised to militiamen as a reward for their loyalty. In addition, there was some resentment of the government policy which prevented justices of the peace from administering oaths of allegiance to American settlers coming into the province; as a result, Americans would be unable to secure title to land and further immigration from the United States might be discouraged. The colonial executive, which controlled provincial expenditures and the land-granting system, was perceived to be the source of these grievances and during the 1817 sessions of the Assembly opposition to the administration appeared in the persons of Robert Nichol and James Durand. Nichol, an officer during the War and a large landholder from Niagara, was especially critical of the government for its policies on compensation and American immigration. He introduced a series of resolutions on the state of the province which were critical of the government and before they could all be passed the Lieutenant-Governor, Sir Francis Gore, prorogued the Assembly. Gore believed that such criticism of the administration would weaken the society and ultimately convey "this devoted Province to the United States of America."[63]

The controversy which centred on Nichol was primarily economically based but during the next session, James Durand, an Ancaster merchant, drew upon the same basis of discontent to pose a constitutional challenge to the government. In his electoral address in 1817, Durand attacked the military rule of Upper Canada during the War which led to the suspension of habeas corpus and the introduction of martial law and compelled "the people to bear the kicks and cuffs of those who are used to overbearing tyranny."

He posed as the defender of the liberty and prosperity of the independent yeoman farmer against the further corruption of executive encroachments upon the rights of the people. Durand's
opposition was largely personal and he was expelled from the Assembly; even Robert Nichol labelled the address as a "false, scan-
dalous and malicious libel." By the end of the session though, only
Jonas Jones and Philip Van Koughnet consistently supported the
administration, while the four members from Niagara, Nichol and
Mahlon Burwell from the Western District, plus Zacheus Burnham,
John Cameron, Alexander McMartin, and Isaac Fraser, often opposed executive measures and began to proclaim the legitimacy of
combining to oppose the government. The spectre of such a significant opposition in an Assembly of just twenty-three members
pressured Gore into again proroguing the legislature.[64]

It was against this background that the Gourlay agitation met
such a sharp response. Robert Gourlay was an erratic Scot and an
agrarian radical who came to Upper Canada in 1817 to gather information for a statistical account of the province as a prelude to
his sponsorship of an emigration scheme from Britain. Gourlay
travelled the province and concluded that the most significant problem facing the society was the exclusion of American settlers. He
wrote later: "On this journey, I found that four-fifths of the settlers
had come from the United States, and that there was not one British-born subject among twenty ... The monstrous conduct of the
Government, forbidding free ingress from the States, had keenly
wounded the feelings of these people."[65] Gourlay's conclusion was
supported by many prominent Upper Canadians, including William Dickson, a relative of his wife; Robert Nichol; and Thomas
Clark – men who were among the largest land holders in the province and thus most critical of the ban on the migration of prospec-
tive settlers from the United States. Gourlay also compared the
development of Upper Canada unfavourably to that of the United
States; the settlers "see the property of their neighbours in the
United States advancing in value while theirs is on the decline;
they see everything in motion there, while all is here at a stand
..." He believed that the subsequent discontent threatened the British connection and so he laid the blame for the problems facing
the province at the feet of the government which pursued "a system of paltry patronage and ruinous favouritism" in its land-granting policies.[66] The nature of Gourlay's criticism is not surprising
given his perceptions of the ideal society. He envisioned an organic
rural community dominated by virtuous yeoman farmers. This ideal
society was constantly threatened by the existence of a landed aris-

tocracy which sought to maintain its privileges and thus oppress the lower orders. This was the situation which he believed had developed in Great Britain; when he came to Upper Canada he applied the same analysis and accordingly found significant grievances to be redressed.[67]

Gourlay articulated many of the themes current in the radical ideology of early nineteenth-century Britain. His appeals were to the past; he sought a restoration of the true Constitution in the face of governmental corruption which diverted people from political issues and kept them in ignorance. Gourlay was concerned with due respect for the Crown and protection for its lawful authority, but he sought to restrict the prerogative of the executive to achieve constitutional balance and guarantee the rights of the people. He wrote: "The British Constitution sets the law above all men; and that the law may be reverenced and implicitly obeyed, it has anointed a King to be its grand Executor ... [In] proportion to the intensity of sentiment which directs our love and regard for the King, should be our watchfulness over those delegated by him to discharge the sacred trust of the laws; and preserve them inviolate." Gourlay also appointed himself as the guardian of the people's rights: "In politics, I hold myself as having to do with men; and to guard against their tyrannical dispositions, consider it my sacred duty to watch and resist, if required." Like many other British radicals, Gourlay believed that the most important measure of popular opinion was the public meeting and the petition.[68] But his calls for township meetings and later for a provincial convention to catalogue grievances in a petition to the Prince Regent were perceived to be extra-constitutional by the administration and thus a threat to the existing political system. The new Lieutenant Governor, Sir Peregrine Maitland, labelled Gourlay's activities as "sedition"; as a result, public opinion began to turn against the Scottish radical.[69]

The Tory case against Gourlay focused upon two interrelated themes. The first was an old argument which stressed the vulnerability of Upper Canada and the subsequent need for internal unity; the second offered a new position – that the province was not developed sufficiently to permit opposition to emerge. The Attorney General, John Beverley Robinson, took up the first question; he believed that Gourlay's activities were "dangerous to this country, chiefly from their example, as they point out the mode by which popular movements on pretences less specious than the present, can be effected, and ... we have no adequate military force in this Province, which it has often been found necessary to resort to in

England to check the tumults excited by artful & discontented demagogues." John Macaulay, a member of the Kingston elite, shared the same view about opposition. It has been suggested that he believed "in the special need for order, due morality, and proper subordination in a province so vulnerably situated as Upper Canada. To support government was not to be truly partisan but to be truly loyal; to oppose it on principle was to be factious and even subversive of good order, and hence was to menace the existence of the colony."[70]

The Tories also began to argue in the post-war period that the infant state of the province simply would not permit opposition to emerge. In a letter to the Kingston *Gazette*, "A Traveller" noted that Upper Canadians "have not had sufficient experience in politics to know, that a man may be firmly, and ardently attached to that government which he accuses of defects and inconsistencies." John Strachan wrote that Gourlay "has done a good deal of mischief in the province by his seditious publications, exciting discontent amongst the people ... A character like Mr. Gourlay, in a quiet colony like this, where there has been little or no spirit of inquiry, and very little knowledge, can do much harm ..." Strachan firmly believed that the infant state of Upper Canada required political unity. The province was weak and a strong government was essential if the province was to continue to develop. Therefore Tories concluded that the administration should not be criticized; dissent simply misled the population.[71] The growing antagonism directed against Gourlay by the administration caused many of his former supporters to back off; men like Nichol and Clark realized that their commercial interests linked them to the patronage web centred in York and consequently they came to support the administration. Even James Durand believed that Gourlay's attempts to change the system of government were unconstitutional.[72]

The controversy grew increasingly bitter by 1818 as Gourlay's critics became vehement in their attacks upon him. William Dickson portrayed the Scottish radical as "an evil-minded, and seditious person" who was endeavouring "to alienate the minds of our subjects in the Province from our person and Government ... [and] to raise a Rebellion ..."[73] Gourlay himself exacerbated the situation; he was not prepared to compromise and he rejected out of hand any criticism of his activities. He felt that he was being persecuted, particularly by that "monstrous little fool of a parson," John Strachan.[74] Yet Gourlay did recognize that loyalty was being used as an ideological weapon against him. Upper Canadians were afraid to support him openly: "by a strange perversion of sentiment, some of them seem to fancy, that openly to speak out would be a declaration of disloyalty ... Every sensible man *must* know that this country cannot be retained to Britain without a radical change of management." Gourlay did not associate loyalty with "passive obedience" and neither did his supporters; an address by one George Adams stated: "True loyalty did not consist in mere passive submission; it consisted in watching over every part of the constitution, at once, with jealousy and affection."[75] Gourlay and his supporters drew upon the opposition tradition in Upper Canada to emphasize their loyalty through appeals to constitutional principles. One observer noted that Gourlay's supporters had proven their loyalty; they "were not under the influence of any disloyal or disaffected views ... All these men, as it is generally allowed, were before this event as faithful subjects of His Majesty as any in the country, and had given ample proof of their loyalty in the recent combat with the United States."[76]

The collapse of Gourlay's agitation as a result of his imprisonment and subsequent expulsion from the province certainly indicated that the idea and practice of opposition had not as yet been accepted in Upper Canada. The perceived weakness of the society prompted the Tories to cling to their traditional values and attempt to crush any internal threats such as that posed by Robert Gourlay; dissent was still equated with disloyalty. Gourlay had failed to make the case that opposition was legitimate – that loyalty to constitutional principles did permit dissent. His efforts were hampered by the limits which he himself placed upon legitimate dissent. He did not accept the idea of political parties and he rejected altogether the propriety of armed opposition. That left him with the right of British subjects to petition the Crown directly, bypassing the provincial administration if necessary. It was a logical position but so entirely impractical that it did not enable him to defend himself, let alone the cause of reform.

In conclusion, the period before 1820 saw the development of two distinctive definitions about the nature of loyalty. The first was based on the experiences of the oppositionists like Thorpe and Gourlay and would provide the ideological foundations for the Reform movement. It was assimilative rather than exclusive; loyalty could be earned but it also could develop naturally through good behaviour in the society. There was also the belief that loyalty was directed towards seventeenth-century English constitutional principles rather than simply to the administration. Moreover, there was an acceptance of the legitimacy of dissent; loyalty did not require acquiescence in abuses. In his electoral address in 1820, W.W. Baldwin stated that even "the purest Administration requires a vigilant activity on the part of all its constitutional checks."[77]

The Tory definition, on the other hand, stressed the exclusive nature of loyalty and, drawing upon the Loyalist tradition, the commitment to the British connection. In addition, the Tories totally rejected the legitimacy of opposition; dissent was disloyal because it disrupted the social equilibrium and political harmony of the province. Dissent was illegitimate for several reasons: Upper Canada remained vulnerable after 1815 and unity had to be maintained; the province was still politically immature; abuses were unthinkable under the British system; and finally, oppositionists were selfish, with suspect motives. Dissent had to be crushed and the Tories were largely successful in their attempts to silence opponents of the administration. As a result, some ideological conformity was imposed in the province. John Macaulay, for example, stated: "While the great body of the people continue loyal, and zealous as they now are in their attachment to the parent state, faction and discontent can never operate successfully among us ..."[78]

The early critics were unable to counter these arguments because they put limits on their dissent and their alternatives were not very practical. While the oppositionists would justify expressions of dissent on loyal grounds, they did not have a program to make dissent effective either by justifying rebellion on the grounds of popular support or by claiming that the Assembly could legitimately be organized to oppose the administration or still less by claiming that it could be organized to control the administration. The dissent which their view of loyalty could legitimize was the dissent of the independent legislator. W.W. Baldwin said: "I ... profess to you an affectionate regard for British liberty and the British constitution ... I know ... that ... it is not the duty of your Representative to oppose, through a spirit of faction, the fair, beneficial and legitimate objects of the Administration ..."[79] That dissent was not likely to accomplish much, quite apart from the fact that it was under Tory attack; and any combination of dissenters went beyond what the oppositionists' idea of loyalty allowed them to justify. But the basis of the debate over the nature of loyalty had emerged by 1820 and these two positions – the Tory and what was to become the Reform – were articulated in more depth as a consequence of the controversy over the Alien Question.

CHAPTER THREE

The Alien Question and
the Debate over Loyalty

In the mid-1820s a letter printed in the *Colonial Advocate* commented on the impact of perhaps the most important political issue of the decade in Upper Canada: the "public mind... seems occupied with nothing else at present; – the *Alien Bill* is the general topic of conversation."[1] The controversy generated by the Alien Question focused upon the status of the largest group of inhabitants in the province, the settlers who had come from the United States after 1792. Although this had been a contentious problem since the end of the War of 1812, it became an important political question in the 1820s when the British courts decided that the American settlers were not legally subjects of the Crown but aliens; as such, they were unable to hold property or enjoy political rights in Upper Canada. The desire on the part of both the administration and its opponents to settle the question produced a long, bitter, and revealing debate.

Two distinct aspects of the Alien Question emerged during this debate. There was the legal controversy during which the Tories claimed that the American settlers had to be naturalized because they were aliens. The Reformers, on the other hand, appealed to prescriptive rights and convention to confirm the claims of this group to be recognized as subjects of the Crown. But the issue developed into far more than a legal question; it became a debate over the nature of loyalty in Upper Canada. The Tory position rested upon arguments which had been developed before 1820. The Tories believed that the province was vulnerable because of the settlement of a large body of potentially disloyal Americans within it; and they looked to the imperial connection to guarantee the continued existence of the province. Tory loyalty was also exclusive; it required adherence to the idea of Upper Canada as a special

Loyalist bastion governed by a Tory elite. Throughout the 1820s this view was challenged by spokesmen of what was to become the Reform movement. Reform loyalty was assimilative rather than exclusive; it was argued that American inhabitants could become loyal subjects through the process of settlement in Upper Canada. This sentiment was accompanied by the development of provincial feeling expressed with nationalist rather than Loyalist rhetoric; as a result, the definition of loyalty was broadened by the Reformers.[2]

The experiences of the War of 1812 crystallized pre-war suspicions and resentment of the American settlers in Upper Canada into fear and hatred. These attitudes produced a major change in government policy towards that group. The perceived vulnerability of Upper Canada as a result of its proximity to the United States and the large American-born population within the province prompted harsh measures from the administration; loyalty oaths were imposed on those suspected of disloyalty, Americans were denied patronage, and immigration from the United States was limited after 1815. John Strachan reflected official attitudes about the American settlers and the Tory vision of the future development of Upper Canada as a British society: "it was deemed wise to check emigration from the United States for a time, until the passions on both sides were cooled, and until a sort of foundation, or nucleus, could be formed of emigrants from the mother country in the new settlements by which they might acquire a British tone and character."[3] The administration believed that if the pre-war pattern of heavy immigration from the United States continued the province would become completely American; therefore British immigration was encouraged and it became more difficult for Americans to establish themselves in Upper Canada. Magistrates were not allowed to give oaths of allegiance to Americans, making it nearly impossible for them to secure title to land. As a result, the proportion of inhabitants of American origin began to decline after 1815.

But a substantial body of American settlers remained in the province and the administration sought to define their legal status. Although the Chief Justice of Upper Canada, William Dummer Powell, believed that they were, by law, British subjects, the Attorney General, John Beverley Robinson, presented an opinion in 1818 which declared that settlers who had remained in the United States after 1783, and had not been naturalized in Upper Canada, were aliens. These inhabitants would not be entitled to hold property or enjoy political rights in the province. Robinson was not prepared to pursue the question to its legal conclusion because the consequent insecurity over land titles, which would be faced by both the American settlers and British subjects who may have purchased property from Americans in Upper Canada, would produce significant unrest in the province.[4] Consequently, no action was taken and the status of the American settlers remained unresolved.

This question was raised again after the victory of Barnabas Bidwell in a by-election held for the constituency of Lennox and Addington in 1821. Bidwell was an American settler; he had been born in Massachusetts in 1763 and had remained in the United States after the American Revolution. He subsequently became attorney general for Massachusetts, a member of the United States Congress, and Treasurer of Berkshire County. Accusations of forgery and embezzlement while Treasurer forced Bidwell's emigration to Upper Canada in 1810. His by-election victory was challenged by several constituents on the grounds that Bidwell was both a criminal and an alien. The petition stated that he had taken an oath of allegiance in the United States in which he abjured his status as a British subject; moreover, it was asserted that Bidwell did not consider the oath of allegiance that he had taken in Upper Canada to be binding because it was compulsory.[5]

The petition was supported by the administration because Bidwell had been an active and vocal opponent of the local Tory elite in Kingston and he had contributed to Gourlay's statistical account. John Strachan, now a member of the Executive Council, had written to John Macaulay before the by-election: "I hope Bidwell will not get in because it would be a disgrace to the Province ..."; after the result was known he remarked: "It positively made me sick to hear of old Bidwell's return."[6] The prospect of eliminating an opponent like Bidwell was quite appealing for the Tories, and John Beverley Robinson initiated proceedings in the House to disqualify the new member. Although the debate over his eligibility touched upon the larger question of the status of American settlers in the province, Bidwell was eventually expelled from the Assembly on the grounds of "moral turpitude" rather than because he was an alien. As the Kingston *Chronicle* reported: "his malversations in office" had forced Bidwell to flee from the United States "into the wilderness of Canada, in order to avoid the swift vengeance with which he was threatened by the uplifted arm of justice."[7]

Barnabas Bidwell was prevented from running again by a statute passed by the Assembly in 1822 to disqualify him; but his son, Marshall Spring Bidwell, did contest the new by-election. The son's qualifications were challenged "upon the ground of his having been born in the United States" and thus he was an alien. As a result, the Returning Officer rejected all votes for Bidwell.[8] Marshall Spring

Bidwell petitioned the Assembly to have the decision overturned; the result was voided and he was declared eligible to sit in the House. At the same time the Lieutenant Governor, Sir Peregrine Maitland, referred the question of the Bidwells' qualifications to the imperial government for resolution and a decision was to be made on the basis of the judgment in a case already pending in the British courts.

The status of the settlers of American origin remained unclear to many Upper Canadians and the legal framework within which the Alien Question was debated was complex. W.W. Baldwin, a lawyer himself, stated: "There is a great difficulty in ascertaining what legal provisions, if any, have been made, between Great Britain and the United States, with a view to separate the mass of the people, under the peculiar circumstances of the revolution into American citizens and British subjects."[9] A significant amount of turmoil was generated by the fact that contradictory legal opinions could be brought to bear on the status of the American settlers. The Reformers based their legal position on the concept of perpetual allegiance – they argued that British common law declared that "a natural-born subject could not shed or lose his nationality by unilateral action of the subject of the Crown." Moreover, two British statutes, passed in 1731 and 1773, stated that "children and grandchildren born abroad of British fathers might retain the status of British subjects." Although Great Britain gave "formal recognition of the severance of allegiance" at the conclusion of the American Revolution, opponents of the administration argued that the Americans who came into the province had remained loyal British subjects.[10] Barnabas Bidwell, for instance, based this contention on the Blackstonian concept that the natural allegiance of a British subject could not be severed; the oath that he took in the United States provided only local allegiance. He remained a subject of the Crown. Marshall Spring Bidwell defended his status on the grounds that he was both the grandson and son of natural-born British subjects.[11]

Although the legality of the Reform position was undermined by subsequent decisions of the British courts, opponents of the administration continued to defend the rights of the American inhabitants. They presented a strong case based upon good conservative appeals to the prescriptive rights of the settlers. They stressed history and precedent, custom and usage, to buttress their position; resolutions passed by the Assembly in December 1825 stated: "from the earliest settlement of Upper Canada ... [Americans] with the knowledge and approbation of His Majesty's Government, came in great numbers to this Province, and were immediately admitted and uniformly considered to be entitled ... to all the rights and privileges ... of natural born subjects." Earlier legislation made "no provision for the naturalization of such persons" and implied, as a consequence, that the "natural allegiance" of the American settlers "have never been in anywise destroyed."[12]

Reformers also appealed to convention to strengthen their arguments; John Wilson stated in the Assembly that: "Governor Simcoe sent proclamations throughout the U. States of America, calling upon all those who wished to retain their allegiance, to come in and renew it, and every Person who came in received lands, upon renewing their allegiance ..."[13] Marshall Spring Bidwell, now a member of the Assembly, said that "Americans were invited to come in, buy lands, build homes and expend their money and industry upon that property to which they are now told, they never did, and never would have title." The policy which now declared the American settlers to be aliens was "inconsistent ... with the uniform uninterrupted practice for years past: at every election Americans have been permitted to vote; they have been elected and have served as Members of Parliament, and not a doubt has been hinted of their eligibility."[14] The Reformers argued that because the American settlers had long enjoyed both property and political rights in the province they were to be considered as British subjects. There would be disastrous consequences if these rights were withdrawn, as the *Upper Canada Herald* noted: these inhabitants "have heretofore not only considered themselves, but have been uniformly considered and treated by His Majesty and by the Provincial authorities and statutes as subjects." To consider them as aliens "will disenfranchise a large proportion of free holders of every district throughout the Province, to their grievous disappointment and injury; and will, in their view at least, be a breach of the public faith."[15]

The administration simply did not accept the Reform position; settlers who had remained in the United States after the American Revolution became citizens of the new nation and were, as a consequence, aliens when they arrived in Upper Canada. The Tory spokesman was John Beverley Robinson, who stated during the debate over the status of Barnabas Bidwell that Bidwell was an alien because under "the constitution of the U. States, those who had taken the oath of allegiance, were called adopted citizens." Bidwell had taken this oath and therefore "abjured his allegiance to the Crown of Great Britain ..." Moreover, Robinson countered the perceptions of his critics about the policy of the Simcoe administration. The Governor did not invite all Americans into Upper Canada;

he sought only the loyal subjects still residing in the United States. The Attorney General had examined Simcoe's Proclamation and concluded that "his Excellency merely said he would give grants of land to settlers, but not a word about their coming from the United States." He also asked: "Did the proclamation invite all persons without distinction? No; the proclamation expressly invited such persons only whose loyalty, and good conduct in the country where they resided, entitled them to encouragement." Accordingly, Robinson rejected appeals to historical convention on this question; he was "anxious ... to set at rest" the erroneous assumption that Americans "should be allowed to cross the river, and enjoy all the privileges of British subjects ... The Americans were always treated as aliens by the government ..."[16]

Tory opinions were confirmed in 1824 by British legal authorities who decided that the Bidwells, father and son, were aliens because Barnabas had acknowledged the independence of the United States and had taken an oath of office which abjured his allegiance to the Crown; and the son of an alien was also an alien. In the same year the British courts also decided that persons remaining in the United States after 1783 were no longer British subjects.[17] These decisions had important consequences for Upper Canada because all inhabitants of the province who had immigrated from the United States, except those registered as Loyalists, were declared to be aliens, and thus unable to hold property or participate in the political life of the province, unless they were naturalized. Throughout the entire debate over the legal status of the American settlers during the Alien Question the Tories maintained this position.

Lieutenant Governor Maitland had recognized that if the American settlers were declared to be aliens "more than half of the possessions of the colony would be unsettled."[18] In order to resolve the situation, the Colonial Secretary, Lord Bathurst, instructed Maitland to secure proper naturalization legislation which would confer "the civil rights and privileges upon such citizens of the United States as, being heretofore settled in Canada, are declared ... to be Aliens ... although they have hitherto enjoyed, without question, the rights of British subjects."[19] The Governor also wanted to conclude the Alien Question because he was aware of growing discontent among the American settlers, which "diminishes their confidence in the protection of the Government." Although Maitland believed that they had proved "their attachment to the British Government and constitution ... by a long residence, and by faithful and valuable services during the late War ...," he felt that they remained potentially disloyal. Their American background made them susceptible to the spread of "godless republicanism" in the province. His solution was to confirm the security of land titles held by the American settlers but deny them political rights because they were aliens. The Legislative Council passed a Naturalization Bill in November 1825 which conformed to Maitland's views.[20]

Maitland may have intended a compromise rather than a partisan solution, but to Reformers his bill was a concrete and dramatic example of how extreme and how unpalatable the exclusiveness of Tory loyalty could be. They also attacked the Tories for changing the rules in the middle of the game to suit the political purposes of the government. Drawing upon traditional opposition arguments, the Reformers appealed to English constitutional principles. They rejected the official position that property rights could be confirmed but the corresponding political rights denied; the two could not be separated. The Reformers saw themselves as the "watchful guardians of the people's rights" and perceived a Tory "plot" designed to neutralize opponents of the government.[21] The *Canadian Freeman* reported that "great fears are entertained that some trick is about to be played off by the ministerial party."[22]

In addition to the Reformers' affirmations of loyalty to constitutional principles, there was also a renewed commitment to the British connection. Opponents of the administration believed that the imperial government wanted the provincial Assembly to confirm the status of the American settlers as British subjects but that imperial intentions were being misrepresented by the Tory-controlled administration. A letter to the *Upper Canada Herald* declared: "The Legislative Council passed a bill, which ... contained a declaration that these persons are not subjects, but in its enacting clauses naturalized them so far only as respects the holding of land, but not as to the rights of suffrage and eligibility. The Bill was essentially at variance with the recommendation of His Majesty's Government."[23] This theme was repeated the following year when the administration introduced legislation whose purpose was to naturalize all inhabitants who had resided in the province for seven years and required that "all persons applying for citizenship were to take an oath renouncing their American citizenship and were to be registered as naturalized British subjects."[24] In a letter to Robert Wilmot Horton, the Colonial Under-Secretary, John Rolph, an English doctor and lawyer who was a Reformer from Middlesex County, articulated the suspicion that the Tories were ignoring imperial instructions about the issue. He wrote: "the present ministry has attempted to conceal or misrepresent the gracious intentions of His Majesty; an imputation which has frequently taken its origin from the unavailing ambition of some Gentlemen in the Colony to identify themselves with the Members of the Imperial Government."[25]

Reformers accepted the idea of a court-country dichotomy which was a central theme in eighteenth-century Anglo-American opposition ideology.[26] They did not attack the Crown; rather they focused upon the Governor's advisers who were subverting the intentions of the imperial authorities. Francis Collins, an Irishman who edited the *Canadian Freeman*, developed this argument in some depth in a pamphlet devoted to a discussion of the Alien Question. He wrote: "public opinion acquits both His Excellency and the home government of any design against the liberty of the people, and rests the odium of such a trick upon the backs of a few deep and designing politicians who have long nestled about the Colonial Executive – and who, like the fable of the snake and the countryman, the moment they have been warmed into existence by the fruit of the toils and industry of the American emigrant farmers ... turned round upon their benefactors, and shed upon them the deadly poison of their political malice."[27] It was the Reformers who would protect the rights and liberties of the people against such encroachments by the executive. William Lyon Mackenzie, a recent Scottish immigrant and editor of the *Colonial Advocate*, quickly became embroiled in the political conflicts of the province; he believed that the greatest threat to the loyalty of the population was "in the inclination to despotic sway, previously exhibited by the few governing against the rights of the many governed." By zealously guarding the liberties of the people, the Reformers were strengthening loyal sentiment in Upper Canada: "the possession of political rights, the consciousness of freedom, independance [sic], and a share of self-government, is in itself a great pleasure; and leads to many other enjoyments and exertions, which are at once delightful to the individual and profitable to the community."[28]

The increased insistence with which Reformers separated the provincial administration from the imperial government and from British constitutional principles was met by a corresponding increase in Tory suspicion of their motives. Since Tories held that there were no real grievances in the province, they were "naturally led to inquire, to what circumstance ... such an anomaly is attributable – that the people acknowledgedly possessing greater privileges under their Government, than are enjoyed by any other, should in fact be opposed to that Government."[29] The obvious answer was that opposition was stirred up by dissenters seeking their own selfish goals. Opposition to the administration on the Alien Question was led by "a band of factious demagogues whose Acts perceptibly tend to disorganize society, to subvert legitimate authority, and to alienate men's minds from the constitutional government."[30] The idea of legitimate opposition was still unacceptable because it disrupted social harmony and political stability. The loyal subject would not oppose the government; the *Gore Gazette* noted: "we do *not* hold that ... an admiration of the institutions of our country, are best evinced by a systematic opposition to its government: we conceive on the contrary, that it is the obvious duty of every good member of society to assist in sustaining the constitutional authorities of his country ..."[31]

The Reformers, of course, reacted strongly against this equation of political dissent and disloyalty; their loyalty was to principles rather than to the corrupt administration. William Lyon Mackenzie, when accused of "democracy, disloyalty and *foul* play," responded by questioning Tory conceptions about the nature of loyalty: "It is true, my loyalty has not descended so low as to degenerate into base fawning cringing servility. I may honour my sovereign surely, and remember the ruler of my people with the respect that is due to his name and rank, without allowing my deportment to be equally respectful and humble to his majesty's butcher, or his baker, or to his taylor! [*sic*] ... The doctrines I have advocated will bear any inspection, for they are of a truly British stamp. Loyalty is an odd sort of word, and readily admits of many definitions[;] there is for instance a sort which consists in keeping a connection with the party that have places to give away ..."[32] Captain John Matthews, a half-pay officer and a member of the Assembly for Middlesex County, was accused of disloyalty in 1826 because he requested a troupe of American actors to sing "Yankee Doodle" after a performance. He was blunt in his equation of Tory loyalty and government patronage: "Loyalty, loyalty is all the cry now a-days, but analyze the term as it is now used, and you will find that it is loyalty to the Attorney General which is meant, because he is able to give away a great many good things ..."[33]

The Reformers not only attacked the corruption represented in their eyes by the Tories' attachment to office, they also condemned the partisanship of a measure that would neutralize political opposition by declaring the American settlers to be aliens. John Rolph claimed that American inhabitants "were being required to admit with stoic insensibility, that they have no title to their farms, and no civil rights, but that they seek the honor of an allegiance ... then shall they be considered freeborn men, sufficiently tamed and chagrined to suit the administration of Upper Canada."[34]

The opponents of the administration also feared the social consequences of a government policy which required the Americans to register as aliens. The process of registration would divide the community by segregating this group from the rest of the population. In the debate over the Alien Bill in 1827 Rolph said: "A man is averse for many and obvious reasons to be considered an alien ... To be an alien, it is said, is no shame ... True; it is no shame to have unfortunately contracted the itch, yet no man so afflicted desires to register his misfortunes, or to be told of it wherever he goes ... we should much prefer the honor of being British subjects."[35] Tory policy threatened social harmony because it would divide the population of Upper Canada into two distinct political classes. Again it was John Rolph, now the spokesman for the opposition on the Alien Question, who saw that the government's legislation would draw "an unnecessary line of distinction between British subjects by right and subjects by act of Parliament. The moment that political distinction is created, then invidious feelings will be generated."[36] Francis Collins was even more critical of such developments. He believed that "the Alien Question has been nothing but a snare – a hidden trap, with which to destroy the civil rights of the American emigrants in this colony – an apple of discord, with which first to divide the people, and then rule them with an iron rod ..."[37] John Matthews struck at the heart of the matter when he, too, argued that the ultimate purpose of the Tory administration was to "divide and govern" the population: "[He] had seen Europeans, Scotch, English, and Irish pitted against Americans ... [T]his little province was as much divided by the machinations of certain persons into political parties, as ever the religious world had been by sects, and by setting these parties against each other, the most intolerant becomes the most powerful."[38] The Reformers were drawing upon the old Tory arguments about the need for internal unity in the society and turning them against the government. To the Reformers, the continued existence of Upper Canada was threatened, not by the menacing spread of republican ideas, but rather by a corrupt administration seeking to limit the political rights of the people and to divide the population in order to secure its own power. According to John Rolph, "the seeds of distrust and discontent" which had been planted could soon disturb the political and social harmony of the province. The lack of public confidence in the administration could shake the foundations of the government itself.[39]

The Reform solution was to appeal directly to the imperial government, over the head of the Tory administration, in order to resolve the Alien Question. In 1827 Robert Randall was sent to Great Britain to obtain the disallowance of the Tory naturalization legislation passed earlier in the year. The Reformers' faith in the imperial authorities as a counterweight to the provincial government was rewarded by the success of Randall's mission; the Colonial Secretary authorized the Upper Canadian Assembly to pass a new bill which would naturalize "all persons who had at any time received grants of land from the provincial government, or who had held public office in the province, or who had taken the oath of allegiance, or who had come in before 1820 ... Persons who had settled since 1820 ... could be naturalized upon completing a seven years' residence."[40] Although Maitland and his executive were shocked by their repudiation at the hands of the imperial government, they drafted legislation which confirmed the political and property rights of the American settlers.[41] The Alien Question was finally resolved. The Reformers had achieved a significant political success. They had exploited the issue to attack the administration and to appeal directly to the large group of American inhabitants. The issue was an important factor in the Reform victory in the election of 1828.

The controversy generated by the Alien Question forced Upper Canadians to make explicit their definitions of the loyal subject. As a result of the debate and their defeat over the issue, the Tories became more insistent on the exclusiveness of loyalty. They were now menaced not only by the presence and influence of the American republic but also by the encouragement given to the American settlers in the province and by the appearance of a formed opposition which they could only explain in terms of self-interest and sedition. The Tories therefore insisted more than ever on "constant, unconditional attachment" to the imperial connection[42] and on the idea that loyalty had to be proved. Proof could be earned by imperial service, by acceptance into the Tory elite,[43] but above all by attachment to the Loyalist tradition. Upper Canada was seen as the homeland of people who had sacrificed everything to defend the Crown during the American Revolution and ultimately they were forced to flee from their old homes. The province represented more than just an asylum for the Loyalists, it was given to them as a reward for their loyalty. The original Loyalist expectations of hegemony within the province were dusted off and appropriated by the Tories; in an open letter to the new Lieutenant Governor, Sir John Colborne, "Watkin Miller" wrote that Loyalist principles "have, in most instances, been carefully instilled into the minds of their descendants, so that, at this period, they form a most valuable and immovable mass of faithful and loyal adherents to the British Crown ..."[44]

The leadership of the Tory elite was threatened by the breakdown of the social and political distinctions necessary to preserve Upper Canada as a Loyalist province; Christopher Hagerman, a prominent Kingston Tory of Loyalist background, believed it a "disgrace" that the American settlers were "placed on an equal footing" with the loyal population.[45] A correspondent to the Kingston *Chronicle*, "John Barleycorn," felt a sense of betrayal that the same people who had once driven him from the American colonies were to be afforded equal civil and political rights: "By whom was I robbed of my patrimony ...? Even by such as him [Barnabas Bidwell] who now claims equal privileges with the best of us ... What are ye about, ye sons of Loyalists? Will ye suffer these things."[46] The War of 1812 had reinforced Tory hostility to the American settlers; in an emotional outburst, John Beverley Robinson declared that he would not support the naturalization of this group – he "would suffer death before he would consent to a measure that would confer the rights of a subject on men who, but a few years ago, had *invaded our country – ransacked our villages – burnt our houses – and murdered our wives and children*."[47]

The Tories believed that as a consequence of their loyalty Upper Canada had been preserved as a special Loyalist bastion; but the continued existence of the province as a British colony was threatened by the American settlers. "A True-Born Canadian" asked "[A]re we to surrender to them all the privileges that had been purchased for us by the sacrifice of the blood and the property of those from whom it is our boast to have descended ... This is a *British* Province"[48] John Strachan believed that the ultimate goal of the American-born inhabitants was to see Upper Canada absorbed by the United States, as indicated in his remark that: "It is not however to be concealed that many of these persons whatever their intentions may have been, when they first removed into this province, are now desirous of destroying it as a British colony, and of annexing it to the United States."[49] The Tories concluded that the American settlers could never be assimilated and that they would always pose a threat to the society; "Catharus" developed this theme: "We can never expect that even favours and kindness will make men educated in republican principles ... loyally attached to our government and laws. No, Sir, they wish the American character and party here to stand out in bold relief ..."[50] The same sentiments were echoed by "Watkin Miller"; the Americans would always be a threat because they were potentially disloyal: "There are hundreds of families that settled in this province not from any feeling of preference for British dominions, but with a most unaffected indifference to everything upon earth beyond their own individual interests; who care not a farthing whether they dwell on British ground, or on that of the United States. Such persons, having no natural or hereditary attachment to the British constitution, and having been early habituated to the customs and laws of a republick [sic], form pliant materials in the hands of designing and ill-disposed persons to work upon; who find little difficulty in persuading them that they are subject to much tyranny and oppression ..."[51]

The American settlers were aliens and could only be considered loyal if they sought naturalization and naturalization was a favour that might be conferred upon the deserving, not a right that the deserving could command. Robinson, for example, stated that "naturalization had to be considered an act of royal favour."[52] Tory loyalty remained exclusive because loyalty had to be earned; it was confirmed "by birthright" or proven in defence of the Crown and revealed through attachment to the Loyalist tradition and support for the administration which embraced it.[53] The Tories had a legitimate claim to leadership and they sought to purify the society by eliminating its disloyal elements.

Another result of the Alien Question was that the Tories had more reason than before to distrust dissent. It was no longer merely individual; it had undermined them at the Colonial Office and beaten them at the polls. It was doubly illegitimate; once for existing at all, and again for being based on an organized and seditious appeal to the disloyal part of the electorate. As a consequence, "Upper Canada, in conservative eyes, was not merely challenged, but was under a state of permanent siege ... The apprehended threat from the large American-born element in the population, and the quite genuine danger, military, political and cultural, from the United States, made 'loyalty' the crux of conservative attitudes."[54]

In the debate over the Alien Question the Reformers presented the Tories with a double challenge: with their expansion of the idea of the nature of loyalty and with a more formidable idea of legitimate dissent. While they were a long way from the claim of a legitimate opposition party, in practice they went beyond the individual expressions of dissent which had been all that their idea of loyalty could justify earlier. The creation of the York Central Committee in 1828 marked the first attempt at a formed opposition. Reform politicians also sought more concerted action in the Assembly; John Rolph wrote to W.W. Baldwin: "I have to thank you for the zeal with wh[.] you propose that the more thoughtful politicians shd consult together about the public good: and I will endeavour to ... do my duty as one of His Majesty's faithful opposition ..."[55]

The Reformers made two claims to warrant carrying dissent so far. First, loyalty to constitutional principles justified the defence of the rights of loyal subjects. Second, they accused the administration of being not only corrupt, self-interested, and unjust, but also of seeking partisan advantage through the disenfranchisement of American settlers. In Blackstonian terms, a partisan ministry was as improper as a formed opposition, so that even if the Reformers were as yet unable to find new terms on which to legitimize organized dissent, they were no longer entirely on the defensive when dissent was discussed in Tory terms.

For the Reformers it was essential that loyalty not be closed off by the (partisan) administration. They rejected the exclusive myth presented by the Tories and through their responses to the arguments of their opponents outlined their own definition of the loyal subject. The Reformers' position was far more accommodative than that of the Tories. While Reformers shared the Tory belief that loyalty could be earned or inculcated, they also argued that settlers could become assimilated. Through the process of settlement, the American-born settlers would be transformed into loyal Upper Canadians. Upper Canada, according to Reformers, was not to be the exclusive homeland of the Loyalists and their descendents; the ideal inhabitant was the farmer. A letter from "A U.E. Loyalist" in the *Upper Canada Herald* claimed that the Americans were as valuable subjects as the Loyalists because they: "contributed as largely [as the Loyalists] to the clearing of the settlement, and improving of the country, and during the late war did as much and behaved as well in the defence of it. They are ... faithful subjects."[56] Reform spokesmen believed that the development of the province was dependent upon the industry of farmers; John Wilson stated in the Assembly that "all classes ... from the highest to the lowest, the Governor, the Judges, the Lawyers, the Merchants, and the men in office, were supported by this class ... The labouring class alone ought to be respected in a country like this; where we had nothing but wild woods a few years ago, we have now fine fields, and all this has been effected by the industry and enterprise of our farmers."[57] Marshall Spring Bidwell began to articulate a myth of the independent yeoman based upon the same idea; he argued: "Instead of a peasantry, let us have a yeomanry; and the country, on the one hand, would be more free, and all its liberal and popular institutions be supported with more spirit."[58]

The Reformers looked to the farmers from the United States as a spur to provincial development. Mackenzie believed that only the Tory administration wanted to exclude American settlers from Upper Canada: "persons of skill, capital and scientific information, of industrious habits, and of useful and productive callings" should be welcomed because they stimulated "our agriculture, our manufactures, and our commerce."[59] John Rolph argued that because this group contributed to economic growth they should be recognized as good subjects. The Americans should not be stripped of their rights by a vindictive administration; they "did not come here to act as squatters – not to live on air, or like the Indian, to hunt the wild animals of the Forest, but to become permanent settlers ... They came at this imperial invitation not to be degraded – they came from a free country, elated with the assurance that they should enjoy freedom here ... [T]hey had long been called subjects, and boasted themselves on account of their loyalty; and now all was to be swept away, and violence offered to their feelings ..."[60] To declare them to be aliens in the 1820s revealed only the desire of the government to limit the rights and liberties of the people.

The Reformers did not share the Tory suspicion of the American-born inhabitants; they were not perceived to be a threat to the continued existence of the society. William Lyon Mackenzie scoffed at the idea that the American settlers were tainted by "the principle of liberty, and equality, the antimonarchical notions and ideas ... which it is supposed they would disseminate through our colonies ..."[61] John Rolph also rejected the Tory claim that the Americans would infect Upper Canada with republicanism: "I think there is no danger to be apprehended from Americans. If they came there, they do not leave a bad government and barren soil; No – they come as agriculturalists to subdue not our government, but our forests; to overcome, not our authorities, civil and military, but our wastes, and our desolate places ..."[62] These settlers had no desire to undermine British institutions; they came to the province because "they do not find democracy so palatable in practice as in theory" and they "might desire to live under a monarchy." Consequently, they ought to be considered "as stray sheep returning to the fold, and instead of driving them off, we ought to hail with rejoicing their return."[63]

The Americans had also proven themselves to be good, and loyal, subjects. The *Gore Gazette* praised "their hard industry, their fidelity to their allegiance, by defending the rights and honor of the Crown, with their blood; at the same time they believed they were defending their own farms and firesides, from the grasp and ravages of those whom they then conceived, to be their and their King's *enemies* ..."[64] William Lyon Mackenzie also stressed "their meritorious and loyal conduct, in defence of this Province [during the War of 1812] ... the gallantry with which they encountered the dangers – and the patience and cheerfulness with which they endured the privations of war – proved that they justly appreciate the rights which they have so long enjoyed, and are fully entitled to the confidence, protection and paternalism of His Majesty's government."[65]

The Reformers, then, shared the Tory assumption that Upper Canada was the homeland of those whose loyalty had been proven by defending their community. The American settlers had earned their rights during the War of 1812 just as the Loyalists had during the American Revolution. The naturalization policy of the administration in the 1820s was perceived as a monstrous injustice because it conferred, rather than confirmed, the rights of this group. In a marvellous distortion of the historical process, Francis Collins thundered against the corrupt Tory government in a long editorial:

is it just – is it "equitable" – to reduce the acknowledged subjects of half a century to a level with the alien of last year, when painful requisitions are to be complied with? Is it "equitable" to compel men who waded thro fields of blood and slaughter (many of them without shoes or stockings on their feet) in the late war – men who proved their allegiance at the mouth of a cannon and point of the bayonet ... men, had it not been for whose unshaken allegiance and intrepid valour, the British would not now possess a foot of ground in Upper Canada, from which to drive an alien ... to crouch to an additional attestation of allegiance ... No – such a notion of justice and "equity" could never enter the mind of any man save some degraded hireling whose ideas of "equity" are governed by the caprice of his employers.[66]

The process of developing the loyal subject could be reinforced by other factors as well. Like the Tories, many Reformers believed that loyalty could be inculcated through state-aided education. John Rolph asked of the American settlers: "Will not their children be even as our children? Will they not feel a warm affection for the land in which they are reared? Will not education make them as we are now? and if they are taught by proper instructors, will they not love our institutions and never rebel against them?"[67] The Reformers sought to broaden the loyal base of the society; they believed that the good subject could also become the loyal subject. Loyalty would develop naturally through settlement in Upper Canada; the farmer would become part of the community in which he lived. Again it was Rolph who asked in the same speech: "Will not those who come here, and have property, become attached to us, to a government in the welfare of which they have a deep personal interest, and in which they will have a vote ...?"[68] William Lyon Mackenzie also believed that loyalty had to develop naturally from within the subject – it could not be instilled through coercion or by flooding Upper Canada with British immigrants. Loyalty was the result of the "possession of political rights, the consciousness of freedom, independance [sic], and a share of self-government."[69]

During the 1820s the Reformers began to articulate an assimilative myth in order to define the nature of loyalty; the American settlers could be accommodated within Upper Canada. They would become loyal because, as John Rolph explained: the "flame of patriotism burns with ardour in the breasts of the people ... Their desire to be considered subjects, arises from their attachment to our government, and a preference for it, grounded in causes which all men experience, but cannot explain. This political attachment is the strength of a nation ..."[70] A letter from "A Canadian" to *The Farmers' Journal* summed up the assimilative nature of Reform loyalty. The American settlers did not have "an hereditary attachment" to Upper Canada "but their attachment is wholly where it should be – in the country they live in, and where they have property ..." Moreover, he concluded: " another half century will make their children *Canadians*, at all events; and all distinction of country will then be forgotten."[71]

As the Tory idea of loyalty became more rigidly exclusive, the Reformers' idea became more explicitly assimilative. Furthermore, as a Reform conception of loyalty began to emerge, it was expressed through increased provincial feeling. The perceived mishandling of the Alien Question by the imperial authorities stimulated this sentiment. John Rolph was critical of the Colonial Office in 1826 for requesting naturalization legislation which required American settlers to register as aliens because Whitehall had not taken into account the will of the provincial Assembly.[72] The Reformers also rejected the spiritual and emotional component of Tory loyalty; instead they linked loyalty to the material growth of Upper Canada. The Reformers were stretching the idea of loyalty a little farther and doing so in a way that accords entirely with the logic of their own argument. They accepted loyalty as the test of political legitimacy as well as of social acceptance but by extending the possibility of loyalty to any well-behaved settler they found it necessary to provide some definition of good behaviour; that definition included contributing to the economic development of the province, on the grounds that people will be loyal to what they have helped to build; doing what is good for Upper Canada therefore becomes a way of demonstrating loyalty. While loyalty is still directed towards the imperial connection and British constitutional principles, the province is on the way to becoming the third of the identifiable legitimate objects of Reform loyalty. For the Tories, loyalty was a duty for which provincial welfare was a just reward; but for the Reformers the promotion of provincial welfare was a merit for which the recognition of loyalty was due.

The Tories also believed that loyalty was the test of political legitimacy and the basis of acceptance into the Upper Canadian community. The Reformers, though, did not believe that they were disloyal; in fact they shared many of the Tory perceptions about the nature of loyalty. They were committed to the imperial connection and rejected the idea of annexation to the United States. They accepted the argument that Upper Canada must be the homeland of those whose loyalty had been earned but they broadened the definition of the loyal subject to include the American settlers who had proven their loyalty during the War of 1812. Spokesmen like John Rolph also believed that loyalty could be inculcated through such institutions as schools. A measure of conservative consensus about the nature of loyalty, which was shaped by the Reformers, had emerged by the end of the 1820s.

The emotional responses of both Tories and Reformers to the Alien Question drew other groups into the debate over loyalty. The Methodists, for example, were forced to defend their loyalty in the face of Tory attacks on their connections with American Conferences and their apparent alliance with the provincial Reformers. The responses of prominent Methodist spokesmen, such as Egerton Ryerson, illuminate further the concept of loyalty in Upper Canada.

Born in the Bosom of Loyalty: Egerton Ryerson and the Methodists in Upper Canada

During the controversy generated by the Alien Question, the idea of loyalty became increasingly politicized as Tories and Reformers developed different definitions of the loyal subject in Upper Canada. By the late 1820s other groups, the basis of whose definition was not political, had been drawn into the debate over the nature of loyalty. The most important such group was the Episcopal Methodists whose numbers totalled perhaps as many as 6,100 members by 1824.[1] They were criticized for their disloyalty by Tory spokesmen such as the Anglican archdeacon of York, John Strachan, because they were seen to be ignorant, religious enthusiasts who maintained close connections with American Conferences; the sect was tainted by religious dissent and republicanism. This perception was reinforced by the Methodist association with the growing Reform opposition to the provincial administration. As a result they remained outside the social and political mainstream of the province.

Methodist leaders, and Egerton Ryerson in particular, rejected the Tory charge of disloyalty. In response to their critics they articulated what might be called a Methodist conception of loyalty. This position reflected a complex set of sociopolitical assumptions to which, it has been suggested, "no simple label can be attached ... Their position was ... many-sided and certainly not fixed."[2] Drawing upon the Toryism of English Wesleyanism and the Loyalist tradition, Ryerson sought to demonstrate Methodist loyalty; he stressed as well the argument that loyalty could be inculcated through state-aided education. Moreover, as the increasing radicalism of men like Mackenzie polarized Upper Canada in the 1830s, and as the Methodists' increasing popularity confirmed their desire to be accepted as respectable, Ryerson and others came to support

the administration. Many Methodists became part of the broad conservative consensus which dominated the province.

The conservatism of these Methodists was tempered by their attempts to resolve their opposition to church establishment, and
Anglican pretensions to exclusive control of the Clergy Reserves
and education on the one hand, and their fears of disloyalty on
the other. By rejecting the exclusiveness of the High Tories, this
group of Methodists strengthened moderate conservatism in the
province, and broadened that ideological base.[3] They accepted the
legitimacy of dissent because of their own religious experience; they
accepted the assimilative myth already enunciated by many Reformers and their loyalty became an expression of provincial feeling.
The idea of loyalty was fundamental to Methodist social and political attitudes; Egerton Ryerson continued to stress this theme into
the 1880s when he wrote that "the birthplace of Methodism in Canada was in the bosom of loyalty."[4] Ryerson, who was editor of
The Christian Guardian for much of the period between its establishment in 1829 and 1840, became one of the most prominent spokesmen for conservative Methodist views and one of the most
successful defenders of the Methodists in Upper Canada. Ryerson
was born into a Loyalist family in Norfolk County in 1803. Although his parents, especially his mother, were devout Anglicans,
Egerton, like his three older brothers, sought religious fulfilment in
evangelical Methodism. He became an itinerant preacher and in
1825 was assigned to the York and Yonge Street circuit.[5] Ryerson
always believed that he was more concerned with the spiritual than
the secular affairs of man; in the first issue of the *Christian Guardian* he declared: "we consider it our duty and feel it to be our vo-
cation to devote our limited researches, talents and influence, to
the high and holy interests of morality and religion – to the spiritual welfare of immortal and redeemed men."[6] Religion shaped
Ryerson's political perceptions and ultimately drew him into debate with John Strachan over their differing perceptions of Upper
Canadian society.[7]

Strachan, born a Scottish Presbyterian, had come to Upper Canada to tutor the children of Richard Cartwright. By 1812 he had
joined the Church of England, established a school in Cornwall
where he taught many future members of the elite, and then moved
to York to assume a parish. By the 1820s Strachan was a member
of both the Executive and Legislative Councils and was for a time
the most influential member of the Family Compact.[8] He believed
that the continued existence of Upper Canada was dependent upon
both the continued attachment to the imperial connection and the

development of a conservative society distinct from the United States. He was also a vocal defender of the Anglican establishment in the province and consequently injected his Toryism with a strong sense of religious mission.[9] These themes were the fundamental bases of Strachan's thought and his responses to other questions, including religious and educational ones, were shaped by his High Tory views.

In order to maintain the conservative social order which was essential for Upper Canadian development, Strachan had to ensure that harmony existed between the religious and political institutions of the province. He stressed the importance of a state-supported church: "There should be in every Christian country an established religion, otherwise it is not a Christian but an Infidel country."[10] In turn, the church would encourage loyalty to the state; Strachan asked: "Can it be doubted that it is only through the Church and its Institutions, that a truly English character and feeling can be given to or preserved among the population of any Foreign possession?"[11]

Strachan also saw the school as an agent of socialization;[12] the purpose of education was to produce a talented governing elite which embodied proper moral values, such as Christian virtue, rationality and the discipline of passions; in short, it produced men of respectability: "it is only by a well instructed population that we can expect to preserve our excellent constitution and our connexion with the British Empire – or give that respectability to the Province which arises from an intelligent Magistracy, and from having all public situations filled with men of information."[13] Strachan emphasized the importance of the school as a means to inculcate loyalty; in his address at the last annual examination at his Cornwall school he said: "This we deem an object of the greatest importance; living under the best practical form of government, the only one which, in the present wreck and degradation of nations, can be said to cherish true and rational freedom, it is necessary that those that are born its subjects should be aware of its perfection ... To speak of Great Britain is indeed delightful ..."[14] In addition, education must be directed by "Tutors, not merely eminent for their learning, but for their attachment to the British Monarchy, and to the Established Church ..."[15] He repeated this theme in his plea for a provincial university; such an institution "would tend to establish a most affectionate connexion between this Colony and the Parent State ... [and] would gradually infuse into the whole population, a tone and feeling entirely English ..."[16] Ultimately Strachan believed that the imperial connection was more dependent upon the strength of the established church and the educational system than upon other factors: "It is to be lamented that this great country [England], in establishing colonies, has chiefly confined her views to pecuniary advantage, and seems entirely to have forgotten that the attachment of foreign settlements depends infinitely more upon moral and religious feeling than the political arrangement or commercial profit."[17]   By the 1820s the Archdeacon of York became more insistent that the Church of England was to be recognized as the established church with exclusive control of the Clergy Reserves and the school system.   The Anglican Church, it was argued, had proven its loyalty during the American Revolution and its position had been confirmed by the Constitutional Act.[18] As a result, Strachan was sensitive to any challenge to the exclusiveness of the Church of England, especially from the Methodists.

Anglican opposition to the Methodists was based upon theological and political factors. Antipathy to the sect had been apparent since the early days of settlement in Upper Canada; Bishop Jacob Mountain of Quebec had feared the threat to social stability posed by the Methodists whom he saw as "a set of ignorant enthusiasts, whose preaching is calculated only to perplex the understanding, & corrupt the morals & relax the nerves of industry, & disolve [sic] the bonds of society."[19] Moreover, the loyalty of the group was brought into question because Upper Canada was part of a Methodist Conference located in New York State and many preachers were American. In 1814 General Sir Gordon Drummond called the Methodists "itinerant fanatics, enthusiastic in political as well as religious matters," who came in from the United States to disseminate "their noxious principles."[20]

Although the Methodists comprised a significant proportion of the population, the sect had not been active politically before the War. S.D. Clark suggested that the Methodist appeal was otherworldly and the influence of the preachers "was one directed not so much to making people dissatisfied with their system of government as to make them completely indifferent towards it, and it was in the development of this attitude of political indifference that their influence was most felt as a force weakening a sense of loyalty and attachment to colonial institutions of government and to the British Crown."[21] Many Methodist societies, though, dissolved during the War of 1812 because their links with the United States could not be sustained. G.F. Playter, a nineteenth-century Methodist historian, stated that after the War some itinerant preachers did not return from the United States and those of American origin who remained in Upper Canada were "of moderate politics and prudent conduct."[22] The Methodists had no desire to offend the provincial authorities.

To the Tory mind, already acutely conscious of the American threat, apparent Methodist indifference to the survival of the province was extremely suspect. And John Strachan became the most ardent post-war critic of the Methodists.[23] Before 1820 Strachan was quite optimistic about Anglican fortunes in Upper Canada; it has been suggested that he assumed that "denominational loyalties were in a state of flux and that a tolerant and flexible Church of England would induce most Upper Canadians to sever their connection with dissent."[24] While he had "serious political objections" to the Methodists, he was not prepared to antagonize members of the sect because "they have been useful in preserving a religious feeling in many parts of the Province, where it was becoming dead ... and all must acknowledge their merit, in undergoing many fatigues and privations to reclaim the vicious, and to soften the hardened. Such benevolent exertions ought to be applauded ..."[25] But the continued vulnerability of the Church of England in the face of increased opposition to its established position tempered Strachan's toleration of religious dissent.

The Archdeacon of York had strong theological reasons for being critical of the sect; the Methodists believed that faith alone was the sole means of attaining salvation and their conversion process occurred in the midst of emotional hysteria. He deplored their excesses: "The Methodists are making good progress among us and, filling the country with the most deplorable fanaticism. You can have almost no conception of their excesses. They will bawl twenty of them at once, tumble on the ground, laugh, sing, jump and stamp ..."[26] Strachan emphasized the concept of "rational devotion" and believed that "reason must always be the guiding and ruling faculty – the affections must not lead but follow ..."[27] Salvation was "not to be accomplished in a few minutes or hours or days as it were a miracle – it is the work of time or mature reflection of continued industry of steady perseverance."[28] Therefore Strachan's opinions reflected the belief that salvation was within the reach of all men: "it was attained through faith *and* virtuous conduct ..."[29]

While Strachan's emphasis upon the rationality of Anglican doctrines made him critical of the emotional excesses associated with Methodism, he also opposed the Methodist attempts to separate church and state. He believed that only through an established Church of England could social order be maintained and asked:

"Have not the Methodists in the Province in connexion with the American Conference ever shewn themselves the enemies of the Established Church? Are they not at this moment labouring to separate religion from the State, with which it ought ever to be firmly united, since one of its great objects is to give stability to good Government, nor can it be separated with impunity in any country?"[30] Because of their opposition to the established church, the Methodists were perceived to be dangerous; as well, their close ties with American Conferences made them disloyal. Strachan asserted that the "religious teachers" in Upper Canada, excluding the Anglicans and "a very few respectable Ministers" of the Church of Scotland, "come almost universally from the Republican States of America, where they gather their knowledge and form their sentiments." These dissenting preachers fostered the spread of republican ideas in the province and, as a consequence, "the mass of our population will be nurtured in hostility to our Parent Church, nor will it be long till they imbibe opinions any thing but favourable to the political Institutions of England."[31] Other members of the Upper Canadian administration shared Strachan's belief that the Methodists were disloyal because of their American ties. The Lieutenant Governor, Sir Peregrine Maitland, expressed his fears in a letter to the Colonial Secretary: "if to preserve the allegiance of the people to the government of the Mother Country be held as an object of importance," then the presence of American Methodist preachers in the province could not be "too strongly discountenanced."[32]

In response to official suspicions that the Methodists were "disaffected to the Government and institutions of the country"[33] and to Strachan's accusations of disloyalty contained in his sermon delivered after the death of Bishop Mountain, Egerton Ryerson, a twenty-three-year-old preacher, was drawn into the debate over loyalty. Ryerson did not accept the Tory definition of the loyal subject and developed a more moderate position. Methodist loyalty remained conservative because it was shaped by the English Toryism represented by John Wesley and by the Loyalist tradition embodied by Ryerson himself. Ryerson accepted many Tory views, such as the belief in the benefits of the British Constitution and antipathy to republicanism. The polarization of politics in the 1830s also reinforced Ryerson's fear of radicalism and his distrust of factious opposition to the administration. Consequently, he incorporated many Tory ingredients into the Methodist idea of loyalty.

Ryerson drew heavily upon late eighteenth-century English Toryism as a source for his views. John Wesley, the founder of English Methodism, was profoundly conservative; he believed "God not the people to be the origin of all civil power." He also stressed unquestioning commitment to the Crown: if "a man does not love the King, he cannot love God." Wesley's religious and political views were cemented by his loyalty: "Loyalty is with me an essential branch of religion ... There is the closest connection, therefore, between my religious and political conduct."[34]

In addition to English Methodism, Ryerson's views were shaped by his study of English political theorists like Locke, Blackstone, and Paley.[35] He believed that: "Civil government is a social compact, or voluntary association, formed and established on some general rules, or principles, which are called the *constitution* ..."[36] Civil government was also sanctioned by "God, who is the Fountain of law, order, and regularity" and, hence, "every member of civil society ought to obey the government."[37] Ryerson's support of the British constitution was enhanced by the benefits inherent in its balance; he quoted Dr Adam Clarke to that effect: "this government [of Great Britain] possesses in itself all the excellencies of the three forms. It can only become *Corrupt* when any of the three estates *preponderates* over the rest. In its nature and regular operation, it secures the *prerogative* of the *monarch*; it preserves the honor and *property* of the nobility; it respects and secures the *rights* of the *people*; it is, in a word, a *limited monarchy*, a *popular aristocracy*, and an *ennobled democracy*. God grant it permanence!" The balanced constitution ensured both good government and social equipoise as it provided "a tranquility, a fairness of various emulation, a spirit of public enterprize, a pledge of constitutional security, and an impetus to religious industry ..."[38] Thus, it strengthened the loyalty of the province.

The focus of Ryerson's loyalty was the colonial governor, who symbolized both the balanced constitution and the imperial connection. No opposition to the governor could be countenanced: "[The] civil governor, who administers the laws of a state according to its *constitution* is the *minister of God* ... if he make [sic] no attempt to change the constitution, nor break [sic] the compact between him and the people; there is, therefore, no legal ground of opposition to his civil authority ..."[39] Moreover, Ryerson was not prepared to accept any change in the Constitution because of the explicit threat to political and social stability; he wrote: "I am opposed to the introduction of any new and untried theories of government ... In civil affairs I take my stand upon the established constitution of the country."[40] He resisted the demands of Reformers, such as Robert Baldwin, for responsible government because such a change would weaken the royal prerogative, upset the constitutional balance and ultimately sever the imperial connection. If the executive was to be drawn from the majority in the assembly, "then the Government is no longer administered by the Representative of the King ... the authority and prerogative of the crown are annihilated, and the Province becomes an independent Republic ..."[41] Ryerson's perception that any political change, including the moderate reform represented by responsible government, was a republican innovation, and so disloyal, revealed that this Methodist spokesman shared common ground with the political conservatism of his most severe Tory critics.

Ryerson's conservatism was reinforced by his Loyalist heritage. His father was a Loyalist and many early Loyalists, such as the Hecks, George Neal, and William Losee, were Methodists. The foundations of Methodism in Upper Canada were established "by men who had borne arms in defence of their King and country."[42] During the War of 1812 the Methodists had proven their loyalty once again; Ryerson declared: "not one ... deserted from the army – not one of them turned traitor to his country – some of the local preachers, at the alarm of greatest danger, shouldered their muskets and fearlessly stood forward in the hottest battles to defend their country ..."[43]

The Methodists were loyal and sought to inculcate that sentiment in Upper Canada; like the Tories, they believed that the church and the school were agents of socialization which could be used to buttress the society and the government. The Methodist Conference stated: "Deeply impressed with a due sense of the advantages derived from the connexion existing between this Province and the Mother Country, it will be alike our duty and delight to inculcate, by precept and example, on the numerous people under our pastoral care and institution, those scriptural principles of piety and loyalty which are essential to their peace and prosperity, and to the perpetuation of that connexion."[44] The role of the school, like that of the church, was to inculcate proper moral values. Ryerson believed that civil disorder and disloyalty were linked to ignorance; the purpose of education was to make "this country British in domestic feeling, as I think it now is intentionally at least in loyalty."[45]

While Ryerson accepted many of the components of Tory loyalty, its exclusiveness posed a dilemma. That exclusiveness was directed most explicitly against his fellow Methodists and he was, in fact, drawn into the political arena because of his opposition to church establishment. He made it clear that he would not criticize the Church of England: "I firmly believe in her doctrines, I admire her liturgy, and I heartily rejoice in the success of those principles ..." But the idea of an established church degraded the true purpose of religion: "When we see the heavenly affection which she [the church] infuses into the minds of men represented as nothing more than an attachment to a particular constitution, we are sensible that the religion of the meek Saviour is being made to bleed by a wound more fatal than those which are inflicted by the ravings of infidelity."[46] Drawing upon the Methodist belief that salvation was "free in all and free for all," and, therefore, all men were equal before God, Ryerson argued that all should be equal before the state as well: "The doctrine of universal equality before the law was the natural result of the doctrine of equality before God in both creation and redemption ..."[47] The best means to ensure religious equality within the society was to maintain the separation of church and state. The establishment of one church meant that "one portion or denomination of the social compact" enjoyed "privileges and immunities which are withheld from another."[48] Every man, Ryerson wrote, has an "undeniable and inviolable right of private judgement in all matters of religious faith and duty ... Religion being a spiritual system of inspired truth, must be promoted only by moral and spiritual influences, and not only by the coercion of civil government."[49] The threat to the religious rights of the individual posed by church establishment made the separation of church and state essential.

Supporters of the "state religion" were also more corrupt than members of other denominations; their choice was often influenced by "motives of worldly honor or gain, or both." Their loyalty was ultimately suspect because they would abandon the Church of England if more promising prospects were available. A Methodist, on the other hand, was truly loyal; he "was induced to embrace his system of faith and practice by an honest submission to what he conceives to be the truth, in opposition to the allurements of arbitrary fashion and the seductive maxims of popular policy."[50] The motives of the Methodists were pure because of the moral commitment associated with their religious choice.

The coercion and corruption linked to church establishment weakened Upper Canadian society; moreover, Strachan's claim that only the Church of England could strengthen loyalty was also challenged. Ryerson asserted that the province was loyal without a strong Anglican establishment: "Your general design appears to be to infuse into the minds of the inhabitants of these Provinces a tone and feeling *entirely English* – to give the *Clergymen* of the

Church of England the *sole direction* of education and to bring the whole population of these Provinces into the *communion* of the Church of England. [Yet] ... the tone and feelings of the population in these Provinces are already British, and to intimate the reverse, is a barefaced slander upon their tried loyalty."[51] A report of the Assembly emphasized the same theme; church establishment, it was argued, "cannot be necessary for the security of the Government [because] the loyalty of the people is deep and enthusiastic ... Religious instruction ... will promote and strengthen loyalty ... but no more when communicated by clergymen of the church of England than by those of any other sect, and probably less if they are ... political teachers and servants of the state ..."[52]

With a loyal population the attempts of the government to support the exclusive claims of the Anglicans simply created social and religious inequalities in the province; the administration's actions were "an infringement and absolute outrage"[53] upon the rights of the people and thus disturbed the social harmony necessary for political tranquility. Ryerson believed that the best means to ensure loyalty was to oppose the divisiveness of church establishment and encourage a policy of "Equal religious rights and privileges among all denominations of His Majesty's subjects."[54] He reinforced this argument by linking it to the Loyalist tradition: "it was the Loyalists of America, and their descendents in Upper Canada, who first lifted up the voice of remonstrance against ecclesiastical despotism ... and unfurled the flag of equal religious rights and liberties for all religious persuasions."[55] Consequently Ryerson's views reflected both Toryism and some of the traditional arguments of the provincial oppositionists.

Ryerson was convinced that the Methodists were attacked because they sought "to promote liberal policy in the administration of the government";[56] in other words, it was due to their hostility to the idea of close church-state relations. The Tory administration equated religious dissent with political dissent: "[In] ... worshipping God according to the dictates of their consciences, they [the Methodists] differ in some of their religious opinions from a Sect, the principle members of which, possessing a controuling [*sic*] influence in the Executive, have laboured to identify their religious notions with the Civil Government and to saddle their articles of faith and form of worship upon the people as the *established* religion of the country, and consequently that all who did or should *dissent* from this so-called Established Religion, must be viewed and represented as enemies to our Civil Institutions."[57] Ryerson refused to accept this argument on Tory terms; while he opposed the Anglican establishment, he was, and would remain, loyal to the government: "however many and great objections I may have to a religious Establishment in Canada, I have no objections to the civil government. I am a British-born subject; and by my paternal and personal feelings, I am unwaveringly attached to the British Constitution."[58]

Accordingly, Ryerson included the concept of legitimate religious dissent within his definition of loyalty; true loyalty, he argued, "does not imply a passive submission to all those measures which may be introduced and pressed forward by professed subjects, or ministers, or functionaries." Political dissent "when the object is to *improve a deficient and inadequate state of the supreme Government*," was not disloyal.[59] The loyal citizen could be defined as follows: "None are so truly loyal and obedient to the laws under which they live as those who feel that, under the government of those laws, they are not only men, but *free* men. Such is every Briton, whether he be born or live in Great Britain or in Canada."[60] This justification for dissent was not limited to individual expressions and it needed only to be secularized to be equated with the position the Reformers had been working out in the debate over the Alien Question.

Methodists' loyalty was also shaped by their commitment to the society in which they lived; Ryerson embraced the assimilative myth which had been articulated by the Reformers during the Alien Question. He defended the Methodist attachment to Upper Canada: "As to patriotism and loyalty, we shrink not from a comparison, paternally and personally, with any of our slanderers, and we may venture to affirm that those preachers who faced the winter's storm and the summer's heat, followed the first influx of emigration into the country, kept pace with the sound of the axe through the tractless forests, and scattered *cots* of the wilderness, and planted the pure doctrines of Methodism in every township in the province; – such preachers have given much more substantial proofs of their patriotism and love of Wesleyan Methodism than any cooped-up growling polemic, whose greatest labour consist in 'slanderously accusing' those whose self-denial and industry, and devoted zeal, he has no disposition to emulate."[61] Ryerson further believed that, in spite of the heterogeneity of the population, settlers in the province would become Canadian: "From whatever part of Great Britain or Ireland a man may emigrate, when he settles in Canada, are not all his interests Canadian? Is it not in Canada, then, that his all becomes invested and involved? CANADA is their HOME in whatever part of the world they may have been born, and any attempt to excite feelings from the place of their birth against those who have been born in the place of their adopted residence, is unpatriotic, unchristian and unnatural."[62] His loyalty became an expression of provincial feeling as well as a commitment to the British connection.

Ryerson broadened the Tory definition of the loyal subject to include the Methodists. By rejecting the exclusiveness of Toryism through an affirmation of the legitimacy of religious dissent to protect individual rights and an emphasis upon the accommodative nature of Upper Canadian society, Ryerson contributed to the development of a moderate conservative ideology by the early 1830s.[63] During his trip to England in 1833, the differences between the High and Moderate Tories were reinforced and confirmed Ryerson's place in the moderate camp; he wrote: "An English ultra tory is what we believe has usually been meant and understood in Canada by the *unqualified* term *tory*; that is, a lordling in power, a tyrant in politics, and a bigot in religion. The other branch ... is what is called the *moderate* tory. In political theory he agrees with his high-toned neighbour; but he acts from *religious* principle, and this governs his private as well as public life – he contemplates the good of the nation and the welfare of mankind, without regard to party measures, and uninfluenced by political sectarianism. To this class belongs ... a great majority of the Wesleyan Methodists."[64]

In spite of the apparent conservatism of spokesmen like Ryerson, the Episcopal Methodists continued to be viewed with some suspicion because of their lack of respectability and their American origins. These problems had plagued the sect since the end of the War of 1812 and the Reverend Fitch Reed noted in the 1820s that: "A general prejudice existed against the Society – really, no doubt, because of the obscurity of their social position ... [and] because they were subject to a foreign ecclesiastical jurisdiction, and their ministers and people suffered many annoyances by reason of this foreign element."[65]

The desire to improve the social status of Upper Canadian Methodism characterized the activities of the sect in the 1820s and 1830s. The belief that respectability demonstrated loyalty shaped their social, religious and political responses in this period. The Methodists were becoming integrated into the social mainstream; S.D. Clark suggested that this development was the result of the increasing institutionalization of the sect within the province. There was a decline in camp meetings exhorted by itinerants and a moderation of the evangelical appeal in favour of urban churches led by educated professional preachers.[66] The social status of Methodist congregations also began to change in this period; when Ryerson was preaching at York in 1825 he noted: "Our morning congregation fill the chapel, which was never the case before; and in the evening the chapel will not contain but little more than three-quarters of the people. Last evening, several members of Parliament were present."[67] In the 1830s, the Reverend Benjamin Slight was "amazed" at the social composition of his Amherstburg congregation: "The most respectable people in the town attend, and *all* the most respectable & they regularly attend Sabbath after Sabbath; they also hear with deep and fixed attention. I am given to understand that they have not been accustomed to do so in times past."[68]

As the Methodists became more respectable they also became more fully accommodated within the social structures of the province. In the 1820s the Methodists were viewed as ignorant enthusiasts; by the 1830s they had become another group included in the conservative coalition. Ryerson noted these developments in an editorial published in 1835:

the Methodists were an obscure, a despised, an ill-treated people; in several instances their Ministers were unjustly used and shamefully persecuted by the local authorities of the Government under which they lived, and of which they had always shown themselves faithful and loyal subjects. They were not suffered to solemnize matrimony even in their own Societies; nor had the Church the security of law for a single chapel, parsonage, or acre of land ... *Now* the political condition and relations of the Methodist Connexion are pleasingly changed. It has the law of the land for the security of its chapel property; its Ministers solemnize matrimony to the same extent with Clergymen of the Church of England; the rights and privileges of the body are respected in the highest quarters, as well as by the public generally; and the Government itself proposes the removal of every remaining cause of complaint and dissatisfaction.[69]

In the same editorial Ryerson also noted that the American origins of the Episcopals "excited jealousy and alarm in the minds of many private individuals, as well as the civil authorities." The claim that they were disloyal was rejected; Henry Ryan, the presiding elder of the Genesee Conference, asked: "Who has ever proved any of us to be rebels? ... Can it be proved that any of us has not been conscientious in praying for Kings and all that are in authority?"[70] Ryerson asserted that Methodist preachers "are not republicans; neither are they infected with republican principles; nor have they come 'almost universally from the republican States of America.' Seven-eighths of the teachers are British-born subjects ..."[71] But the Episcopals continued to be attacked and as the numbers of British immigrants to the province increased, their critics included the more conservative and more respectable English Wesleyans.[72] As a result, an Episcopal spokesman like Ryerson became more willing to make compromises in order to ensure denominational harmony.

The period after 1815 had witnessed a struggle between the Episcopals and the Wesleyans over control of the province. The English Methodists were quite willing to adopt Tory tactics to achieve their ends and they attacked the Episcopals over their American ties. The Episcopals noted the activities of Henry Pope, an English Wesleyan missionary in the Niagara District: "Mr. Pope used every means to prejudice the minds of the people against us. He preached 'Loyalty' 'British Authority,' etc. He succeeded in drawing a few away. But his adherents were, chiefly, persons who had been shorn of their spirituality by politics and war."[73] Some Upper Canadian Methodists did not feel that Wesleyans were any better than the Episcopals and asked: "Why should we cast off our preachers that God has owned in the Salvation of our Souls and be to a vast expense in fetching over Preachers from England barely because they were Brittish [sic] born?"[74]

The rivalry between the two groups continued until 1820 when a compromise was reached. The Episcopals were to maintain control of Upper Canada west of Kingston, while the Wesleyans were restricted to Kingston and the Eastern District. Pressure continued to build on the Episcopals to sever their American connection and at the annual conference of Methodist preachers held at Hallowell in Prince Edward County in 1824, a declaration seeking a separate Canadian Conference was passed. Finally, in October 1828, autonomy was achieved with the creation of the Methodist Episcopal Church in Canada.[75] Ryerson believed that such developments removed much of the popular suspicion of the Methodists; only the administration still perceived the Episcopals to be disloyal. A report prepared by the Upper Canadian Assembly seemed to confirm Ryerson's view: "Their influence and instruction, far from being ... a tendency hostile to our institutions, have been conducive in a degree which cannot be easily estimated, to the reformation of their hearers from licentiousness, and the diffusion of correct morals, the foundation of all sound loyalty and social order. There is no reason to believe that, as a body, they have failed to inculcate, by precept and example ... an attachment to the Sovereign and a cheerful and conscientious obedience to the laws of the country."[76]

The attacks on the Episcopal Methodists did not end with the creation of an independent Canadian Church or with the Assembly's stamp of approval. Their loyalty, and hence their respectability, continued to be questioned. Ryerson argued that the Methodists were labelled as disloyal in the hopes that their support among recent British immigrants would be transferred to the Church of England: "Much has been said and re-said about 'Yankee Methodists' in this Province – their 'republicanism, revolutionary principles,' &c. and numerous other frightful things, truly alarming to those strangers among us who are possessed of loyal feelings and have a regard for British rule in Canada, and who have not been long enough in the country to know the real state of things."[77] The desire for increased respectability led some Episcopal leaders, like Egerton Ryerson, to compromise by seeking a union with the Wesleyans whose numbers were ever-increasing as a result of massive immigration from Britain in this period. The pressures of demography and politics produced a union of the two groups in 1833.[78]

The accusations of disloyalty levelled against the Methodists did not end in spite of the developments of the early 1830s. The Kingston *Chronicle* noted that the existence of American Methodists would continue to undermine the British values shaping the society: "The British Conference are no doubt deceived as to the true state of the case, although the motives for their proceedings were meant to be good. They have intended to advance the cause of Religion, by the connection of two denominations ... The one class have been taught to cultivate British feeling and, when necessary, to appeal to British generosity for aid; the other [the Episcopals], have derived their existence, many of their preachers, and in a good degree their support from another people than the British."[79] The loyalty of the British Wesleyans was confirmed, but the Episcopals remained suspect.

Political developments had reinforced the suspicion that Episcopals were disloyal. Until Ryerson made explicit his support for the Tories in 1833, he had been an acknowledged spokesman for the Reform movement because of his opposition to the administration on the question of Anglican exclusiveness. A letter from "An Anglo-Canadian" to the Kingston *Chronicle* expressed support for meetings which would afford the Tories "an opportunity of expressing our abhorrence of the seditious principles of Mackenzie, Ryerson, & Co. ..."[80] Ogle Gowan, the Grand Master of the Orange Order in Upper Canada, believed that Methodist preachers were spreading republican ideas among both inhabitants of Loyalist origin and recent British immigrants: "A large portion of the old Loyalists, having unfortunately deserted the principles, which sustained their Fathers under the privations incident to the first settlement of the country, and many of the European population, being compelled to 'fall in' with the instruction given them in the back Townships, were led over by political preachers of a foreign and hostile sect, and the weekly instructions of their favorite 'Guardian' to embrace revolutionary doctrines, and to seek eagerly after that portion of the press, which the *new light* they observed in religion and politics, told them was *'independent* and liberal'."[81] Even some opponents of the administration distrusted the Methodist-dominated Reform movement; Francis Collins, the Roman Catholic editor of the *Canadian Freeman*, was a constant critic of the "saddlebags" faction in the Assembly.[82]

Ryerson and others recognized that critics of the government were labelled "'Yankees,' 'rebels,' 'demagogues,' 'revolutionists,' &c to make them odious."[83] Accordingly, he sought to dissociate the Methodists from Reformers like William Lyon Mackenzie. Using good Tory arguments, the *Christian Guardian* (edited by James Richardson in Ryerson's absence) accused the radicals of disturbing constitutional balance and social stability by generating a "turbulent spirit" in Upper Canada: "[We] will soon be governed, not by a Monarchy, Aristocracy, or Democracy, but by a *Mob-ocracy*, alike fatal to Religion, good morals, order, peace, and the happiness of society."[84]

Ryerson's suspicion of political radicalism was reinforced during his trip to England in 1833. The radicals, led by Joseph Hume, were both republican and irreligious: "Radicalism in England appeared to us to be another word for Republicanism, with the name of King instead of President ... And perhaps one of the most formidable obstacles to a wise, safe and effectual reform of political, ecclesiastical and religious abuses in England, is, the notorious want of religious virtue or integrity in many of the leading politicians who have lamentably succeeded in getting their names identified with *reform* ..."[85] The close links between the English radicals and those in Upper Canada posed a serious threat to religious and political stability in the provincial society and to the imperial connection. As a result, Ryerson believed the Upper Canadian radicals to be disloyal and his suspicions were confirmed by the publication of Hume's "baneful domination" letter: "Lately the King's ministers were respected and honoured, now they are insulted and abused. Lately attachment and loyalty to the British Government were professed; now *Independence* from its 'baneful domination' is recommended as the motto and watchword of *reformers* ... [I]n so grave a question as whether a country shall remain a monarchy or become a republic – whether it shall remain an appendage of Great Britain or become an American state – every Christian and patriot has a duty to discharge ..."[86]

Ryerson's break with the Reformers, which reflected his own conservative inclinations, produced a tremendous outcry in the province and a split among the Methodists. Although Egerton was supported by his brother, John, who was also "ankious [*sic*] to obtain the confidence of the government & entirely disconnect ourselves with that tribe of villans [*sic*] with whom we have been too intimate ...,"[87] other Methodist preachers, including his younger brother, Edwy, were opposed. They wrote Egerton to say that they "were meeting a 'torrent of opposition' on the circuits, with subscribers cancelling the *Guardian* ... They stated that they and their 'brethren in the ministry' had not changed their political views, that they still felt themselves to be connected with the reformers, and implored Egerton to abandon the quarrel."[88] But as a result of the polarization of politics in the 1830s Egerton Ryerson was no longer prepared to countenance the apparent disloyalty of the radicals; he argued that his views were: "a two-edged sword, that cuts all the representations which have been made in years past against our *loyalty* to the British Government on the one hand, and the misrepresentations of Mr Mackenzie and his partizans on the other. They show the consistency of our *principles* with our professions, and of our *practice* with our duty."[89]

Although the Methodists maintained a lower political profile after 1833, many continued to support the Reform cause. Joseph Stinson, the Wesleyan Missions Superintendent, noted caustically: "There is not a radical meeting in the country at which some of the Methodist leaders and Local preachers are not the most conspicuous characters."[90] Moreover during the "loyalty election" of 1836 seven of the eighteen Radical members elected were Methodists – the largest religious group among the radicals.[91] There was still a strong link between the Episcopals and the radical movement, in spite of the efforts of many Methodist leaders.

The Methodists had gained a large measure of social and political respectability in this period. Their spokesmen articulated more forcefully the traditional Tory interpretation of events. The election of 1836 was seen as a contest of loyalty: "The real question seems to be, whether we shall retain our *colonial relation*, or *govern ourselves* by *elective institutions*. In other words, shall we abide under *British rule* or become a *Republic.*"[92] The editor of the *Christian Guardian* at that time, Ephraim Evans, fully supported the administration of Sir Francis Bond Head and he urged voters to declare "for the continuation of that unrivalled national blessing, the British constitution."[93] Some observers, such as Francis Hincks, believed that the Methodists played a decisive role in the Tory victory in 1836.[94] Although this perception was probably incorrect, the new Assembly did contain a new group: three Canadian Methodist Tories were elected.[95] The Methodists had become another element in the conservative coalition in Upper Canada.[96]

The increased social and political respectability of the Methodists in the 1830s reflected their growing ideological respectability. In response to Tory critics, Methodist spokesmen demonstrated their loyalty and articulated a position which could be accommodated quite easily within Upper Canadian conservatism. Egerton Ryerson, especially, believed that the existence of a distinctive provincial society was predicated upon respect for the Sovereign and the Constitution, "freedom of our institutions, and the excellencies of our civilization; it was strengthened by the imperial connection." Years later, in an address presented to celebrate the battle of Lundy's Lane, he came back to these "true principles of loyalty"; Ryerson said: "Canadian loyalty is a firm attachment to that British Constitution and those British laws ... which best secure life, liberty and prosperity, and which prompt us to Christian and patriotic deeds by linking us with all that is good and noble in the traditions of our national history."[97]

Ryerson and others steered the Methodists between the radicalism of Mackenzie on the one hand and the High Toryism of Strachan on the other. In resisting an Anglican monopoly of the Clergy Reserves and Anglican control of education they defined the issues on which the Compact ultimately lost popular support, but by their social conservatism and defence of the Constitution they also strengthened the moderate conservative element in the province. The defence of Methodist loyalty did not challenge Tory insistence upon the necessity of loyalty but it necessarily rejected exclusiveness as one of the components of loyalty. The Methodists brought into a Tory context an acceptance of the legitimacy of dissent, if only in religious terms; and they adopted the Reformers' concept of the assimilative nature of loyalty in Upper Canadian society. As the Methodists became integrated into the social and political mainstream they became an important part of the conservative consensus that was to dominate the political culture of the province. They broadened the definition of loyalty and therefore made possible the emergence during the early 1830s of moderate Toryism as a significant development in the politics of Upper Canada.

"We Seek Tranquility and Good Government, According to Our Constitution": Moderate Toryism in the 1830s

Not all Upper Canadians were happy with the ideological emphasis that had characterized the political debate of the 1820s. The editor of the Kingston *Chronicle* hoped that politics in the new decade would cease to concentrate "on nice and fanciful distinctions between freedom and prerogative – questions of little or no utility, while the substantial interests of the country were neglected ... Let this Parliament proceed to measures for the improvement of our roads, the increase of our commerce, and the advancement of agriculture." But what he deplored as "the reign of theory"[1] continued in the 1830s: the definition of the loyal subject remained at the centre of political contention.

Upper Canadians became more concerned with the political rather than the ideological components of loyalty in this period. It became the means to differentiate the supporters of two irreconcilable value systems – British monarchy and American republicanism. The Tories framed this debate; loyalty was discussed on their terms and as a result attitudes began to crystallize. Tory loyalty reinforced its emphasis on the imperial connection and on Upper Canada's dependence upon the mother country for its political stability, its defence and its material prosperity. The loss of dependence was equated to the loss of identity; and that loss was threatened by the alarming appearance of a formed opposition to the exclusive leadership of the Tory elite. This view of loyalty excluded the legitimacy of dissent; all Reformers became associated with the radicalism of William Lyon Mackenzie and they were portrayed as factious demagogues seeking to destroy the society. By the time of the "loyalty election" in 1836 the Tories had simplified politics: there were but two choices, loyalty or disloyalty. Explanation of attitudes was no longer necessary. Rhetoric replaced analysis; labels and symbols became the staples of political debate.

This polarization of politics attracted the support of a broad coalition of groups which accepted the central importance of loyalty. Yet within this apparent Tory consensus new ingredients had been added to the concept of loyalty – ingredients which were to prove irreconcilable with the exclusiveness to which the Tory leadership was committed and which gave an ideological basis for the development of moderate Toryism. Moreover, these ideas reflected an increasing acceptance of some moderate Reform assumptions. The definition of the loyal subject became less exclusive; it was broadened to incorporate the belief that loyalty could develop through the process of settlement and the consequent commitment to the community. It was also argued that loyalty could be earned through respectability. The Methodists had staked out a claim to a measure of political legitimacy in this manner and the Orange Order was soon to follow them. Moderate Toryism also developed a more provincial view. There was less unquestioning acceptance of imperial governance and increasingly loyalty was expressed with colonial nationalist rather than Loyalist rhetoric. By the end of the 1830s, the moderate Tories had shaped much of the ideological basis for conservative ideas of loyalty in the province.

To the Tory, Upper Canada was a battleground between two conflicting value systems: on the one hand there was the social and political stability represented by the British constitution and the imperial connection; on the other, the turbulence of American democracy. The Reformers' victory in the elections of 1828 appeared to usher in an age of uncertainty because of the prospect of the triumph of democracy. The *Upper Canada Herald* revealed some of these fundamental fears in an editorial in the mid-1830s: "The present age has been properly characterized as an age of *movement*. Of movement there is plenty; though in some instances it is retrograde. Individuals and bodies of men are in continual motion, which is more or less rapid according to circumstances, yet in few cases so rapid as the ungovernable spirit of the age impetuously requires. In politics the movement is certainly retrograde, for it goes to place power in the hands of those who are least entitled and qualified to use it, and thus only enables them to injure themselves and society, by pulling down the temples of social order on their own heads and on all who are unfortunately included with them in the edifice. The greatest political struggle of the present time is to establish the absolute rule of *democracy* ..."[2] Tory fears about the advance of democracy were directly related to their pessimism about the nature of man. The *Herald* argued that "a great majority of men are ignorant and more or less wicked." Democracy was really "mobocracy" and presented the threat of tyranny of the majority; the editorial continued: "If there is any principle more absurd than another in much of modern legislation, it is the principle that political questions are to be decided by mere numbers; for it assumes that all men are in every respect equal ... With the liberals a man whose mind is but one remove from idiocy, is as competent to legislate as a Newton would be ...Wonderful discovery of modern liberalism! *quantity is* everything – quality nothing!"[3] The perception of a stable, hierarchical society governed by the Tory elite was threatened by the forces of political and social equality. To prevent further decay the Tories demanded loyalty to their vision of Upper Canada.

They further looked to Britain to buttress that vision because the province was perceived to be immature both economically and politically. The imperial connection was necessary for the material progress of Upper Canada; the British Constitutional Society, a Tory organization re-established in 1836 to marshal the forces of loyalty, declared that Upper Canada "principally owes its rapid development in population and wealth to that connexion ..."[4] The province was a society which still required "the most careful nursing" by the mother country. Thomas Dalton, the English-born editor of *The Patriot* and defender of the Compact, believed that the society was evolving, but remained dependent on Britain for "men of intelligence and enterprise ... for a few years longer."[5] The immature state of the society made comparisons with the rapid development of the United States unfair; the *Upper Canada Herald* attacked radicals who "compare the present state of the two countries, but never avert to the *time* which they have respectively taken in order to arrive at that state. Yet to compare the two countries absolutely without reference to time, is as wise and just as it would be to compare a boy of ten years with a youth of eighteen, without any reference to their age ..."[6] The Hamilton *Gazette* echoed that sentiment; the province, it was argued, "cannot stand alone ... United with Great Britain in the fullest and firmest affection, she [Upper Canada] must become great, powerful, prosperous and happy. British capital will flow in, converting the swamps of the country into corn-fields – the forests into meadows and orchards, mines will be dug – canals cut – fabrics erected – new channels of commerce explored – old ones improved, and property ... materially enhanced ..."[7] The Tories looked to the mother country to strengthen the society and make it more attractive in comparison with the apparent prosperity of the United States.

They also saw the imperial connection as a means to ensure the political stability of Upper Canada. The mother country protected the province from "the horrors of revolution, the insecurity of their persons and property, and the experience and tyranny of would-be rulers."[8] The Tories depended upon Britain, according to the *Upper Canada Herald*: "As a people we are minors under guardianship, and can no more expect the entire control of our affairs, than a youth under age could expect the entire control of his estates. Our natural guardian, Great Britain, has always been desirous of promoting our interests and of preparing us for a wise and happy maturity." The British government, it concluded, *"is the Government of Canada."*[9]

In addition to providing political stability, Britain provided a constitutional model for Upper Canada. The *Patriot* praised the "equipoise" in "the settled and admirable Constitution and Government of our country";[10] Ogle Gowan, editor of the Orange journal, *The Antidote*, also stressed the benefits of the balanced constitution: "it defines more accurately and confirms with more certainty, the powers and privileges of all ranks of men ... It allows to every individual some share of power, as well as privilege; and it makes the powers of all to co-operate towards the security of all. It possesses the strength and despatch of monarchy, the wisdom of aristocracy, and the public spirit of democracy."[11] The superiority of the British Constitution was apparent to the Tories; it represented the stability and continuity necessary for social development. Upper Canadians were protected by "a constitution, which has stood the admiration of past ages, and will forever defy the ravages of time."[12] It provided the people with "as much liberty as any people under heaven."[13] Consequently, "the Constitution conferred on us by the Mother Country is well adapted to secure our peace, welfare and good government ..."[14]

Because of the political and material benefits associated with the imperial connection, many Tories believed that the continued existence of the province required British support. In an emotional outburst to the Kingston *Chronicle* "A Subscriber" wrote: "The connection between this Province and the parent state can never be dissolved ... since there exists sterling loyalty in the country ... Upper Canada shall continue to be governed under the mild and paternal rule of the British Crown ..."[15] Chief Justice John Beverley Robinson also believed that "if their independence were granted to them," Upper Canadians "could not maintain it." But loyalty to the British connection would permit the province to continue its development within the imperial context. The people, he argued, "do not waver in their allegiance. This country [Britain] has not the feeling of attachment to create. It is there; it has taken strong root, and has a generous growth; she has only to cultivate and shelter it."[16] In his electoral address of 1836 W.H. Draper, the victorious Tory candidate in Toronto, had announced his determination "to preserve inviolate the connexion of this Province with the beloved Mother Country ... We seek tranquillity and good government, according to our Constitution."[17] The electorate was only too happy to respond in kind; in the Johnstown District the people also sought no "disruption of the happy connexion existing between us and the Mother Country."[18]

Yet many Tories no longer accepted the imperial connection without question. In the 1830s the focus for Tory loyalty was beginning to shift from the mother country to Upper Canada.[19] Tory confidence in British officials was sometimes shaken; in 1833, for example, the Colonial Office ordered the dismissal of the Attorney General, Henry John Boulton, and the Solicitor General, Christopher Hagerman, as punishment for the repeated expulsions of William Lyon Mackenzie from the Assembly. In response, George Gurnett, editor of Courier of Upper Canada, exploded in a fury: "The minds of all the well affected people of the country ... begin to be unhinged. Instead of dwelling with delight and confidence upon their connection with the glorious Empire of their sires, with a determination to support that connection, as many of them have already supported it, with their fortunes or their blood, their affections are already more than half alienated from the Government of that country and in the apprehension that the same insulting and degrading course of policy towards them is likely to be continued; they already begin to 'cast about' in 'their minds eye,' for some new state of political existence, which shall effectively put the Colony beyond the reach of injury and insult from any and every ignoramus whom the political lottery of the day may chance to elevate to the Colonial Office."[20] Even John Beverley Robinson, the archetypal High Tory, believed that Britain should not interfere in the internal affairs of the province; the mother country should only control obvious imperial concerns such as defence and foreign policy.[21] Therefore Tory loyalty was beginning to express a sense of provincial feeling by the mid-1830s.

Upper Canadians reinforced this provincialism by drawing upon their own past for traditions which strengthened loyal sentiment. The example of the Loyalists remained paramount. In an address delivered at a town meeting in Kingston in 1832, J.S. Cartwright, the son of the Loyalist merchant, Richard Cartwright, explored this theme: "The American Loyalists, a set of gallant men, many of whom, were the greatest Landholders in the United States – Excuse me sir for exhibiting any feeling at the mention of these noble Britons, it may be that they are considered as foolish, and visionary enthusiasts in the cause of loyalty ... They contended for the constitution, and the rights of the Crown – they had been taught to regard the supremacy of parliament as co-extensive with the British dominions; and they hazarded their lives and fortunes, in attempting to put down Rebellion and preserve the unity of the Empire ... [They chose] to find a home in the wilderness under the sanction, and protection of their Sovereign, than remain citizens of a nation whom they regarded as Rebels."[22] The belief that the Loyalists had sacrificed everything to prove their loyalty to the crown and constitution was central to Tory thought. The idea of Upper Canada as a special Loyalist homeland remained, as did the hope, articulated by the *Upper Canada Herald*, that the Loyalist example might "serve to inculcate the noble sentiments and principles for which they contended ..."[23] The qualities exhibited by the founders of the province were required of the population in the 1830s as well; they formed "the sheet anchor of a conservative government."[24]

Yet within this loyal society dissent continued to exist. The Tories feared that the fundamental nature of the changes sought by radicals like Mackenzie, including "the overthrow of the whole imperial-colonial structure and the creation ... of a 'social democracy' in Upper Canada,"[25] would destroy their conservative community. Radicalism would lead to the "subversion of monarchical institutions – and the certain introduction of democracy ..."[26] More important, though, was the fact that the Tories saw no need for any changes; Upper Canadians enjoyed the full benefit of their rights, liberties, and properties. In an extended address on passing the sentence of death upon Samuel Lount and Peter Mathews after the rebellion, Chief Justice Robinson gave striking evidence of how persistent and unqualified was the Tory belief that there were no real grievances in the province. He said:

A few months ago, you were, both of you, living in the enjoyment of health and liberty, under circumstances as favourable, perhaps, to happiness, as the condition of human nature admits of ... A long residence in this Province had given you the opportunity of acquiring property, and had enabled you to find a suitable field for your exertion. You were not the tenants of rigorous and exacting landlords; you were not burthened with taxes for the State ... you held that middle station of life that which none is happier; you were your own masters ... You have lived in a country where every man who obeys the law is secure in the protection of life, liberty, and property; under a form of government, which has been the admiration of the world for ages ... In short, you were living in the enjoyment of as full a security against injury of every kind as any people in the world.[27]

If Upper Canadians were blessed with every natural advantage, in Tory eyes, the emergence of discontent was the result of factious opponents to the administration who introduced dissension and discord into the society. A letter from "A Subscriber" to the Kingston *Chronicle* argued: "There exists in the public mind many discordant materials and conflicting sentiments which form the fuel for continual excitement ... It must be admitted, however, that this state of affairs is not owing to any innate quality – any constitutional bias in the people, but is altogether an affair of habit. The proneness to excitement – the fondness of controversy – the devotion to party purposes, manifested on the part of the public, is entirely artificial ..."[28] The Tories simply could not accept the concept of legitimate opposition; the *Upper Canada Herald* noted that "In every community there are some discontented spirits who will strive to obtain power by flattering and deceiving the people. These selfish and crafty wrigglers for power will surely though slowly destroy the people's fidelity to the established principles of the best policy existing ..."[29]

Tory fears of opposition were intensified by the fact that their critics were no longer acting as individuals as Thorpe or Gourlay had done; the Reform movement presented the spectre of a formed opposition – of a party.[30] Since the late 1820s, with the creation of the York Central Committee, the Reformers had become increasingly organized, with predictable consequences according to the Tories. Party destroyed the social harmony and political consensus necessary for stability. Furthermore, as the American historian, Richard Hofstadter, has noted in his study of Anglo-American views of opposition, party was thought to be "the instrument with which some small and narrow special interest could impose its will upon the whole of society, and hence ... become the agent of tyranny."[31] Accordingly, Upper Canadian Tories, like Thomas Dalton, editor of *The Patriot*, vowed to remain "detached from party ... I have clearly understood what is meant by PARTY. I take it to be a knot here, a junta there, or a cabal anywhere, opposed to the settled and admirable Constitution and Government of our Country, with views of appropriating power and emolument to themselves, at the expense of long-established, and generally venerated institutions."[32]

Party was also perceived to be an American innovation; it was "anti-British and of a republican tendency." Consequently, the activities of the opposition were not only a danger to the Constitution but were disloyal as well. The population of Upper Canada was warned "against the machinations and intrigues of a few individuals, who unfortunately, are led by those, whose hostility to the British Constitution is such, that they would sacrifice any and every thing to pull it down, in order that they might build up a Republic on its ruins."[33] The Tories continually returned to this theme: the success of their opponents would mark the end of Upper Canada as a British colony. The radicals, according to the former King's Printer, Charles Fothergill, in his electorial address of 1834, were "deceivers and *would be destroyers* ... seeking to blast the fairest hopes of this great and rising Colony, and erect their own fortunes amidst the general devastation their mad schemes must create." The opposition was thus disloyal because they sought to tear Upper Canada away from "the greatest empire at this day upon earth ..."[34] The Hamilton *Gazette* also attacked "The Faction" of Bidwell, Rolph, and Mackenzie; it was viewed as the "greatest impediment to rendering Upper Canada what it ought to be" because it pursued its party goals with impunity "at the *sacrifice* of the peace, prosperity and all the best interests of the Province." The "*half-civilized* republicanism" of the radicals threatened to subdue the "indomitable spirit of the British population."[35]

The continued existence of Upper Canada as a British society was further jeopardized because the opponents of the government were "mostly of American origin" and they were supported by the inhabitants of American background.[36] Sir John Colborne, the Lieutenant Governor, believed that support for the radicals was greatest "among settlers who entered the Province about 25 years ago from Pennsylvania, and the American population of the Townships of Markham and Vaughan in this country, connected with them ... Mechanics who lived for some time in the States before they settled in the Province. The Colonial Advocate published by Mackenzie is taken in generally by the American population, and has made them discontented."[37] The Tory suspicion of the potential disloyalty of·the American settlers in their midst had not abated; in fact the political controversies of the 1830s merely confirmed their view that the Americans were republicans whose values could infect the loyal population. George Gurnett, editor of the *Gore Gazette*, argued that this group was by inclination disloyal; American inhabitants "who were born and educated under republican institutions, and who ... have been thought to view those institutions as the perfection of political Government ... have also been taught to despise and ridicule the monarchical system. Such persons – whatever may be their protestations of loyalty – cannot in reality appreciate our institutions or feel an attachment for them ..."[38]

By labelling their opponents as disloyal, the Tories sought to polarize the population over the issue of loyalty and, as a result, isolate the radicals. As early as 1832 a Tory political meeting in Middlesex County emphatically concluded that Upper Canada was divided into two groups: "The one will be composed of Loyal men – the other of Disaffected men, of Republicans, of Revolutionists, and of Rebels. Let every man therefore ask himself this question. Shall I stand up on the same side with these Revolutionary Republicans – on the same side with these Rebels – or shall I stand up on the side of Loyalty?"[39] During the election of 1834 the Tories focused exclusively on the issue of loyalty in response to both the increased radicalism of men like Mackenzie and the publication of the English radical Joseph Hume's "baneful domination" letter which called for the separation of the colonies from the mother country. In a masterful display of overstatement, the Kingston *Chronicle* thundered that the election would "stamp the political character of a rapidly improving country ... it will either encourage or annihilate forever the artful and heartless schemes of a disorganizing junto and their duped adherents." It was a contest between two parties: "one steadily supporting the colonial government, in the general policy of administration, and invariably upholding the connection with the parent empire – the other always opposing the government ... and treating with cold indifference the ties of union which bind the colony to Great Britain."[40]

The exploitation of loyalty as an ideological weapon proved unsuccessful in 1834 and reflected the basic weakness of the Tory position; but the Tories were not deterred and they continued to attack the disloyalty of their opponents. By 1836, moreover, they had the support of a powerful and vocal ally, the new Lieutenant Governor, Sir Francis Bond Head. Although Head had dismissed his Council over the question of ministerial responsibility, he interpreted the subsequent election as a contest between monarchy and republicanism. The election marked the final opportunity to maintain the British character of the province and check its drift towards republicanism; the contest was a "moral war ... between those who were for British institutions, against those who were for soiling the empire by the introduction of democracy." Head concluded that if he did not overpower "Democracy ... it would overpower me."[41]

Head also realized that he had to crush the radicals before they gained more strength. The existence of factious opposition disturbed both the political tranquility and the material progress of the province; as a result, the insecurities of the population about their future were increased and their doubts about the benefits of the imperial connection were fed. Head was determined to prove the strength of the government and reinforce the loyalty of the people; he wrote to the Colonial Office: "as long as the people in the remote Districts are allowed to believe that the Government of this Province feels itself insecure, so long will they be led to attach themselves to whatever they conceive has Stability and Strength, but if their own Interests be appealed to, if they find that we are anxious to infuse among them Capital and Population (both of which they ardently desire), and that nothing but Dissension prevents it, they will, I firmly believe, very quickly correct for themselves the greatest of all their Grievances, namely a Factious Opposition to the British Government."[42] The Lieutenant Governor also believed that he had a vast reservoir of loyal support upon which he could draw. He declared that "The people of Upper Canada detest democracy; they revere their Constitutional Charter, and are consequently staunch in their allegiance to their King." Therefore, if they "were disposed to join heart and hand with me, in loyally promoting the peace and prosperity of the Province, they shall find me faithfully devoted to their service. In the mean while I will carefully guard the Constitution of the country."[43]

Sir Francis Bond Head became the rallying point for the Tories in 1836; he symbolized both the authority of the Crown and the strength of the imperial connection. *The Patriot*, for example, suggested: "If there be on earth, a condition supereminently enviable, it is that of a Governor, feeling the wants and imagining the good, of the beings he is set over in authority."[44] The people of Upper Canada were prepared to support the Governor because he represented the link between the province and the mother country. A political meeting in Lanark resolved, in 1836, that: "as subjects of the British Crown and BORN on BRITISH SOIL, we hold it the first of our constitutional duties to preserve inviolate the rights and prerogatives of our Sovereign, as well as to watch for the liberties of the subject and on all occasions to strengthen the link of connection with our Mother Country ..."[45]

By the time of the loyalty election of 1836 several themes which had shaped Tory assumptions had been drawn together and were crystallized. To the Tory, loyalty was not just a set of attitudes; it had become the central, indeed the only, political issue. It polarized the population of Upper Canada. The loyal forces were to be maintained and strengthened while the disloyal elements had to be eliminated from the political spectrum. The overwhelming Tory victory in 1836 seemed to confirm the strength of loyal forces in the province. The Toronto *Albion* noted that the success of the Tories was due to "the appeal made to the people by our excellent Lieutenant Governor, [which] has been responded to with becoming spirit and patriotism." *The Patriot* stated that the Upper Canadian had been summoned "to the support of his King and Constitution, and to the defence of all that is dear to him in life ..." John Neilson, editor of the Quebec *Gazette*, who had broken with Papineau over the same issue, observed the results as an outsider: "The inhabitants of Upper Canada have nobly vindicated the character of loyalty which they acquired during the last war ... They have repudiated the connection which their representatives had formed with the disaffected in Lower Canada, and disavowed the coalition of Bidwell, Perry, McKenzie & Co. with Roebuck, Papineau & Co., against the rights of the British Crown, the supremacy of the Imperial Parliament, and the connection of the North American colonies with the United Kingdom ... They adhere to the constitution as by law established, to their ancient loyalty and the countries of their birth or of their ancestors ... The conduct of the people of Upper Canada, on this occasion, shews that there is no danger in their enjoying the freedom of the British constitution."[46]

Tory appeals to loyalty apparently made a deep impression upon the population of the province. But Lieutenant Governor Head also appealed directly to the economic interests of the settlers. In a reply to the inhabitants of the Newcastle District, he warned Upper Canadians that "if you choose to dispute with me you will, to use a homely phrase, only quarrel with your own bread and butter."[47] His decision to stop supplies, thereby cutting off support for public works during the summer of 1836, created tremendous discontent. Head, moreover, was prepared to use his government's powers of patronage to ensure the loyalty of the population at this critical time; for example, since their arrival in Lanark County in 1818, the Scottish settlers had demanded the settlement of claims to cover the expenses of emigration. The threat of the massive emigration of this loyal community to the United States in 1836 prompted the government to make an award of 22,000 pounds sterling shortly before the election. The Scots were praised as "a class of persons who, though hitherto unsuccessful as agriculturalists, are represented to be universally industrious, temperate and moral, and faithfully attached to the British Government." Coincidentally, Lanark returned a Tory candidate in the election.[48]

The appeal to loyalty during the 1836 election suggests that a simple issue was necessary to unite the increasing heterogeneous population of Upper Canada. The Tories were successful because they were able to construct a broad coalition of conservative groups in support of the Governor.[49] Included within this coalition were two important political groupings: moderate Tories and some former supporters of moderate Reform. A moderate Tory, according to the Kingston *Chronicle and Gazette*, was devotedly attached to the government, "but is wedded to no abuses, and wishes to improve the condition of the people without encroaching upon the prerogatives of the Crown." The Reformers – "in general men of good sense and commendable enterprise" – were "anxious to extend the power of the people, and wish to a great extent the privilege of ruling themselves without the interference of the Home Government." Although they had been linked with the radicals in the past because of "their zeal for improvement," they were left with no alternative but to support the administration when loyalty became the central issue.[50] The emergence of these moderates was one of the most important political developments of the 1830s.

Moderate Toryism also broadened the conservative ideology of Upper Canada by contributing new ingredients to the concept of loyalty. Loyalty became more accommodative, for example, as moderates began to resist the exclusive claims of the Anglican Church. They tempered their acceptance of a social hierarchy with the belief that Upper Canada offered equality of condition and thus the society could assimilate new settlers; they also accepted the belief that loyalty could be demonstrated through respectability. In short, the moderate Tories had adopted some of the ideas about loyalty articulated by their old Reform opponents.

Political observers in the 1830s had noted the existence of different groups among the supporters of the government when they commented upon the lack of unity among Tories in the Assembly. *The Patriot*, for example, lamented the inability of "the administration party" to dominate the legislature between 1830 and 1834; they "have no acknowledged leader – no mutual understanding – and no common or uniform system of action ..."[51] On questions of church establishment and control of education the High Tory policy of Anglican exclusiveness was unacceptable to dissident Tories,

like William Morris, a Presbyterian from Perth. Moderates first settled on the idea of "Christian establishment," which would see the
proceeds from the sale of the Clergy Reserves divided among all
religious denominations, and then, on state-aided education.[52] The
official position on other issues, such as the principle of primogeni-
ture, banking legislation, and internal improvements, was also challenged by Tories in the Assembly.[53]

Moderate Toryism had appeared in the legislature as early as
1816 when Robert Nichol criticized the administration for its failure
to settle claims for war losses. Robert Nichol did not envision an
idealized, British community developing in Upper Canada; he recognized the "great dissimilarity" between the province and the
mother country.[54] By the 1830s, the nature of these differences was
analyzed in more depth; moderates began to outline the importance of the formative impact of the North American environment
upon the provincial society. There was a limited acceptance of the
concept of equality of condition in Upper Canada. In a pamphlet
written by an anonymous "J.K.," it was suggested that "The inequalities of condition and wealth, – the characteristics of an old
and densely populated country, – are not as yet known in UPPER
CANADA." This theme was illustrated at some length:

The humblest and most uneducated labourer who emigrates to this Province from the Mother country, is able, by the honest sweat of his brow, to
raise himself to the rank of an independent farmer in the course of a very
few years. From the renter of a cottage, and the possessor of a single pig,
he is converted into the master of two hundred acres, of a comfortable
dwelling, barns, cattle, and horses. Instead of a smock-frock he wears the
finest broadcloth. His English meal of potatoes, rarely diversified by a
piece of meat, is here succeeded by the varied produce of the farm ...
[He] enjoys the solid sweets of Canadian independence blended with the
loveliness of his native spot. If he be a man with natural powers at all
above the common, the House of Assembly and Legislative Council are
open to his ambition.[55]

It was as a land of opportunity that Upper Canada could lay claim
to the loyalty of its inhabitants.

Some moderate Tories even adopted the Reform belief that loyalty could develop naturally through the harsh process of settlement in the community; Tory loyalty became more assimilative. The
Loyalist, for example, reprinted an article entitled "The Love of
Country" which stated: "the love of country [may] be styled the
universal sentiment ... for there is no region where humanity can

exist, that it is not found to flourish ... It even appears to grow more intense in proportion as a country labours under natural disadvantages; but the reason is, that where physical circumstances make it difficult for man to sustain his existence, the dangers, the toil, and the incessant activity of rude enterprise, which occupy and support life, produce hardihood of mind and body, which give to all the affections a more decisive energy than they can have where greater opportunities of repose and luxurious enjoyment soften down the human character..."[56] Although Upper Canada offered everything required by its inhabitants, it remained a society threatened from both within and without. These natural disadvantages could be overcome by building up the provincial community; the process of settlement, moreover, required a commitment to the land. It strengthened "the love of country" and thus reinforced loyalty.

Yet the moderate Tory did not believe that all settlers could share this sentiment; while the definition of the loyal subject was broadened, it remained more exclusive than that of the Reformers. The "patriot passion" was more intense "in the boisterous and inclement regions of the north."[57] Therefore, in Upper Canada, loyalty could be restricted to "English, Scotch, and Irish Emigrants, together with the descendents of the U.E. Loyalists ..."[58] The belief that recent British immigrants were more loyal than other groups in the society was noted by observers like Patrick Shirreff who wrote, as a result of his tour through North America in 1835, that: "A feeling of toryism pervaded most people in the Canadas ... more especially those lately arrived from Britain. Whig and Radical in the mother country, after becoming possessed of a few acres of forest in Canada, seem to consider themselves part of the aristocracy, and speak with horror of the people and liberality."[59] Loyalty was not automatically confirmed by the processes of immigration from Great Britain and settlement in Upper Canada. It still had to be earned – loyalty had to be demonstrated by respectability.

This problem proved to be particularly acute for the Orange Order, which asserted its loyalty but had to establish its legitimacy in the 1830s before it could earn a place in the Tory coalition. After 1815, there was massive British immigration to Upper Canada, of which perhaps some 60 per cent were of Irish origin. It is estimated that about three-tenths of Ontarians were of Protestant Irish stock by the time of Confederation.[60] Some of these Irish immigrants were Orangemen and during the 1820s, a couple of lodges were established in eastern Upper Canada, in Huntley Township and at Perth.[61] Almost immediately there was an outcry from the small Irish Roman Catholic population, which appealed to Sir Peregrine Maitland, the Lieutenant Governor, "to put an end forever to party feeling and distinctions grounded upon religious differences in this country."[62] Many of the old inhabitants of the province were also apprehensive about the growth of the Orange Order; they wanted no part of imported Irish quarrels reflected by the turmoils of the 1790s. Christopher Hagerman, a Tory of Loyalist background, declared: "In this country differences of religion imposed no political distinction, Protestant and Catholic were justly and happily entitled to the same privileges[;] to encourage degrading distinctions, therefore, was impolitic and unjust."[63] Upper Canadians feared that the Orange Order was a party which would unnecessarily divide the population and so disturb social harmony. W.W. Baldwin, an Irishman himself, rejected attempts to label the Roman Catholics in the province as disloyal; he asserted that "the loyalty of all classes of people in this country was undoubted – and why make division when there was no difference – there was no necessity for parties of this kind – when the people of the Province were lately called on to defend it, there were no different feelings – all classes united heart and head in the general defence of the country ..."[64] John Macaulay and eight other justices of the peace from the Kingston area echoed Baldwin's complaint seven years later; they rejected the argument that "any class of their Protestant brethren should ever have deemed it advisable to transfer to this happy portion of the British Empire, public exhibitions commemorative of the ascendancy of one religious body over another or societies assuming a higher degree of loyalty than their brethren of another faith."[65] While the Orange Order represented a threat to political tranquility, it also was not respectable; the Brockville *Gazette* pointed out that "the most enlightened and influential individuals in the community" were not Orangemen. The lodges were generally composed of Irish immigrants "of the opposite description" who displayed "less discretion and moderation."[66] Thus the Orange Order lacked social respectability as well as political legitimacy.

The attempts to overcome these disabilities were directed by Ogle Gowan, a Protestant Irishman from County Wexford who immigrated to Leeds County in 1829.[67] Gowan, who had been active in the Orange movement in Ireland, established the Grand Orange Lodge of British America on 1 January 1830 and was installed as the Grand Master. Although the organization was formed to support "the principles and practice of the Protestant Religion," Gowan began to temper the society's religious exclusiveness in favour of its loyalty; its purpose was "to maintain the Laws and Constitution off [sic] the country."[68] This approach had been advocated earlier by "A Subject" in a letter to the Brockville *Gazette* who believed that there was some necessity for an organization dedicated to strengthening loyal sentiment in the province: "I could never see the necessity of their [the Orange Lodges'] establishment here, while their only effect was annoyance to the feelings of the Roman Catholics. They are not necessary, most certainly, to secure the State from Popish ascendancy in this Province, but in another respect they may now, perhaps, be eminently useful; inasmuch, as they tend to encourage and cherish a feeling of loyalty and attachment to our King and Constitution, and may, perhaps, at some future day, be the salvation of this Province from Republicanism ..."[69] By 1832, resolutions passed at the annual meeting of the Grand Orange Lodge omitted any reference to Protestant exclusiveness; the society became a political organization dedicated to the ascendancy of British principles and the permanence of the imperial connection "against the traitorous and wily machinations and schemes of a pack of united Democrats, headed by Messrs. Ryerson, Bidwell and McKenzie ..."[70]

Gowan also began to publish his own journal, *The Antidote*, in the same year; he articulated a conservative conception of loyalty which reflected many Upper Canadian Tory attitudes. Gowan believed that the economic and military weakness of the province, combined with its proximity to the United States, meant that the continued existence of Upper Canada could only be maintained within the imperial context. The province would be forever dependent upon the mother country: "We, by no means, assent to the proposition that the Canadas must necessarily, in process of time, be seperated [sic] from Great Britain; ... on the very contrary, we hold, that every successive year, tend [sic] to knit us more closely together; for as the resources of the Colony are developed, the absolute necessity of an intimate connexion with and dependance [sic] on, England, becomes more and more apparent. What other nation would buy our grain? Where is our lumber to be disposed of? and even if we were independent (!!!) what country are we to look to for protection from our powerful and ambitious neighbours ... We are debarred from access to the sea, for five months in the year, and in the event of invasion have nothing but the rigors of our climate to look to for protection." Gowan's perception was totally colonial; the British connection defined the province's status: "The fact is," he wrote, "we have not the requisites of nationality, and, therefore, cannot obtain it ... The idea of *a Canadian nation* ... is ... preposterous..."[71]

Gowan also argued that loyalty required adherence to the idea of a stable, hierarchical society reflecting constitutional balance. This social model was threatened by republican principles imported from the United States; when "the people arrogate to themselves all power ... [they] oppress and injure the rest of the community."[72] Prominent Reformers, especially Mackenzie, Bidwell and Ryerson, were attacked because they "were exerting every nerve, and taking advantage of every opportunity, to infuse into the minds of the lower orders, the most preposterous notions, and the most treasonable ideas."[73] Republican agitators disturbed the idyllic harmony shaped by British principles when they misled the people into believing that they "should govern themselves. That they are deluded and misled by men in authority, that the standard of Democracy should be raised upon the ruins of Aristocracy; that the title of '*Excellency*' applied to any man, violates the darling principle of equality ..."[74] The activities of these grievance-mongering demagogues, spreading their revolutionary rhetoric, were supported by "almost all the American rabble that have settled amongst us."[75] Thus Gowan was drawing upon traditional Tory arguments to establish the political legitimacy of the Orange Irish. It was no longer Roman Catholicism but rather republicanism which posed the gravest threat to social order and political tranquility in the province. Gowan's ideas were defined to ensure that Orange loyalty could be incorporated within the dominant conservative consensus shaping the political culture of Upper Canada.

During the early 1830s Gowan's efforts were hampered by his belief that the Irish immigrants had to be protected from the majority of native Upper Canadians. Consequently, loyalty also became the means to reinforce the immigrant identity, and it was a political wedge with which the Orange Irish could meet their sociopolitical demands.[76] Gowan hoped to divide the population into two camps, using birthplace as the main criterion. In 1830, for example, he ran as an independent immigrant candidate, after he had been rejected by the Reformers in Leeds County. The recent immigrants in the area were praised for their devotion to the British Constitution, while native Upper Canadians were attacked for their "*apathy*, indecision, and *disloyalty*."[77] Gowan continually pointed out instances of "native prejudice" directed against the immigrants. Marshall Spring Bidwell was labelled as disloyal when he accused the British government of shipping pauper emigrants to the province;[78] a Mr Keele, an English attorney, was the victim of "monstrous" treatment because he was required to apprentice for five years with an Upper Canadian lawyer.[79] Like many conservatives, Gowan made no distinctions among his political opponents, either Reformer or Tory. In reference to the Keele petition, he attacked Christopher Hagerman, the Solicitor General, because Hagerman spoke against English attorneys practicing in the province. The Solictor General "considered it no hardship to exclude Lawyers from a FOREIGN COUNTRY!!!" Allan N. MacNab was also criticized because he stated that "it is not reasonable that this Province should be open to a FOREIGN LAWYER!!!" Gowan's response was sharp: "has it come to this! Are we in a British colony?..."[80] This "Yankee impudence" would not be tolerated, and the Irish immigrants were assured: "We can never forget the writings of McKenzie ... and Ryerson, and the speeches of Bidwell, Hagerman and Boulton. Their language needs no explanation."[81]

The exclusiveness of Tory loyalty was also attacked in *The Antidote*; political appointments and land grants were monopolized by the descendants of the Loyalists at the expense of the Irish immigrants. In a letter to the newspaper, "Hibernicus" noted that the sacrifices made by the Loyalists "entitled them to lasting gratitude and ample remuneration." But he asked: "have they not been amply remunerated? Has not the entire porvince [sic] been placed under their feet: Judgeships, Colonelcies, Sherivalties, magistracies, all offices were in them, or whosoever they wished. – The first situations in this Province – Mill- seatd [sic] and town seats were given to reward their loyalty, and to command their interests ... Interest, not worth, was the sole recommendation to office. They accumulated thousands of acres of the best, and most advantageously situated lands, which they suffered to be waste and uncultivated, till the axe of the hardy emigrant, who purchased it at double price, rendered them valuable."[82] Gowan believed that the immigrants were perhaps more deserving of rewards because they were "the true fountains, from which sprang the streams and rivulets of British ascendancy and British feeling (as contradistinguished from Canadian) ..."[83] Orange loyalty was thus more accommodative than that of the Tory; the definition of the loyal subject was broadened to include the immigrant, who was to be the foundation of loyalty in the province.

There was a backlash to Gowan's attempts to polarize the population according to birthplace. "A Native of Upper Canada" protested Gowan's efforts to create an immigrant party; such a development was "unjust because it casts the *natives* of the country into the shade, and seems to class us with the *anti-British faction;*

while all the old country born stand in the opposite light. This were doubly unjust, for not only are all the natives *not* revolutionists, but some of the very worst of the faction are of British birth and education." He concluded that *"principles* – and not country or birthplace should divide the population."[84] Gowan also found that Irish candidates were unable to win elections on immigrant support alone;[85] as a result, he moderated his position in an effort to attract other conservative groups. By 1833 he was no longer simply a defender of the Irish.

Gowan persisted in exploiting loyalty to achieve his goals. He wrote: "We shall continue to fight under BRITISH COLOURS, and to unite ... all the British population under the same Ensigns: – Country or Religion causes no difference with us, in the grand struggle ..."[86] But Gowan had accepted the Tory interpretation of developments; the electorate was no longer to be divided according to place of birth, but between loyal and disloyal groups. The Reformers, who represented both republican and anti-immigrant sentiment, became the focus of Orange opposition.[87] The Irish had been drawn into the coalition of conservative groups which dominated the politics of the province; Gowan was prepared to support the Tories because they were "ready and willing to counteract the organised system of anti-British feeling that unquestionably prevails."[88]

The Orange Irish were also attracted to Toryism because it seemed to confer the respectability which the immigrants lacked. Samuel Thompson, who immigrated to the province in 1832 and later edited the Orange journal, the Toronto *Herald*, wrote in his reminiscences that he supported "the Conservative side of Canadian party politics, in which I found so many of the solid, respectable, well-to-do citizens of Toronto ..."[89] Ogle Gowan also commented on the desire for political legitimacy; he expressed disappointment that while the Orange Order possessed "the full confidence of His Excellency the Governor, and the Executive ... [we] have not a vast number of the *Gentlemen* & *Clergy* in the Province enrolled in our ranks ..."[90] Gowan's prospects did improve by the mid-1830s – he gained a strong measure of political respectability when his Tory running-mate in 1834 was the new Attorney General, Robert Jameson, and both were elected for Leeds. In 1836, Gowan was paired with Jonas Jones, a member of the local elite, and again, both Tories were returned after Head's "loyalty" campaign.[91]

Although he had been unable to create an immigrant party which would allow him to dominate locate politics, Gowan was drawn into a political alliance with the Tories for ideological as well as practical reasons. Orange spokesmen, like Gowan, accepted without question fundamental Tory assumptions about the importance of the imperial connection and the threat of republicanism to the British character of the province. But Orange loyalty was, in its principal object, the reverse of Tory exclusiveness: it was by claiming loyalty that Irish immigrants sought title to participate fully in the society of Upper Canada. Unless the concept of loyalty was assimilative and could be demonstrated by the achievement of respectability, it could not provide the Irish immigrants with the *entrée* that they sought. They were attracted to a concept which broadened the definition of the loyal subject and to assumptions which drew them into the coalition of moderate Tories.

It has been suggested that the Tories accepted the Orange Order out of political necessity; they exploited the loyalty of the Irish immigrants to defeat their Reform opponents in 1836. S.R. Mealing has hypothesized that "the lines of communication and patronage which linked local Tories to Toronto were increasingly ineffective in the face of the heavy British immigration of the 1830s, and increasingly inaccessible to the members of that group who aspired to political activity. Swamped with this human flood, and resented by those whose ambitions it blocked, the Tory system was in fact crumbling and could only save itself by falling back on inflammatory appeals to loyalty."[92]

The latent weakness of their political system intensified the exclusiveness that the Tory elite attached to loyalty; it required the unquestioning acceptance of the leadership of that elite and of its assessment of events. The elections of 1836 seemed to establish that the electorate of the province equated opposition with disloyalty; then Mackenzie's rebellion in early December 1837 seemed to confirm the equation of disloyalty with republican subversion. Thomas Rolph wrote to the Hamilton *Gazette* that "it was not *reform* which they sought, but *subversion,* and the transfer of the Government to them. Notwithstanding their repeated assertions that they were loyal ... we discovered that their actions invariably belied their professions ..."[93] Chief Justice John Beverley Robinson believed that the rebels were simply selfish and discontented; they should have left the province rather than attempt to overthrow the government. The radicals had "too long and unreservedly indulged in a feeling of envy and hatred towards your rulers – which was sure to undermine every just and generous sentiment, and to lead in the end to the ruin of your happiness and peace ..."[94]

The Tories also argued that the response to the rebellion proved the loyalty of the provincial population; the disaffected comprised a very small element. Egerton Ryerson said that the uprising revealed a "'universal substratum' of loyalty to law and order; the country at large was loyal to the heart's core ..."[95] Not all the inhabitants responded loyally though; the traditional Tory suspicion of the American settlers was reinforced. It was reported that the character of the rebels could be seen "in the *Hirams*, the *Elijahs* and innumerable other scriptural names; we have without further inquiry, sufficient evidence that the disaffected of the country were principally Americans or descendants of Americans."[96] R.B. Sullivan, an Executive Councillor, presented a "Report on the State of the Province" to the new Lieutenant Governor, Sir George Arthur, which stated that the American settlers were "formerly quiet and orderly, as many of them are at present but they never had as a body an active principle of loyalty or attachment to England ... [I]t is not surprising to find the American settlers and their Children taking the side in Politics which tended most towards their favourite republican institutions."[97]

Although the rebellion strengthened Tory beliefs that opposition was disloyal, the flights of William Lyon Mackenzie and Charles Duncombe and the executions of Samuel Lount and Peter Mathews appeared to purge the province of its dissidents. As a result, Upper Canada could develop as a model British society which required no changes. The Kingston *Chronicle and Gazette* addressed an editorial to the residents of the United States: "we never wished your help to detach us from the Mother Country – to take us from the British Constitution ... we tell you ... that nine-tenths of our population prefer the form of government we have to yours – we tell you that we are not an ill-governed or oppressed people, we are almost wholly free from taxation, we enjoy FULL, FREE and PERFECT LIBERTY."[98] R.B. Sullivan was more succinct: "So long as the Queens [*sic*] Government are sincerely desirous of doing justice to the Colonies there seems little occasion for organic changes."[99]

Consequently, by 1838, the Tories looked to the loyal responses of the Upper Canadian population as proof that their view of the nature of the community and their interpretation of its loyal subject were generally accepted. The Kingston *Chronicle and Gazette* believed that the future of the province was settled: "Democracy which has so proudly reared its head ... has been weighed in the balance and found wanting."[100] The polarization of politics in the period had crystallized the clearly defined assumptions about loyalty. It excluded the legitimacy of dissent; the belief that opposition was radical and subversive was confirmed. Moreover, Tory beliefs about Upper Canada as a special Loyalist society dependent upon the imperial connection were not shaken.

While the Tories had framed the debate and simplified politics to a choice between loyalty and disloyalty, the 1830s did produce a broadening of the conservative consensus in the province. The breakdown of the High Tory system and the emergence of moderate Toryism added new ideas to the concept of loyalty. As new groups, such as the Methodists and the Orange Order, were incorporated into the Tory coalition, the definition of the loyal subject also broadened. Loyalty remained a necessity for social as well as for political acceptance; even W.M. Harvard, the chairman of the Methodist Conference, wrote: "should any person apply hereafter for admission into our church who may be ill-affected to the Crown under which we live ... tell him kindly but firmly that it is a commodity we do not deal in – that he has applied at the wrong door."[101] But the concept did become more accommodative; loyalty no longer had to be earned through attachment to the Loyalist tradition or through acceptance into the Tory elite. Loyalty was strengthened by social or political respectability. "The love of country" could also develop through the commitment to the land acquired through the process of settlement. Moderate Reform beliefs about the nature of loyalty had become part of the conservative mind.

Moderate Tories also developed a more provincial outlook. Political events of the 1830s had shaken their faith in the British government to some extent and tempered their unquestioning acceptance of the imperial connection. They could envision a distinct Upper Canadian community within a larger imperial framework. An ideological gulf had thus developed between the formal spokesmen of the central Compact and the moderate body of their political supporters. That gulf was the opportunity for an accommodation between moderate Tories and moderate Reformers, once the emotional atmosphere of the rebellion had passed.

CHAPTER SIX

The Controversy over Legitimate Opposition: Reform Loyalty before the Rebellion

The polarization of Upper Canadian politics during the 1830s had important consequences for Reform as well as for Tory conceptions of loyalty. Since the Compact Tories succeeded in framing the debate, loyalty was discussed on their terms. Moderate Reformers could not escape being tarred with the brush of disloyalty because they did constitute a formed opposition and because it was hard for them to dissociate themselves entirely from the apparent republicanism of radical spokesmen like William Lyon Mackenzie. Charges of disloyalty were effective precisely because loyalty was as important to them as it was to their opponents. The Irish immigrant Francis Collins reflected bitterly that Upper Canadians were "over anxious to be considered *loyal*, and too much alarmed at the sound of *radical*, to act the intrepid part of old country patriots ... The first thing that sickens a European subject on entering the province is the incessant hum of 'loyalty! loyalty! loyalty!' – from both Whig and Tory."[1] The mere exchange of charge and counter-charge suited the defence of the Tory administration and it reduced the Reformers to ineffectiveness in the political arena by 1836.

Nevertheless, moderate Reform survived the rebellion with a concept of loyalty that had been sharpened during the controversies of the 1830s. Reform loyalty stressed different values from the Tory idea; it insisted that constitutional change was called for by British traditions and that true loyalty required application of those principles to Upper Canada. The moderate Reformers portrayed themselves as defenders of the rights of the people in a contest against a powerful and corrupt executive; they sought to restore the constitutional balance necessary for social harmony. Drawing upon their perceptions of British practices and forced by the Tories to define limits to the extent of their opposition, the moderate Reformers articulated a concept of loyalty which permitted political dissent based upon the constitutional rights of British subjects, the independence of legislators, and the scope allowed to the Assembly by a balanced constitution. The legitimacy of a formed opposition to the administration was also accepted. While they concurred with the idea of provincial development within an imperial context, the Reformers rejected the Tory argument that Upper Canada was an infant society dependent upon the mother country. Their loyalty reflected a commitment to greater local autonomy. The moderate Reform position gave the society an intellectual and emotional basis for loyalty which was to shape the political debates of the Union period.

The 1830s were marked by the growth of a strong Reform movement in Upper Canada. The electoral success of 1828 had been tempered by the opposition of the Lieutenant Governor, Sir John Colborne, and the rejection of Reform measures by the Legislative Council, a factor which led to the Tory victory in 1830. But developments in both Great Britain and the United States in this period stimulated a sense of optimism among Reformers. The election of a Whig ministry in the mother country and the passage of the Great Reform Bill were greeted with much enthusiasm.[2] The political and economic progress of Jacksonian America was admired by envious Reformers, especially when the United States was compared with their own province. William Lyon Mackenzie, the editor of the *Colonial Advocate*, praised the economy, harmony, and progress experienced under republican state governments: "One great beauty in American State governments is the harmony of their movements resulting from the absence of all conflicting elements in their compositions. The Governor, the Senate, and the Commons' House all derive their power from the people ... The paramount influence of public opinion in the Republican State Governments, and the harmony of their movements, and the unparalleled spirit of improvement and general prosperity which have grown up under their auspices are standing provocations to discontent now ..."[3] Mackenzie had noted in 1824, shortly after his arrival, that Upper Canada lagged behind its American neighbour in economic, as well as political, development: "If a farmer, merchant or manufacturer of Canada, has business in the United States ... he observes that certain mark of prosperity, an abundance of precious metals ... [while] the colonies are impoverished, drained of specie, in debt ..."[4] Dr Charles Duncombe, a Reformer of American birth, developed the same theme over a decade later in a letter to the Colonial Office: "The People of Upper Canada have constantly before them, on the one hand, in their immediate vicinity a Republican Government, highly flourishing, contented, peaceable, and prosperous ... while, on the other hand, they are suffering from ... Discontent and Excitement prevailing to a great Degree, their own Agriculture in a depressed State, without Commerce and without Manufacturers, the Province deeply in Debt, and no Provision made for its final Payment."[5]

The slow political and economic development of Upper Canada was due, in the opinion of Reformers, to the fact that the province was poorly governed[6] and poor government was due to the fact that the constitution was unbalanced. The Reformers argued that the constitution was dominated by a corrupt executive. They embraced the concept of a "Patriot King" who would promote the welfare and prosperity of the entire society; their loyalty was directed towards this symbol: "The true sense of loyalty in this country is *true to the father of his people* – The interests of our King as such, is [*sic*] identified with the interest of his subjects."[7] In Upper Canada, the Patriot-King was represented by the colonial governor. It was his duty to maintain domestic harmony: "To reconcile jarring interests, to unite all hearts, and invigorate every man, is the first and best task of a virtuous provincial governor; The love of his King and country is ever uppermost in his mind, and inciteth to a patient and laborious, yet effectual co-operation with his parliament in every thing that is good and noble."[8] Upper Canadians were required to be loyal to this "virtuous provincial governor" because, as the St Thomas *Liberal* suggested: "Loyalty is the devotion of the heart and powers of the Subject to a Sovereign who *deserves* that devotion ... [It] is a *passion* awakened and called forth by a *conviction of elevated* excellence."[9]

The governors of Upper Canada fell far short of this ideal; they were the products of imperial patronage, with little skill in the art of governance: "Needy favourites succeeding needy favourites, were successively sent out to govern ... who in their turn, harrassed [and] oppressed [the people]."[10] The threat of oppression was compounded by the prospect of official corruption. Sir Francis Bond Head's "bread and butter" appeal during the loyalty election of 1836 was vehemently attacked by the *Correspondent and Advocate*: "The people of Upper Canada would rather live upon 'potatoes and salt', than eat and drink corruption ... in the greasy and dirty shape of your 'bread and butter'."[11]

Moreover, the governors were invariably military men who knew little about the province they were to administer; therefore, they had to rely upon the advice of their Tory councils. The Hamilton

Free Press criticized Sir John Colborne because he exhibited these flaws. An editorial asked: "What can Sir John possibly know of the Province besides the information he gets from persons whose interest it is to deceive him? Nothing at all. He never travels out in the country, and being a stranger among us what can he know from experience? Like Maitland, too, instead of standing out firm for the country, and keeping free from faction's influence, he allows his mind and opinion to be prejudiced and formed by the advice of the York executive – a faction conspiring to uphold their own arbitrary and exclusive view of things."[12]

The Reformers attacked the Tory officials who surrounded the Governor; drawing upon traditional Anglo-American theories of opposition, they saw the executive as a clique of evil advisers seeking their own aggrandizement at the expense of the people of Upper Canada. Mackenzie wrote: "The family compact surround the Lieutenant-Governor, and mould him like wax, to their will; they fill every office with their relatives, dependants and partisans ... they are the paymasters, receivers, auditors, Kings, Lords and Commons!" The domination of Upper Canadian Tories produced "a system of favouritism, nourishes flattery and sycophancy ... and degrades the common mass of mankind in the scale of political consequence."[13] The exclusiveness of the official party – its "tendency to confine political knowledge and consequently political power to a very few" – upset social harmony and, thus, it was disloyal: the practice "weakens the political mind by destroying that affection and good understanding, which ever ought to exist between the governors and the governed."[14]

The Family Compact was also attacked because it was a party. Most Reformers in the early 1830s shared the conservative fear that parties divided the society and disturbed political stability; they represented selfish interests seeking to impose their will on the people and thus raised the spectre of tyranny. Francis Collins, the editor of the *Canadian Freeman*, stated: "We want no parties ... neither ministerial or popular ... we want steady honest men who will put their shoulders to the wheel and endeavour to develope [sic] the resources of the country, going hand in hand with the Executive when right, and checking it coolly, when wrong."[15] The same argument that the Tories used to deny legitimacy to a formed opposition was thus turned against them, to deny the legitimacy of a partisan administration.

The Reformers' ideology was built upon the foundation of assumptions drawn from British traditions defending a virtuous opposition in contrast to the corrupt and disloyal administration.

During the controversies of the 1830s their concept of loyalty, which accepted the legitimacy of dissent based upon the defence of the constitutional rights of British subjects, crystallized. The Reformers remained loyal to the system of government but opposed "the tyrannical conduct of a small and despicable faction in the Colony"[16] which caused the Constitution to become unbalanced. They fully exploited the issue of Mackenzie's repeated expulsions from the Assembly in the early 1830s to illustrate their view. The editor of the *Colonial Advocate* was accused of libelling the Tory-dominated legislature when he wrote that it had degenerated into "a sycophantic office for registering the decrees of as mean, as mercenary an executive" as existed in British North America.[17] Tory spokesmen, like the Attorney General, Henry John Boulton, saw Mackenzie as "a Sword which severs apart the bonds which cement society together" because he introduced "party spirit" into the province.[18] But the Reformers pictured Mackenzie as the victim of "the great influence of the Executive in this province."[19] A letter to the *Canadian Watchman* stated that he had become "the John Wilkes of Upper Canada"; the administration had "clothed him with an attractive robe of popularity, and armed him with the sympathy which a generous public always feel for a bold defender of popular rights, borne down by the arm of power."[20]

The Reformers continually had to defend the rights of the people against the encroachments of the executive: "their constitutional rights are invaded and trampled upon."[21] The *Canadian Correspondent*, in an emotional outburst, proclaimed: "Canadians, you were born FREE-MEN! – Will you give up your glorious birth-right ... Will you bend down your necks to the yoke of a hateful, heartless oligarchy? But you will say that liberty is as dear to you as the apple of your eye – that you are ardently attached to free institutions – that you are deeply impressed with the multifarious grievances that press like an incubus on the energies of the country."[22] They believed that in Upper Canada the British Constitution was no longer in balance; it had been tipped in favour of the executive at the expense of the popular branch. During the loyalty election of 1836, the Reformers argued that "our CONSTITUTION was designed, and is calculated to secure ... equal rights and privileges to all men."[23] But the balance necessary for social harmony had been corrupted by the administration, and so the question was asked: "Shall we have the British Constitution which SIMCOE declared that it was intended that we should have administered in this Province in all its forms?"[24] An independent legislature was seen as the best means to defend the rights of the people. John Rolph asserted: "let the people, through their representatives, have a constitutional control over the public purse and general expenditure, and then ... shall we enjoy the 'blessings of the English Constitution,' and the very 'image and transcript' of it."[25] There was no desire to overturn the Constitution; they just wanted to reform the system in Upper Canada so that it conformed to what they believed was the British model. The *British American Journal* stated: "REFORM simply implies, a change from worse to better: to grow better. Political reform may be defined to be, a prudent but *cautious* improvement in the existing form of government; not to destroy its specifick [sic] character, but to adapt it, in its better administration, to the wants and interests of the governed. A *change* of government, is revolution. A change in the *system* of administering a government, if it tend to promote the national welfare, is reform ..."[26] The Cobourg *Reformer* believed that when reform sentiment had completely "diffused itself over our population," Upper Canadians would "have less to complain of; our grievances will then have an end; our civil and religious liberties will be secured; equal laws and equal rights will be administered; and peace and prosperity and contentment will bless our happy land."[27] Consequently the Reformers portrayed themselves as the true defenders of the British Constitution.

Reformers' attempts to strengthen the rights of the people were accompanied by the belief that there should be increased local control over the internal affairs of Upper Canada. Unlike the High Tories, who believed that the province was still an immature society dependent upon the mother country for its continued existence, the Reformers argued that Upper Canada was sufficiently developed to allow the people increased control of their own affairs. The *British Colonial Argus* described the society in terms remarkably similar to those articulated by the Tories; it was "unrivalled" in its "immense natural resources ... for agricultural and commercial purposes ... The interior every where presents the appearance of a country peculiarly adapted to supply the wants created by civilization, and where enterprise and industry would be sure to meet an abundant reward."[28] Although full development was hampered by a dependence upon British "trading and manufacturing interests," the province would be completely transformed if the people were allowed to manage their own affairs and unleash "that spirit of enterprise which transforms the wilderness into fertile fields; that speeds the plough, the shuttle and the hammer; plants cities, towns and villages; paves the streets; rears the college dome and academic hall; gives life and energy to trade and commerce ... that gives impetus to the axle, and expansive force to steam; ... and spreads the sail of commerce to every breeze ..."[29] Marshall Spring Bidwell, one of the most prominent Reform leaders, stated this idea in its simplest terms: "It was a sacred principle in all free governments that the people should have a voice in making the laws by which they are governed."[30]

Few Reformers evinced any desire to eliminate the imperial connection; the St Thomas *Liberal* believed that Upper Canadians were "satisfied ... with paternal England."[31] In the mid-1830s, William Lyon Mackenzie still believed that provincial development should continue within the imperial context. He wrote: "Under the protection of Great Britain, the province may arrive at a very great height of prosperity ... We cannot be independent. Three hundred thousand settlers, thinly scattered over a vast extent of territory and far distant from the sea could not possibly set up for themselves ..."[32] "Reformers," according to the Brockville *Recorder*, "wish to preserve unimpaired the advantages which they derive from being connected with a country possessing the power and resources of the British Empire."[33]

The Reformers were as insistent as the Tories that the special importance of the imperial connection lay in its provision of a constitutional model for Upper Canada. They hoped to obtain "for the people all those advantages which they conceive themselves entitled [to] according to the true meaning and spirit of the British Constitution."[34] Under the leadership of the Baldwins, this hope passed beyond generalities about the balance of the Constitution and even beyond the mere legitimization of dissent. So long as the administration was unresponsive to public opinion dissent within constitutional bounds was unlikely to be effective. The best means to make the administration more receptive to public opinion and, at the same time, facilitate greater internal self-government, was through the introduction of responsible government. The reform would, it was argued, make the provincial constitution conform more closely to that of the mother country – it would give Upper Canada "the image and transcript of the British Constitution."

The Baldwins' position, simply stated, was that the Governor should accept the advice of his council on local matters and that the executive should have the confidence of a majority in the Assembly; when the ministry lost that confidence it was to resign.[35] The St Thomas *Liberal* reflected Reform confidence that this plan was no innovation but the application of traditional British practice; it stated: "every Governor wo'ld have his council to whom he may refer for advice given ... To require that his council in Canada should be accountable to the country is asking no more than is required of the Privy Council in Britain."[36] Graeme Patterson has concluded that this moderate Reform position embraced the belief in the natural rights of British subjects; it was designed to solve local political difficulties and it was "part of a larger insistence upon an inalienable right of colonials to *full* parliamentary government."[37] More specifically, it was shown by W.L. Morton that the Baldwins' support for responsible government was grounded in the Irish Whig theories of local ministerial responsibility developed in the 1790s.[38]

Robert Baldwin insisted that his support for responsible government reflected his own loyalty; he wrote to Baron Glenelg, the Colonial Secretary, in 1836, that he was: "Educated in the warmest attachment to the Monarchical Form of Government, believing it to be the best adapted to secure the Happiness of the People, and fully sensible that it can be maintained in Upper Canada only by means of the Connexion with the Mother Country ..." Moreover, the introduction of the principle "calls for no Legislative Interference; it involves no Sacrifice of any Constitutional Principle ... it involves no Diminution of the paramount Authority of the Mother Country..."[39] Executive responsibility conformed to British constitutional practice; it was not a radical innovation but rather a loyal measure. In any case, it was an article of Reform belief that change was an integral part of the Constitution. The *Correspondent and Advocate* wrote: "Any man with the slightest acquaintance with English history cannot be ignorant that the British Constitution is the result of successive improvements advancing with the intelligence of the people. It has been well compared to a tree of magnificent growth in which decayed parts have at intervals appeared, and been partly abscinded, and new and more perfect branches engrafted ..."[40] In a letter to Lord Durham after the rebellion, Baldwin repeated the same themes. The introduction of responsible government would guarantee the rights of the people and maintain the imperial connection: "Your Lordship must adapt the Government to the genius of the people upon and among who it is to act – It is the genius of the English race in both hemispheres to be concerned in the Government of themselves ... You must place the Government in advance of public opinion you must give those in whom the people have confidence an interest in preserving the *system* of your Government, and maintaining the connection with the Mother Country..."[41]

Many of these Reform attitudes about loyalty had crystallized in the mid-1830s. During the election of 1834 they portrayed themselves as the defenders of the people's rights and liberties in the face of a corrupt administration; the Brockville *Recorder* stressed the importance of the contest: "members then to be chosen will, in a great measure, depend whether the people of this province are to become hewers of wood and drawers of water to a petty dominant faction, or whether they will be allowed to exercise that salutary controul [*sic*] over their own affairs which is at all times so necessary to promote a healthy administration of the laws and a close attention to the public good."[42] William Lyon Mackenzie's address "To the Reformers of Upper Canada" developed the same themes: "It is to you who call yourselves the friends of freedom ... the defenders of the rights of Englishmen, the admirers of all that is noble and generous in the institutions of Britain ... [who] are to decide, whether a few factious and aspiring men shall yet a little longer mar the happiness of its inhabitants, or whether an honest and intelligent House of Assembly ... will go hand in hand with the King and his excellent ministers in perfecting our political institutions."[43]

The Reformers argued that they would check the corruption of the Tory faction dominating the administration and allow the province to develop fully; as a result, loyalty would be strengthened. In his address to the electors of Stormont County in 1834, William Bruce declared that the Reformers "would effectually stem the torrent of bribery and organize a patriotic House of Assembly, whose members, instead of seeking places and self emolument, would labour for the commonwealth. Trade would flourish: the farmer might then rejoice over the fruits of his industry. Legitimate Government would become agreeable to the people, and the loyal spirit of their ancestors which now languishes in the bosoms of their children thro' misrule and corruption & would be renovated."[44]

Their victory in 1834 was interpreted as a confirmation of both the ideas and the loyalty of the Reformers. The St Thomas *Liberal*, in a mood of elation, interpreted the victory as the result of the people "becoming sensible ... that they are the fountain of power; and they only have to maintain their allegiance firmly and exercise their powers constitutionally, to enable them to defeat the machinations of their political enemies, and subvert the foundation of corruption."[45] John Rolph, on the other hand, was not so optimistic; he was unsure that the population had truly embraced Reform principles when he expressed these sentiments before the election: "I shall not, however, conceal my apprehension that these movements on the part of the people may be merely the transient ebullition of feelings temporarily excited by the injuries lately inflicted upon their civil and religious liberties throughout the country, and that they may not be grounded on rational and settled principles. It is a vain thing to indulge in the loudest outcries against the administration of public affairs, when the evil, by whatever epithets it may be denounced, can be traced to the hustlings [*sic*]." [46] For the moment at least, these prophetic doubts about the solidity of popular Reform could be set aside. The Reformers had asserted the legitimacy of dissent and had seen their assertion vindicated at the polls. The new Assembly, replying to the speech from the Throne in 1835, declared that the existence of opposition did not entitle the executive "to impeach the loyalty, integrity and patriotism" of its opponents. [47] In an address to the king, the Assembly also assured him "of their devoted Loyalty, and their sincere and anxious desire to maintain and perpetuate the connexion with the Great Empire of which they form so important a part." [48]

The election of 1834 seemed to the Reformers a victory of common sense with the true principles of the British Constitution at last applied to the public interest in Upper Canada. Peter Perry, a farmer of Loyalist descent from Lennox and Addington, was blunt in his equation of reform and loyalty: he "had lived long enough to learn that there were abuses in the administration of the government of Upper Canada, and while seeking to remedy them he did not think that the charge of disloyalty applied to him." [49] He was wrong because the Reformers' success in legitimizing opposition was met by the blanket charge of disloyalty; and their response to it, being merely defensive, was ineffective. It did not help to call the Tory tactics unfair, as the Brockville *Recorder* did when it attacked the attempts of the administration "to impeach the loyalty, integrity and patriotism of those who conscientiously dissent from them on questions of public policy and expenditure – thereby creating observations and dissensions, destructive of the peace, welfare and good government of the country." [50] The efforts of Reformers like Peter Perry, who believed that "it is not the loyal portion of the subjects who are continually crying out loyalty, loyalty ...," [51] were also unsuccessful. And accusations that the administration was simply desirous of power were no more effective than the attempts to question the loyalty of those who cried loyalty; the *Correspondent and Advocate* argued that "the Tories care neither for King nor constitution, nor the Parliament of Great Britain or Upper Canada ... [T]hey want to keep the Freemen of Upper Canada under their 'baneful domination' by the exercise of unconstitutional power." [52] It did not even help to maintain a Reform claim to share in the Loyalist tradition; Peter Perry, of Loyalist background himself, "considered the loyal to be those who were native of Upper

Canada, and had borne the heat and burden of the day ..."[53] W.B. Wells, a lawyer of Loyalist background who represented Grenville County, also looked with pride to these traditions which he believed strengthened the desire for reform; the Loyalists did not come to Upper Canada "to live without liberty! ... He [Wells] owes it to *his* memory – to *himself* – to his beloved country, not to submit to the usurpations of the few at the expense of the many – not to continue tyranny in any shape or form."[54] In the identification of the loyal subject, rhetoric had replaced analysis. As a consequence, the assimilative concept of loyalty which Reformers had worked out in the 1820s, and which moderate Tories were coming around to, was inoperative in political dispute. It was not crude or inflammatory enough to compete with the stark dichotomy of High Tory rhetoric, which allowed only unqualified support for the administration on the one hand or seditious opposition tainted by republican sympathies on the other.

Tory rhetoric was fortunate that its most obviously appropriate target was now the loudest voice attacking the government. William Lyon Mackenzie had been the focus of Tory wrath throughout the 1830s.[55] The Kingston *Chronicle and Gazette* thundered that the vocal newspaper editor was "inseparably connected with the party we oppose. We rejoice that it is so. The banner that has floated over ... the 'Reform' party in this province is indelibly inscribed with the name of Mackenzie, and there let it remain, as glaring as infamy can make it ... [I]t is a worthy name connected with slander, tyranny and treason. It is in vain that some, especially the more respectable of his party are beginning to be ashamed of him and seek to disown him ... [T]hey cannot."[56] During the election of 1834, Joseph Hume's "baneful domination" letter to Mackenzie gave the Tories the opportunity to denounce the Reformers as "wretched conspirators" who were now "gibbeted together, TRAITORS IN THE FIRST DEGREE."[57]

Mackenzie's politics were becoming more radical in this period and his disenchantment with the colonial administration increased. Others were also drawn to radicalism; men like Marshall Spring Bidwell, of American background, and John Rolph, an English doctor and lawyer, believed that fundamental changes in, rather than simply the reform of, the social and political system were in order. They also based their position on the traditional Anglo-American opposition appeal to the rights and liberties of the people. Another spokesman, W.J. O'Grady, a former Roman Catholic priest and then editor of the *Correspondent and Advocate*, wrote: "we are that *vile thing*, called a radical reformer ... We hold it as a first principle, that the people alone are the true source of legitimate power – from which it follows, that true loyalty in a Government like ours, consists as much in securing the rights of the people, as in defending the honour and dignity of the Crown."[58]

The radicals offered the same justifications for change as the moderate Reformers had because, of course, men like Mackenzie, Bidwell, and Rolph played important roles in shaping the responses of the opposition in the 1820s and early 1830s. They continued to seek the restoration of a balanced constitution, for example, by restricting the prerogative of the Crown and eliminating the corruption which surrounded the executive branch. But by 1836 the radicals were beginning to argue that the Colonial Office was also actively seeking to restrict the rights of the people. In a long examination of the "State and Colony" during Lieutenant Governor Head's "loyalty election," Mackenzie added to the catalogue of grievances developed by the opposition throughout the 1830s: "if freedom and security be the design and end of good government, we certainly had it not ... [The] real object [of the Colonial Office] ... was, and now is, to nullify all that is really good in the constitution of 1791 ..."[59]

As Mackenzie's dissatisfaction with the mother country grew, his admiration for the United States increased.[60] It had a tremendous appeal for radicals, in both Upper Canada and the mother country, because "The Republic had most of the liberal virtues – apparently free institutions, a rule of law, the constitutional protection of individual rights and liberties, religious toleration, and minimal government."[61] Radical arguments were based upon two fundamental assumptions. The radicals believed that Upper Canada was no different from the United States because both societies were North American. They also believed that political institutions shaped the character and development of a society; the inferior position of Upper Canada in relation to the United States lay in the defectiveness of its political institutions.[62] It has been suggested that after his tour of the United States in 1829, Mackenzie was attracted by "the cheapness and efficiency of American ... government, and the domestic simplicity and accessiblity of American officers of government."[63] Therefore, he and other radicals began to look to American political solutions to correct the problems which faced Upper Canada; in particular, they advocated the adoption of the elective principle. Marshall Spring Bidwell, for example, favoured an elected Legislative Council because it would be infused with "the principle of responsibility to public opinion."[64]

Although the radicals looked to the United States as a political model, there remained a certain ambivalence in their thought. They were also preoccupied with the achievement of a responsible ministry in Upper Canada. Peter Perry criticized the composition of the executive council: "the principles of the British Constitution were not put in practice as it regarded this Council ... we allude to the fact that persons had been appointed, or continued as Councillors, whose political opinions and principles were in opposition to those of the people and their representatives, and in many cases to the expressed wishes and intentions of His Majesty's Government ..."[65] This ambivalence in the radicals' thought reflected its twin sources: they drew upon American republican arguments and English opposition theory to buttress their arguments. The radicals believed that constitutional balance could only be achieved through a defence of the liberty of the people and the maintenance of the privileges and authority of the Assembly against both the prerogative power of the Crown and the corrupt faction surrounding the Governor. Loyalty could be strengthened if these aims were attained. Bidwell said: "The way to preserve the connexion is not to keep an irresponsible body there – particularly in view of the attractions of the United States. Gain the affections of the people, and you draw bulwarks around the government much better than those of armies and fortifications."[66] Charles Duncombe emphasized the same theme; in his address to the electors of Oxford County, in 1836, he stated that he "opposed every measure tending to produce a separation of this Province from the Parent State"; he supported political reform "by every constitutional means ... [and was] firmly and decidedly opposed to revolution and revolutionary principles."[67]

Their acceptance of American republican solutions confirmed the disloyalty of the radicals for both the Tories and the moderate Reformers. Moderates totally rejected the radicals; the *British American Journal* declared radicalism was "remote from reform." It "is the practice of those who ... are inveighing against the government ... in every variety of style and vituperative invective. Such a course ... may serve to keep the publick [sic] mind in a constant state of ebulition, mislead the judgement and inflame the passions of the people, alienate their affections from the legitimate and lawful sovereign, annihilating all reverence for laws and respect for its administrators ..."[68] The moderate Reformers sought to dissociate themselves from Mackenzie; they rejected the Tory claim that the fiery Scot represented the mainstream of reform. The St Thomas *Liberal* stated: "It is true that Mr Mackenzie has many friends among liberal minded men, but the Tories are mistaken if they suppose, for an instant that he is the rallying point and sole dependance [sic] of Colonial Improvements."[69] The Cornwall *Observer* interpreted the election of 1834 as a contest between moderates and radicals; it was a fight between "Reform and revolution ... A reformer is continually on the watch to guard against every innovation, and maintain the constitutional rights of every member of society ... not throwing off approved institutions, but correcting every abuse that may creep into them ..."[70] The Grenville *Gazette* developed similar themes: "Reform and revolution are as dissimilar in the objects they aim at, as light is to darkness. The former has always been to the British Constitution, what a burnishing steel is to a soldier's firelock, a polisher and not a destroyer ..."[71]

The political debates of the 1830s in which the Tories linked dissent with disloyalty forced the moderate Reformers to put limits on the extent of their opposition. The moderates were not prepared to countenance the use of extraconstitutional means to achieve their goals. The *British Colonial Argus* argued that the best means for "the people of Upper Canada to proceed in order to obtain a government suited to their condition ..." was to follow traditional British political practices. They were to establish Reform newspapers which would "disseminate correct political knowledge"; the people were to create "*political* UNIONS" and "unitedly petition His Majesty and the Parliament of Great Britain, for a constitution in which the right of the people to self-government should be acknowledged and surrendered."[72] Yet increasingly, all Reformers were linked to the radicalism of the leading oppositionist, William Lyon Mackenzie.

The completeness with which the moderate Reformers failed to dissociate themselves from Mackenzie was revealed in the "loyalty election" of 1836. Moderates were either drawn to the coalition of loyal groups supporting Sir Francis Bond Head or squeezed out of the political arena; Robert Baldwin, for instance, declined to run in the election. The Reformers did not lack organization,[73] but their organization lacked support. The results of the election confirmed the administration's view that the population was overwhelmingly loyal in Tory terms and that republican "principles and views do not belong to any save a few designing radicals ..."[74] The moderate Reformers, though, had a more realistic view; the Tories, led by the Lieutenant Governor, had fully exploited the potential of the loyalty issue. W.W. Baldwin wrote to his son, Robert: "By appeals to their [the electorate's] fears and patriotism, and other means quite as effective, but less widely advertised, Sir Francis won the elections."[75] But Marshall Spring Bidwell, who had been defeated in the election, believed that the Tory strategy could back-fire; no good would be accomplished "by denouncing any man as disloyal, a revolutionist, a traitor who happens to differ from the Provincial government on questions of expediency or constitutional principle."[76]

The politicization of the loyalty question, and their crushing defeat in the election, increased the radicals' frustration after 1836. They attributed the Tory victory to "bribery and corruption" and continued to press their attacks against the administration. Radical perceptions about provincial misgovernment and the oppression of the colonial system led to a rejection of the imperial connection. As early as 1835, Mackenzie had written to John Neilson, the editor of the Quebec *Gazette*: "If the English government had done its best to ensure to this colony the advantages contemplated by the [Constitutional] Act ... I should have remained a contented plodding individual, loyal from inclanation [*sic*] *as well as duty* ... [But] I have seen enough to convince me that we shall continue to have the very *worst possible government in Upper Canada* until we get rid of *the system* which binds us to the earth. I therefore am *less loyal* than I was."[77] Charles Duncombe echoed similar sentiments in a letter to Robert Baldwin: "if ever they [the people of Upper Canada] have good government ... they must look among themselves for the means of producing it, for they [the British Government] care very little for the people of Canada other than as a source of patronage or revenue."[78] The *Correspondent and Advocate* drew a sharp contrast: "In the United States the people are everything ... here the people have scarcely the shadow of power."[79]

Before 1837 Mackenzie had always rejected extraconstitutional means of change. Like Robert Gourlay he had relied upon the techniques of English radicalism – township meetings, petitions to the Crown, and personal meetings with imperial officials. His Canadian Alliance Society had advocated an elective legislative council and a written constitution but revolution was not among the American models that it had adopted. After the debacle of 1836 his emphasis shifted towards popular sovereignty. "Government," he argued, "is founded on the authority and is for the benefit of a people." He declared that "the duty we owe our country and posterity requires from us the assertion of our rights and the redress of our wrongs."[80] During the summer of 1837 the radicals adopted a declaration closely modelled on the American Declaration of Independence,[81] and Mackenzie, finally rejecting the possibility of constitutional change, declared that Upper Canadians had a legal right of rebellion in defence of their liberties.[82] The ease with which his rising was crushed did nothing to lessen the Tory conviction that his disloyalty was the common attribute of all their opponents, nor to mitigate the embarrassment of moderate Reformers whose dissociation from any radical character or sentiment was incomplete.

The failure of the rebellion did, however, eliminate radicalism as a serious political alternative in Upper Canada. The republican element in the political spectrum had been removed; in Sir Francis Bond Head's words, "The struggle on this continent between Monarchy and Democracy has been a problem which Upper Canada has just solved."[83] For a time Tory revenge was given free rein: mail was opened, the arrests of Reformers were tolerated, and "disloyal" government officials, such as the postmaster of Toronto, J.S. Howard, were dismissed.[84] The state trials of 1838 culminated in the hanging of Samuel Lount and Peter Mathews. The threat of invasion from the United States strengthened the administration's desire to eliminate all disloyalty.[85] As a result of the increased harassment, many of the supposedly disloyal either engaged in such displays of formal loyalty as joining the militia or they simply left the province.[86]

Moderate Reformers had to remain on the defensive, vying with one another in condemning a resort to arms. "We are advocates of Reform so far as is consistent with the true principles of British Constitution ...," wrote the Brockville *Recorder* on 14 December 1837. "We go no further ..."[87] But as the narrowness of Mackenzie's support became evident,[88] the lesson increasingly drawn was that the population of Upper Canada was, and would remain, fundamentally loyal. Deprived of its spectre of sedition, the exclusiveness of High Tory loyalty lost much of its point; and moderate Reformers could again proclaim their faith that Upper Canadians were "worthy of all the privileges which the British Constitution is intended to confer ..."[89] Before the end of the rebellion winter, the Niagara *Reporter* had drawn the conclusion that rebellion was a danger only from Tory exploitation of it: "There is danger in imagining we are safe – the loyalty we have recently exhibited, may be made the means of enslaving us. Let us convince our rulers, that it was not for the purpose of perpetuating their tenure of office that the people of this province buckled on their armour. There is danger of a re-action on the part of that 'family influence' which has so long ridden rough shod over the liberties and interests of this glorious appendage of the British empire. Now is the time ...

to demand the enactment of liberal [laws] ... now is the time for REFORM."[90]

With their confidence restored, moderate Reformers could once more dispute the exclusiveness of the Tory concept of loyalty and reassert their own assimilative and more accommodating model. They could deny that loyalty to the imperial connection implied limitations on the rights or political role of any respectable inhabitant of the province, so long as he accepted that loyalty. They looked to the mother country as a constitutional model for the province, and believed that there was imbalance in Upper Canada. In an effort to counter the "tyranny" of corrupt administrations they drew upon traditional English and American opposition theories to assert the legitimacy of dissent based upon the constitutional rights of British subjects, the independence of legislators, and the scope allowed to the Assembly by a balanced constitution.

Reform loyalty also incorporated the concept of a formed opposition within the political system. Such a legitimized opposition, especially if linked to the idea of responsible government, would restore the constitutional balance that Tory domination of the administration had upset in Upper Canada. For Baldwinites at least, constitutional balance was acquiring a meaning that reflected British parliamentary reform quite as much as the much-praised eighteenth-century model: its object was to ensure, not that one branch of government would check the others, but that public opinion, reflected in the Assembly, would be able to influence the administration. Responsible government would also strengthen local self-government because the Governor would be required to accept the advice of his council on domestic matters. Reform loyalty incorporated the belief in the need for greater provincial autonomy within the imperial system. The Reformers suggested that the province was sufficiently mature to allow the people greater control of their own affairs. Accordingly, "an intense local patriotism" began to emerge and loyalty became an expression of Upper Canadian nationalism.[91]

While the implications of loyalty to the imperial connection were different for Reformers and Tories, the views of both groups were essentially conservative. Both assumed that the society of Upper Canada was and should be hierarchical; and if the Reformers envisaged a looser structure with easier access, they had no more sympathy than the Tories with attempts to upset it. As Graeme Patterson has argued: "Ideological conflict in Upper Canada was less a contest between 'conservative' and 'progressive' schools of thought than a struggle between warring conservative traditions that came into conflict when transplanted from Europe and other parts of North America to the new colony."[92] This conflict would continue into the 1840s with loyalty remaining the centre of the debate.

CHAPTER SEVEN

Loyalty and the Idea of Party in the 1840s

Once tempers had cooled after the rebellion, there seemed for a time to be no argument left over loyalty. During the post-rebellion period Upper Canadians of both Tory and Reform backgrounds continued to emphasize their preference for British symbols and sentiments, as well as their attachment to the imperial connection. By the end of the 1840s there was little difference between the editorials of a Tory journal like the Toronto *Patriot* which criticized the American judicial system, the concept of written constitutions, and popular democracy, and the views of Robert Baldwin, now Attorney-General for Canada West, who "believed the English constitution to be the best in the world – infinitely superior to that of the United States."[1] The diminishing ideological tensions between moderate Tories and moderate Reformers and "the emergence of a larger degree of consensus" was "a reflection of the movement toward a two-party system in the British North American provinces."[2] This development, though, was accompanied by continued debate over the nature of loyalty. Throughout the entire period before the rebellion, and across nearly the whole of the political spectrum in Upper Canada, the concept of loyalty remained the basis not only of political legitimacy but also of acceptance into the provincial society. Loyalty was a complex of ideas. Tories and Reformers adhered to different combinations of its components and those components themselves evolved over time. During the 1840s, when changing political, economic, and social circumstances had dramatic consequences for fragile party groupings, a consensus, in which loyalty remained central, began to emerge. While the Tories still had differences, nevertheless they came a long way towards redefining their views of loyalty and its definition was at last the common property of moderates of both parties.

The most important feature of the mid-century consensus was that it accepted the legitimacy of a formed opposition in politics and therefore of party government which, in turn, was the instrument of expanding colonial autonomy. That consensus, when first examined by historians with a focus on constitutional forms, was characterized as the triumph of Reform in the "struggle" for responsible government.[3] Recent historiography has emphasized its conservatism and even its class basis, especially beyond the realm of party politics.[4] Yet a straightforward emphasis on growing conservatism is not borne out by the evolution of loyalty, the central conception of Upper Canadian politics. As the Baldwinites pressed for the introduction of responsible government issues such as the constitutional role of the Governor General, who represented and symbolized the imperial connection, and the development of parties came to the fore. While the Tories forced the moderate Reformers to define the limits of their dissent as a result of the rebellion, most of the political evolution during the early 1840s consisted of the acceptance by moderate Tories of positions already worked out by moderate Reformers.

In the wake of the rebellion the attitudes of the Upper Canadian Tories about the nature of loyalty were strengthened at the expense of those of their Reform opponents. The loyal response exhibited during the winter of 1837-8 was integrated into the Loyalist tradition which shaped the conservative mind and had been previously expressed after the American Revolution and the War of 1812. There were numerous professions and public displays of loyalty.[5] In 1840 there was a ceremony at Queenston Heights which honoured the hero of the War of 1812, Sir Isaac Brock; the *Patriot* believed that after the rebellion such an event would confirm Upper Canadian "feelings of allegiance to our Queen and country ... they wish to enjoy ... the protecting influence of the Crown – and the desire to preserve inviolate on our part, the happy connexion ..."[6]

Others could play the same game, with variations. Ogle Gowan, the Grand Master of the Orange Order, also sought to broaden the interpretation of the Loyalist myth in an effort to include the Orange Irish within that tradition. The loyal response of that group in 1837 proved their commitment to their new homeland. The Orangemen believed that they had earned their place in the Upper Canadian community; Gowan wrote: "Well do the bulk of the people of Upper Canada deserve that free and glorious constitution, and rationally and nobly have they defended it ... And are not the Emigrant Britons, as well as those who forfeited their all, rather than their connexion with Britain, and who braved foreign foes and domestic traitors, in perpetuation of that connexion, entitled to some respect? Do they not deserve all the rights of Empire, for the integrity of which they have so nobly, so successfully struggled?"[7] Attempts to broaden the Loyalist tradition were accompanied by increased emphasis upon the belief that the continued existence of Upper Canada could only be assured through the imperial connection; loyalty to the mother country remained as important as ever.

The Tories continued to feel vulnerable in spite of their success during the rebellion because of continued tensions along the border with the United States. The publication of Lord Durham's *Report* intensified their fears. To the Tory mind the rebellion was a conflict between "the loyal and the traitorous ... between the monarchists and the republicans ..."[8] But Durham offered a different interpretation. He was critical of the failure of the administration to resolve the Clergy Reserves question and to promote the economic development of the province. Moreover, the Governor General attacked the exclusiveness of the "'family compact'," which had enjoyed a "monopoly of power so extensive and so lasting [that it] could not fail in process of time, to excite envy, create dissatisfaction, and ultimately provoke attack ..."[9] Durham thus blamed the High Tories for the outbreak of the rebellion. His solution to the political tensions which plagued Upper Canada was anathema to the Compact. Durham recommended the introduction of responsible government as the means to restore tranquility: a colonial governor must draw his councillors from the party which could command a majority in the Assembly. The problem of maintaining British control over the colony was resolved by differentiating between local and imperial issues; the Colonial Office would continue to control the structures of local government, foreign relations, trade, and the disposal of Crown lands. The result would minimize discontent and strengthen the imperial connection: "The British people of the North American colonies are a people on whom we may safely rely, and to whom we must not grudge power."[10]

News of the *Report* did not reach Upper Canada until April 1839, although John Beverley Robinson, who was in England at the time, had examined the document when it was released in February. He wrote to the Lieutenant Governor, Sir George Arthur: "It absolutely made me ill to read it ... You said rightly to me once 'Lord Durham is a bad man' – I should try in vain to find words to express the contempt I feel for him." Other High Tories were also disturbed by the attacks on the Compact; Christopher Hagerman complained to Arthur: "[U]nless Lord Durhams Report – and the principles and theories it advocates, are openly – plainly – emphatically *denounced* ... these Noble Colonies ... will cease to be appendages of the British Crown in a very few years ..." Responsible government would destroy both the Constitution and the imperial connection.[11] These themes were continually repeated in the months following as the High Tories embraced their traditional precepts. It was believed, for example, that the province was still immature in comparison with Britain; the Anglican journal, *The Church*, proclaimed: "When in Canada we have the same social organization ... when we have a hereditary peerage, a wealthy country gentry, and the same powerful diffusion of commercial influence; when we have the benefit of a healthy system of education, and the full operation of the principle of an established religion, we might venture thus to entrust the destinies of the country to the 'will of the people' – without endangering prerogatives of the Crown or the supremacy of the Mother Country."[12] Moreover, responsible government would lead to the emergence of parties which would exacerbate social and political instability in the fragile Upper Canadian community.[13] But the anger and disillusion which marked their response to the Durham *Report* failed to spur the High Tories to actively defend their position because they were left with no route to follow. As a result they became increasingly impotent in the politics of the post-rebellion period.

The Compact watched with alarm the resurgence of their old opponents. The Reformers in Upper Canada were elated with the *Report*. Francis Hincks wrote in the Toronto *Examiner*, the newspaper he established in 1838: "No document has ever been promulgated in British North America that has given such general satisfaction as this."[14] Responsible government had long been the goal of moderates like Robert Baldwin, and he had written to the Colonial Office in 1836: "being an English principle it would strengthen the attachment of the people to the connexion with the Mother country; and would place the Provincial Government at the head of public opinion, instead of occupying its present invidious position of always being in direct opposition to it."[15] After the publication of the Durham *Report*, Baldwin intensified his demands for the practical application of constitutional principles and the administration of local affairs in Upper Canada; the result would be, in Durham's words, the restoration of "harmony ... where dissension had so long prevailed."[16] The moderate Reformers who had been discredited because of their association with Mackenzie in the 1830s were renewed as a political force; they organized Durham meetings and Durham clubs to pursue their goal.

The Reformers had to counter continued Tory claims that their activities were disloyal. Robert Baldwin argued that responsible government was based "on monarchical principles, in contradistinction to republican, and in conformity with the essence and spirit of the British constitution."[17] William Hamilton Merritt articulated the same sentiment when he was a supporter of Baldwin in the early forties: "This is no Republican or elective institution. Here is no upsetting the foundations of society among us ... here is the simple application of the tried principles of the British Constitution in a British province ..." As well, the introduction of responsible government would be "an effectual prevention against the introduction of Democratic or Republican principles among the inhabitants. Give us the *full benefits* of the British Constitution and we will become the admiration and envy of the United States."[18]

On the issue of responsible government, in fact, the moderate Reformers succeeded in legitimizing it against Tory charges of disloyalty by tactics which had become standard since the debate on the Alien Question. The rebellion of 1837 had intensified the hostility of most Reformers to the process of extraconstitutional change in Upper Canada; but they were still faced with the problem that the Tories refused to recognize the idea of legitimate opposition. Opposition to the Crown had traditionally inferred disloyalty. The Reformers did not dismiss or evade the question of loyalty, but met it by a direct rebuttal; and the grounds on which they relied for that rebuttal were precedents drawn from British practice and appeals to British constitutional principles.

The growing acceptance of the legitimacy of opposition was linked to the development of parties in the province. While the Tories viewed the party system as a republican innovation and thus a threat to the continued existence of Upper Canada as a British province, the Reformers argued that it could be accommodated within the political system. The most articulate spokesman in favour of party development was Francis Hincks, a businessman, journalist, and skilled political tactician. (Between 1839 and 1841, for example, he laid the groundwork for the alliance of Reformers from Upper and Lower Canada, led by Robert Baldwin and Louis LaFontaine.)[19] Hincks did not draw his ideas about party from American examples but rather from British sources. Party was not a republican phenomenon; it drew its inspiration instead from British Whiggism. Hincks's newspaper, *The Examiner*, copied an article from the *Edinburgh Review* entitled "Present State and conduct of parties." The *Review* rejected the concept of the aristocratic basis of politics – the domination of government by a Tory elite. The base of political power, it was argued, rested upon "the whole mass of the population ... It is the diffusion of power among all classes which constitutes the real strength of the state."[20] Parties were the inevitable and necessary instruments of free politics. Hincks opposed attempts to block the development of parties because "there cannot be a greater delusion to imagine that in a free country, enjoying representative institutions, all the people can be got to be of one mind, and of course of one party." He wrote that the Tories were "of late endeavouring to deceive the people into a belief that parties can be amalgamated ... There must be two parties, each ... united in the promotion of great objects; the one carrying out 'Progressive Reform,' the other in thwarting and opposing it." Upper Canada would benefit from the competition between parties.[21]

Hincks was referring to attempts by the new Governor General, Charles Poulett Thomson, assisted by the moderate Tories, to create an effective government party to replace the old Compact. Thomson, from a wealthy merchant family, had entered politics in 1826, rose rapidly in the Whig party, and had served five years as President of the Board of Trade. When appointed Governor General of British North America in 1839, he was not yet forty. Thomson (soon to be raised to the peerage as Baron Sydenham and Toronto) was to be the instrument of imperial policy in the colonies; he was to organize the proposed union of Upper and Lower Canada and govern effectively without conceding responsible government. The Melbourne administration was weak and wished no problems with its colonial policy; it had distanced itself from Durham and his recommendations, although there was general support for a union as a means to attain stable government by overwhelming the French Canadians in the lower province. The imperial authorities had to appear to be doing something; but they remained firmly opposed to the "movement for what is absurdly called responsible government." The Colonial Secretary, Lord John Russell, believed that the Governor must obey the Colonial Office rather than follow the advice of his executive; power could not be divided between imperial and local authorities or separation would be the result.[22]

While the British government would not accept responsible government, it did wish to minimize political conflict between the executive and the legislature by introducing the harmony principle and the concept of majoritarianism. This envisioned the creation of coalition, not party, governments. The Governor would act as his own Prime Minister and select his executive from the groups in the Assembly which supported his policies and could command a majority of the seats.[23] Thomson wrote that he would not make the "power of the Governor subordinate to that of a Council" by conceding responsibility; but he did intend "to govern the Colony in accordance with the wishes of the people ... in all merely local matters ..."[24] Yet Thomson was not really concerned with philosophical debate; he saw successful politics as a question of administration. Like Durham, he recognized that economic prosperity was essential if loyal sentiment in Upper Canada was to be strengthened after the rebellion; the benefits of the imperial connection had to be shown, especially in the expansion of public works, which would speed up the settlement of the country and stimulate prosperity for all the inhabitants.[25] To ensure this goal, and consequently reinforce loyalty, the Governor had to play a central role in the political process. He sought to put together a coalition in the Assembly, headed by S.B. Harrison, which could attract support from both moderate Tories and moderate Reformers, and at the same time, exclude the others. Thomson said: "I will take the moderates from both sides – reject the extremes – and govern as I think right, and not as they fancy ... I can make a middle reforming party."[26] He also set out to crush his opposition: "to break up the Exclusive power of the Compact on the one hand, and repress the violent radicals on the other."[27]

Thomson was assisted in his efforts by many of the High Tories themselves. Apart from Robinson and Sir Allan MacNab, most were not prepared to mount an effective opposition; Christopher Hagerman, for example, accepted a judgeship. Others, like R.B. Sullivan and John Macaulay, saw no choice but to support the Governor; they accepted the full implications of their loyalty, as Macaulay noted with resignation when he wrote that it was his "duty to give up my opinions and do all in my power to forward the views of the Government whose servant I am."[28] As a consequence, the Compact Tories became increasingly isolated in the political process.

The decline of the High Tories as a political force was accompanied by the increasing strength of the moderate Tories, led by William Henry Draper,[29] a prominent Toronto barrister who replaced Christopher Hagerman as Attorney General. Moderates rejected responsible government for the same reasons as the High Tories; Draper, for example, argued that it "would virtually abrogate the Imperial authority. I cannot agree with those who think that the principle can be applied to local measures – leaving all others to the Home Government. Who shall decide what is a local measure[?]"[30] Moreover, the loyalty of advocates of responsible government remained in question; James Hamilton, Sheriff of the London District, saw them as "a set of vile agitators who have all to gain and nothing to lose in the hope of ultimately succeeding in making this Province a Republic." Draper expressed the same concerns after the elections in 1841: "I do not fear rebellion – but I do fear a prosecution for political course, which will inevitably shake the connexion with the mother Country."[31]

If the structures of government did not have to be changed, the men who dominated the executive certainly did. David Jones, Chairman of the Quarter Sessions for the Eastern District, affirmed the loyalty of the population but recognized that "it is their ardent desire to see a change in the administration of public affairs ..." Charles Fothergill attacked "The system of exclusiveness ... and arbitrary power of the FAMILY COMPACT ..."[32]

The focus of moderate Tory loyalty continued to be the Governor General, who symbolized the link between Upper Canada and the mother country; he also represented the social stability and economic progress inherent in the British connection. It was argued that Upper Canadians should co-operate with Sir Charles Poulett Thomson "in his march of progressive improvement and reform" because the Governor General sought "the general and real improvement of the country."[33] Thomson's policies promised stability and growth; the Clergy Reserves question was addressed, wheat and timber exports grew, and imperial loans for canal building were promised. In addition, he could best guide the political course of Upper Canada because of his concern for the welfare of the province. Therefore, the Governor General was entitled to the support of "every loyal Canadian, no matter what may be his party principles."[34]

Draper recognized that if the moderate Tories were to succeed they had to act together. He wrote to J.S. Cartwright: "It is not enough to *declare* generally that we maintain the connexion with Great Britain &c. &c. ... We must do more." His solution was to organize a party: "on what are called Conservative principles and frame a plan of operations on some leading questions and give all our political support ... to those who will act in furtherance of that plan ..." Draper concluded: "Combination is indispensible to success ..."[35] If the Tories were unable to eliminate opposition, then they would create a party to deal with it effectively.

The result was that moderate Tories began to adopt what had been a Reform position. The substance of the change consisted of three fundamental developments: the acceptance of a formed opposition as legitimate in politics, the further acceptance of parties as necessary without being necessarily evil, and the consequent ac-

ceptance of party government. These were important changes because they provided both the means in practical politics and a conservative justification in political theory for the expansion of
self-government. Important differences between the moderate Tories
and Reformers remained, especially in regard to the roles of the
Governor and political parties. Yet they had come a long way in
redefining their principles of loyalty. During the debate over the
Harrison resolutions, which reaffirmed the harmony principle rather
than responsible government, Draper admitted that he would "immediately resign" if the Governor acted on imperial instructions
with which he disagreed. This was a big step, even if moderate
Tories like Draper did not then realize it.[36]

The two parallel developments – Thomson's attempts to unite
moderates from among the Tories and Reformers and Draper's attempts to create a Conservative party – prompted a strong Reform
response. Thomson was attacked for acting as his own Prime Minister and becoming actively involved in the elections for the new
Union Parliament. Hincks wrote: "the Governor is strictly the Representative of the Crown, and ... his functions should be analo-
gous to those of his Sovereign." Robert Baldwin also rejected the
political leadership of the colonial Governor; he wrote to LaFontaine: "As to Governors it is I think not only idle but mischievous
to ... profess to rely upon or look to them. Upon our own principles they are to look for their advisors from among those possessed
of the confidence of Parliament, and if the country requires a change
in the Councils it is through Parliament that they must look for
it."[37] The Reformers also emphasized the importance of party.
Hincks prided himself on being a party man, and, in a neat inversion of old Tory arguments against party, he attacked political
moderates who had no principles: "their object is to maintain themselves in power ..." He was especially critical of Thomson's fusion
policy which sought to create a coalition of both Tory and Reform
moderates; there was "no principle, but this – that they support
the Government thro' thick and thin!" The inevitable consequence
would be Tory control of the government.[38]

Yet Hincks was not an ideologue; he supported many of Thomson's economic policies.[39] Hincks also believed that the Governor
General had conceded "*practical* responsibility" through the Harrison resolutions, and was so prepared to join the ministry in September 1841. (This entry into Sydenham's coalition may be
interpreted as an attempt to circumvent the emergence of a moderate Tory-controlled party controlling the political centre or that
Hincks was simply an opportunist whose statements of principle

cannot be believed.) He would not offer "factious opposition" to Sydenham because such a course would "aid the Tories in embarassing [sic] an administration disposed to carry out Reform measures." The creation of a moderate party, with Reform leadership, was Hincks's goal.[40]

Hincks had advocated party unity among Reformers as early as 1836, and initiated correspondence to LaFontaine in an effort to create a party composed of Reformers from both Upper and Lower Canada in the new Union Parliament.[41] The basis of this coalition was to be the pursuit of "liberal and economical" administration through the attainment of responsible government. Such a course would strengthen loyalty in the colony, according to Hincks: "My impression is that a large majority of the people desire British Connexion provided it is consistant [sic] with the entire management of their own local affairs." Hincks also argued that the Reformers had to support the idea of party government if they were to attain their goal: "we as a party should be prepared to crush any administration in which we have no confidence and as a necessary consequence to be prepared to take the government into our own hands if strong enough."[42]

In spite of his criticisms of Thomson's efforts to create a government party, Hincks also worked to establish a coalition of Reformers and Tories. In a letter to LaFontaine he indicated that even some High Tories were preferable to some Reformers: "I would rather however have McNab & I do not scruple to say so. Harrison will be a spy & traitor in our camp, always intriguing with weak men & trying to influence them. I confess I dread such persons worse than our old & now broken down enemies."[43] Three years later he warned Baldwin that patronage must be apportioned to suitable Tories, as well as Reformers, if the party was to prosper. In Hincks's view, class interests were more important than political affiliation in the creation of a strong party: "We are now fighting the battle of the *middle classes* against the aristocracy– All our commissions will be attacked on the score of unfit people that is not *gentlemen*– Now I would select Tories from the *same class* that we take our friends from so that when the cry is raised by the Tories they will *hit their own* friends & unite them on that point with us– I would select men of good character who had done work in the world & were at the head of their own business. The same remark applies to the country– I would try & get some respectable Canadian farmers who have acted with the Conservatives in the country."[44]

But the Reform party in Upper Canada continued to rely on French-Canadian support for its strength during the early 1840s rather than moderate Tories. When Sydenham's successor, Sir Charles Bagot, invited Baldwin and LaFontaine into his administration in 1842, the Upper Canadian Reformers believed that their position had been confirmed. But Bagot had not accepted party government because he thought no Canadian party was strong or united enough to form a stable ministry.[45] The attempts by Bagot, and his successor, Sir Charles Metcalfe, to govern without accepting party government led to increasing tensions with the Reform council and precipitated the resignation of the executive in November 1843 over the question of patronage. Consequently, the defence of party became an important theme shaping Reform arguments after the Metcalfe crisis.[46]

The Tories were, in fact, more successful than the Reformers in building a strong moderate party in Upper Canada during this period, but their success was based on continued support of the Governor, the symbolic head of the government party. Their success also required the continued co-operation with moderate reformers like Harrison and working with enemies like Francis Hincks, who entered Bagot's executive as Inspector General, in order to broaden the base of the conservative coalition.[47] Finally, the Tories recognized that they would have to gain French-Canadian support if they were to remain in power. Harrison had written to Governor Bagot that "french support" must be attained if the government was to obtain "an effective working majority"; he recommended that the Governor negotiate "whilst the controlling power is still in your hands – and do that voluntarily ... [because it] must eventually be done by compulsion." Draper agreed: "when the numerical strength and influence of the French Canadians ... are borne in mind, it is little enough to say that they have reason to expect that they should have a place in the Council ..."[48]

This was a marked shift in attitudes for Draper because only three years earlier he had supported the union of the Canadas as the means to assimilate the French Canadians.[49] From a denial of the cultural integrity of French Canadians, many moderate Tories came to see that their position in the union would not be threatened as they feared. Racial harmony, political stability, and economic development became linked in Tory eyes.[50] Although Draper was unable to break the Baldwin-LaFontaine alliance, moderates came to see that their hopes for the future of Canada might be achieved with the support of the French Canadians.

The "loyalty election" of 1844 focused many of these themes, especially in terms of the constitutional role of the Governor as it related to party development in particular, and the larger issue of the colonial link with the mother country in general. The politics of the Metcalfe administration have been ably described elsewhere;[51] it is important to note, though, that the Governor General, Sir Charles Metcalfe, defined the issues of the election and set the tone for the campaign when he outlined his perceptions of his political role and attacked the Reformers who sought the introduction of responsible government. Metcalfe believed that as Governor General he was responsible to the imperial government. But he also believed that he was implementing responsible government as Durham had envisioned; he was prepared to play an active role in the politics of the colony by acting as his own Prime Minister and building a ministry which was able to command a majority in the Assembly. Metcalfe expressed both his distaste for parties and his perception of his role as head of a coalition government comprised of all political groups in letters to the Colonial Office: "I dislike extremely the notion of governing as a supporter of any political party. I wish to make the patronage of government conducive to the conciliation of all parties by bringing into the public service the men of the greatest merit and efficiency, without any party distinction."[52] Therefore, he rejected attempts by his Reform councillors to gain control of local patronage – this remained the prerogative of the Crown, not the governing party. Accordingly the Governor General approached the election of 1844 on these terms: would Canadians remain loyal to the imperial connection and accept British supremacy through their support of Metcalfe's position?[53]

Metcalfe did attract the support of a broad range of moderate Tories in Upper Canada. Egerton Ryerson, for instance, rallied behind the Governor General; and at a public meeting in December 1843, a young Kingston lawyer, John A. Macdonald, supported "the firm, manly and vigorous manner in which His Excellency has maintained the Prerogative of the Crown and at the same time upheld the just rights of all classes of the people."[54] Isaac Buchanan, a grain merchant and former supporter of Baldwin, also linked support for the Governor General with loyalty: "In rallying around His Excellency, we rally round everything that is dear to us as Britons, or as colonists." He continued: "It is under British monarchical institutions that liberty is protected at once from tyranny and licentiousness ... We love the British Government, not only because it is BRITISH, but because it is the freest and *best* government on earth, not only because thinking so, our fathers fought and died to sustain its philanthropic principles, but because we, their sons, are prepared to do so, too, whether we find them openly assailed in the field, or betrayed by the Judas kiss of the colonial republican." The *British Colonist* printed several loyal addresses to the Governor which concurred with Metcalfe's position.[55]

Metcalfe represented the maintenance of political stability in the face of party development. The traditional Tory fear of opposition parties reappeared in 1844; the Governor General symbolized the final barrier to the emergence of party government. One "U.E. Loyalist," for instance, reminisced in a letter to the *Cobourg Star* about the "Golden Age of Politics" which had existed in the 1820s: "there was no *party* in this Province: every official appointment made by the Governor was grounded upon fitness for office – every member of the Assembly was elected for the same reason. The Governor was considered in the light of a Father to the *people* – distributing justice to *all*, looked up to by *all*, and consequently respected by *all*." The development of party, he continued, was the cause of the "restless and feverish state" of the public mind, and "would ultimately ruin the country ... PARTY GOVERNMENT AND A CONNEXION WITH GREAT BRITAIN CANNOT EXIST IN THIS COLONY."[56]

Tory arguments were based on the traditional fear of "the subtlety of faction" and the consequent disruption and corruption caused by the growth of party spirit. They drew upon British political thought to affirm that parties were evil because they were associations of factious men bent on self-aggrandizement. Political competition was also evil: the ideal society was one where unity and consensus prevailed, where the provincial interest was determined by the Governor and his advisers. The recent rebellion had illustrated most vividly the dangers of faction; therefore, the Tories had to support the Governor as the most effective counterweight to the development of party. They saw in the Governor General, Lord Bolingbroke's vision of the "patriot king" who would unite the people and crush the parties which provoked social divisions.[57]

The Tory fear of factionalism was intensified by the belief that the Upper Canadian political system was not sufficiently developed to accommodate the development of parties. Thus, many Tories were only prepared to support coalition ministries, such as Sydenham's, rather than party government; John A. Macdonald, for example, based his entry into politics as a moderate Tory from Kingston on the promise of protecting "the population against the extremes of party rule." W.H. Draper, the leader of Metcalfe's administration in 1844, also favoured "a broad and national party" which would submerge conflicting factions.[58]

But more important, the Tories argued that the introduction of party government was a republican innovation and, thus, a threat to the continued existence of Upper Canada as a British province. *The Patriot* had asserted its loyalty, for instance, by rejecting the concept of responsible government in the early forties; the newspaper was "the unflinching advocate of British Supremacy, and genuine Monarchical principles, and the unsparing enemy of everything in the shape of Republican innovation or Radical quackery with the Constitution."[59] During the election of 1844, supporters of the Governor argued that the Reformers' attempts to introduce party government were disloyal. Isaac Buchanan wrote: "The difference between the views of the Governor General and those of Mr. Baldwin is, that His Excellency views any party but as a means for the purpose of governing; while Mr. Baldwin would practically degenerate government into a mere means of reward for the purpose of party ... Sir Charles Metcalfe's is the English and Mr. Baldwin's, the American way of it." Party development threatened the constitutional balance fundamental to social harmony in the province because it took political responsibility away from both the Governor and the people. Upper Canadians had to rally around Metcalfe who, as the representative of the Crown, stood above party and therefore could block its development.[60]

The Reformers also fell back on their traditional views about loyalty in 1844. They appealed to the ideal of freedom and the rights of Englishmen; the defence of prescriptive rights in the face of the prerogative power of the Crown was linked to true loyalty.[61] These rights of Upper Canadians were threatened by the arbitrary actions of Metcalfe which led to the resignation of his Reform councillors. James Lesslie, who succeeded Hincks as the editor of the *Examiner*, defined the main issue of the election as "whether the power of our Governor is virtually to be absolute ... or whether that power is to be regulated for local purposes, by local restraints, in accordance with British usage, and the principles ... of our own Constitution." As well, a new Reform journal, *The Globe*, edited by a young Scot, George Brown, appeared in March 1844 and took as its motto: "The subject who is truly loyal to the Chief Magistrate will neither advise nor submit to arbitrary measures." Other journals echoed the same theme; even the Kingston *Chronicle* wrote: "There can surely be no disloyalty in contending for the rights and privileges enjoyed by our brethren in England."[62] The Reformers believed that responsible government provided the best guarantee of the political rights of Upper Canadians. But Metcalfe's arbitrary measures meant that "we have no Responsible Government, we have no political freedom, we do not possess the rights of British subjects."[63]

The Reformers also had to defend the development of parties and did so by looking to the British, not the American, political system. The *Brockville Recorder*, for example, wrote: "Some talk of a No-Party Government. The thing is not possible under any free Government ... Men acting together on any given principle, or having a general object in view, necessarily form a party." And Robert Baldwin Sullivan, writing as "Legion," stated that the Governor must accept the idea of party. According to the British Constitution, Metcalfe had to select his advisers "from one party or the other, not from both." Hincks was more succinct: "Nothing can be accomplished except by means of a party." He also stressed the fact that the resignation of the Reform ministry was over the question of responsible government; the Reformers did not want to control patronage simply "to keep ourselves in office ... We desire to carry out the principles of our party, the principles which would lead to such great results as peace, prosperity, and British connection."[64] During the election of 1844, therefore, the Reformers outlined a position which recognized the necessity of party development and the acceptance of party government as essential components of the British Constitution.

Reformers also believed that responsible government would provide local self-government for the province and even regarded its attainment as a means to that end. R.B. Sullivan argued that the imperial connection would not be weakened: "loyalty to our Queen, and love of our country, is not extinguished by our desire to possess that freedom which was the living spring from which flowed all that country's greatness, prosperity, and honour."[65] With the rules of Canadian politics changed, the Reformers were now attempting to redefine the nature of the colonial relationship; and that involved the infusion into their concept of loyalty of a sense of local patriotism which was not static but growing. Baldwin, in a letter "to the Delegates for nominating a Candidate for the Representation of the County of Middlesex," was specific about his hopes for such growth: "I ... wish to see a provincial feeling pervade the whole mass of our population ... to see every man belonging to us proud of the Canadian name, and of Canada as his country ..."[66]

Baldwin's attempt to redefine the colonial relationship between Upper Canada and Great Britain was seized upon by the Tories as evidence of Reform disloyalty. The desire for local self-government, as expressed through responsible government, was seen as an attempt to separate the province from the mother country. The Reformers turned these attacks back on their opponents; the Kingston *Herald* proclaimed: "The Tories, in their zeal for party objects, inflict irreparable injury on *national objects* ..." A letter from "A Farmer" to the Reformers of Lennox and Addington also condemned Tory tactics: "The burthen of their song is 'Rebel,' disaffected and separationist. And should a reformer be advocating any of the great points of our constitution; or of the privileges arising therefrom, he is taunted with the word 'Rebel'."[67]

Metcalfe and Draper's Conservatives proved more successful than the Reformers in defining the issues during the election of 1844. To do so, however, they had been obliged to confirm the tactics of the election of 1836 and to narrow still further the focus of their conception of loyalty. It was now the Governor, no longer the Tory elite itself, for whom loyalty demanded trust and obedience. During the "loyalty election," for instance, they made the issue quite clear: Upper Canadians were offered a choice between the Governor General, who was the focus of loyalty in the province and represented the British connection, and the Reformers, who sought party development and responsible government and were thus disloyal. The Reformers certainly believed that their Tory opponents, led by the Governor General, had successfully exploited the loyalty issue; Sir Charles Metcalfe had been "the very foremost in the ranks of the opposition in charging his late Executive Council and their supporters with disloyalty." The Reformers had been defeated by a party dependent upon the active political participation of the Governor; the Kingston *Herald* wrote: "The Governor can ... return any kind of Parliament that he pleases ... [T]he whole influence of government is exerted to the utmost in his behalf, and with all this combination of intrigue, power, corruption, and every other engine that can be used, his triumph is secure. What is the power of a Ministry compared to the power of a Governor?"[68]

The Tories, of course, interpreted the victory in a different manner; it represented the "loyal feeling of the people; Upper Canadians had proclaimed to the whole British Empire, that she is sound in her heart and true in allegiance to a loved and honoured Sovereign." Matthew Richey, a Methodist preacher, was even more emphatic about the results: "Truth, loyalty and justice have triumphed over misrepresentation, faction and republican selfishness! Canada is not to be severed from the greatest Empire on which the Sun ever looked in his ample circuit."[69] The Tories had exploited the loyalty question to their benefit in 1844 and were able to attract much of the moderate support in the province; the people bought their version of loyalty, so long as it was tied to a willingness to promote development and attempts at reconciling minorities through coalition. They also benefitted by their control of patronage and their ability to succeed in identifying local grievances so important in the individual constituencies.[70]

The Tories' success was also due to the fact they had adopted in practice a Reform position which they still condemned in theory. In spite of their apparent hostility to the development of political parties, the Tories did adopt party organization as a means to strengthen their position.[71] The new administration, led by Draper, sought to strengthen the moderate Tory party in the Assembly by attracting French-Canadian support.[72] While Draper was still unable to break the almost solid French-Canadian bloc led by LaFontaine (he was only able to attract two old war-horses, D.B. Viger and D.B. Papineau, who brought with them a few "loose fish"), he was able to minimize the dominance of an "upper class of old ruling families and landed gentility" to a large extent. A new generation of moderate Tory leaders began to emerge after 1844 – men like John A. Macdonald, J.H. Cameron, and William Cayley – and this group was, as J.M. Careless has pointed out, "truly bourgeois, representatives of fast-emerging, town-based, capitalist society ... [T]hey remained part of a provincial middle class elite ..."[73]

This new political leadership accepted party as the means by which their authority could be asserted and their goals could be pursued. The moderate Tories were concerned with economic progress rather than ideological conflict.[74] What had once been a standard Tory argument against the legitimacy of opposition was now used to recognize the practicality of party. In order to pursue economic development, the Tories were prepared to modify their traditional beliefs about the exclusive nature of loyalty. The Kingston *Chronicle* wrote: "We do not believe that 'loyalty' is a thing to be put off and on at convenience ... but we *do* believe that a Canadian ... talks not much of his loyalty – it is as much a matter of bad taste and indelicacy as for a lady to decant on her virtue."[75] The Tories had gradually abandoned the belief that opposition to the administration was disloyal; within a party system, dissent could be legitimate. Loyalty simply came to represent the attempt to assimilate the Canadian character and political system with that of the mother country. As a result, the moderate Tories sounded very much like the moderate Reformers. They had in fact accepted the arguments of their opponents; a measure of ideological consensus of the fundamental assumptions which shaped the society of Upper Canada had developed.

The acceptance of concepts like ministerial responsibility, party government, and constitutional opposition paralleled similar developments taking place in the mother country.[76] J.M. Ward has suggested that colonial officials were slow to recognize these developments in British North America and therefore were reluctant to grant such changes as responsible government. Certainly the Tories in Great Britain believed that the concession of party government might weaken the imperial connection.[77] Their desire to keep Canada within the empire led to strong British support for Metcalfe's position in 1843-4. The concept of loyalty underpinned Tory beliefs in Great Britain as much as it did in Upper Canada. Norman Gash notes: "Wellington openly, Melbourne and Peel in the last analysis, considered loyalty to the Crown as the highest political duty of the statesman."[78] But Phillip A. Buckner is more convincing when he argues that British authorities were concerned "with retaining as much influence as possible with the minimum expenditure of Imperial resources." Moreover, the emergence of new political leaders in England who accepted the concept of party government facilitated the process in the colonies. The Whigs, especially the third Earl Grey and Charles Buller, were by 1847 prepared to concede responsible government to some of the colonies as a means to strengthen their British character and institutions, as well as reinforcing their ties to the empire.[79] Accordingly, when Lord Elgin was sent to British North America, Grey's instructions were that he was to draw his ministry from the party which could command a majority in the Assembly, regardless of his own preferences. The new Governor General was also to avoid any partisan identification; he could neither act as his own Prime Minister nor control local patronage. But this decision was also shaped by changing views of the nature of Canadian loyalty. Buckner has suggested that in the early 1840s, the imperial authorities "were reluctant to surrender complete control over the patronage of the Government to men whose loyalty was suspect and to exclude from office those who played the most active part in assisting the Government in putting down the rebellions." He concluded that when "the Whigs returned to power in 1846, the legacy of distrust generated by the rebellions was rapidly receding into the past. Yet it was still perhaps fortunate that Grey and Russell had first to face the prospect of establishing an avowedly party government in

Nova Scotia, where the loyalty of the reformers was not an issue, rather than in Canada, were it was."[80]

These changes in imperial policy, as well as the British adoption of free trade, pushed the Tories to accept the concept of greater colonial autonomy; and again, they used the arguments of the Reformers to define their position. Colonial self-interest increased. W.H. Merritt, for example, said: "If the productions of Canada are to receive no advantage over the productions of foreign countries when admitted to Britain, the manufactures of Britain are not entitled to any advantage over the manufactures of foreign countries when admitted into Canada."[81] The responses to the Rebellion Losses Act and the annexation crisis in 1849 intensified these feelings about increased colonial autonomy and effectively eliminated the last major challenge to the political consensus which was developing in Upper Canada. The last gasp from the High Tories came at the end of the decade and their collapse isolated them from the political mainstream in the 1850s. The High Tories in Upper Canada were not attracted as readily as their English-speaking colleagues in Montreal to the idea of annexation with the United States. They were less affected by the economic distress of the late 1840s associated with the British adoption of free trade and most were not prepared to break the imperial connection over the perceived threat of French-Canadian domination of the Union.[82] But the Toronto *Patriot* did flirt with the idea of annexation because "Canada is left to depend upon herself – Canadian loyalists have to contend as they may with republicanism and disaffection, unaided by the Mother Country ..." An "Annexation Manifesto," printed in 1849, also expressed traditional Tory fears about the threat to social harmony and stability posed by the emergence of political parties: "The bitter animosities of political parties and factions in Canada after leading to violence and upon one occasion to civil war seems [sic] not to have been abated with time, nor is there at the present moment any prospect of diminution or accommodation[;] the prospect of parties becoming daily more threatening towards each other ... [threatened] political revolution ..."[83]

The Reformers, of course, did not hesitate to attack the apparent disloyalty of the Tories over the annexation issue. The loyalty question which had been exploited for so long by their opponents was turned against them with glee. For instance, *The Globe* wrote: "The loyalty of principle is one thing, the loyalty of loaves and fishes another – a constant supply of creature comforts is the greatest nourishment of Tory loyalty." Not only did *The Globe* associate Tory loyalty with the lust for office, it also attacked the exclusiveness associated with their opponents' conceptions and defended the Reformers as the true defenders of the Constitution.[84] Moderate Tory spokesmen in Upper Canada also attacked the concept of annexation. A.N. Bethune, an Anglican clergyman and editor of *The Church*, rejected the idea of annexation to the United States simply because of the economic crisis exacerbated by the removal of British preferential tariffs on colonial staples: "[We] shall not be one of those who would rate their loyalty by a standard of gain, and shift their allegiance with alterations of commerce." The political magazine, *Punch (in Canada)*, was more succinct when it printed a cartoon about loyalty.[85] Moderate Tories were also active in the creation of the British American League to counter the appeal of annexation.[86] They were able to reaffirm publicly their loyalty and at the same time squeeze the last High Tory elements from the party.

By the end of the 1840s there was increasing ideological consensus among Upper Canadian political leaders of both moderate Tory and Reform backgrounds. There was no softening of attitudes towards the republican model presented by the United States by either group; there was also general agreement on the desirability of the British Constitution and the necessity of the continued connection between the province and the mother country. In addition, the emergence of this consensus was the result of tremendous changes in both practical politics and political theory after the Durham *Report*. The moderate Tories survived, and later would prosper, by the adoption of what had been a moderate Reform position. This involved, first, an acceptance of the legitimacy of opposition in politics; dissent, in itself, would no longer warrant the label of disloyalty. There was also an acceptance of the necessity of parties, and consequently an acceptance of party government, which in turn became the instrument of expanding colonial autonomy through local self-government. These acceptances were eased by the concession from imperial authorities that loyalty must be defined in Canada, "without rescripts from the Colonial Office," which left the last and narrowest version of High Tory loyalty inviable in politics.

The acceptance of party, in both ideological and practical terms, was also the consequence of the emergence of a new generation of political leaders – men with an urban and professional background like Francis Hincks and John A. Macdonald – who were prepared to use party in order to attain their political goals. This new political leadership pushed out the old Compact elite and shaped the formation of parties in the 1850s. John Macaulay noted

wistfully: "Conservatism is itself but a diluted Toryism, and it must submit to a further dilution, if it wishes to gain new influence ... For my part ... I am too old to change ..."[87] The emergence of Macdonald's Liberal-Conservatives and George Brown's Grit Reformers was the legacy of the debates over the role and development of parties in the previous decade.

The concept of loyalty, throughout the 1840s, was the means to focus the attitudes and perceptions developed in the political debates of the decade. Beginning as the ideological basis for dispute, loyalty was defined in more assimilative, accommodating, and nationalist terms. The definition was accomplished by compromise among moderate political opponents who shared a belief in the necessity for economic development. Loyalty therefore emerged from the political disputes of the 1840s as the basis for a political consensus in the diverse society of Upper Canada.

CHAPTER EIGHT

Conclusion

By 1850, after decades of controversy over its meaning and implications, there was a large measure of agreement in Upper Canadian perceptions of the idea of loyalty. That agreement was part,
even the central part, of a consensus on which the politics of Canada West were based and which was social as well as political in
its content. The mid-century consensus was basically conservative
but the idea of loyalty which it incorporated was very different
from the Tory definition that had first been ineffectually challenged
fifty years before. For most of that period Tories had more often
than not been able to frame the terms of the political debate over
the nature of loyalty; but from the 1820s, moderate Reformers enunciated coherent alternatives to Tory ideas and during the next two
decades those alternatives were not only further elaborated but
were also increasingly accepted by moderate Tories. The resulting
moderate consensus on the nature of loyalty never had to face a
serious challenge from the left because the weak strain of radicalism in Upper Canada was discredited by its attempt at rebellion.
Those High Tories who clung to their original conceptions of loyalty found themselves, in the end, undermined by changing imperial policy and outnumbered by the steady growth of
conservative moderation. Loyalty to the imperial connection remained the most central of their political ideas and on occasion
still the most formidable of their political weapons; but the erosion
of their position left them unable either to hold political power
themselves or to define the terms on which it would be held. That
erosion was accomplished by an evolution of the idea of loyalty,
not by its rejection as the central issue in Upper Canadian politics.
In the process of evolution the most explicit initiatives were taken
by moderate Reformers. Neither able nor willing to challenge the

central importance of loyalty, they proceeded to redefine it in ways that legitimized their own political goals. Since those goals appeared to lead to a practicable political system, and since they were acceptable to moderate Tories, the revised conception of loyalty retained its utility. It formed the basis for a political ideology more complex, more adaptable, and more widely shared than the Tory beliefs from which it had begun.

The amalgam of beliefs and attitudes from which the concept of loyalty was formed by the 1840s included few questions that would have been new twenty years before but many of the answers were different. Loyalty still required adherence to the imperial connection, but the emotional insistence that the connection was beyond question or modification had become an anachronism. The tie with Great Britain was accepted as beneficial to the province, although investment and immigration had replaced mercantilist regulation as the means of economic support. British constitutional models were as sacred as ever, even if the aspects of the Constitution that were identified as models continued to be matters for debate. Loyalty still included a view of the United States as dangerous but more as an aggressive and possibly expansionist neighbour, as the Oregon crisis had illustrated, than a source of radical subversion. The idea of the province as a special Loyalist homeland was not dead, but it was a nostalgic ornament to loyalty not a vital part of its political implications.[1] The notion of "fortress Ontario" was no longer of use to support the claim of a Tory elite to exclusive political leadership.

It was the exclusiveness of the old Tory loyalty that had been most thoroughly defeated. It had been supplanted by an assimilative concept of loyalty for which Reformers had argued since before the War of 1812 and which even earlier had lain behind Simcoe's land-granting policy. Loyalty did not have to be earned by attachment to the Loyalist tradition or by acceptance into a Tory elite; it was the common property of respectable inhabitants and could be acquired through proper social values and good citizenship as settlement developed. The old Tory faith in the inculcation of loyalty was retained but the instrument of inculcation was to be an educational system under state, not Anglican, control.[2] In the defeat of exclusiveness, however, there was little trace of egalitarianism or of social radicalism. Moderate Reformers were as committed as Tories to a stable, hierarchical society with a rural base in which inequality would not be a problem because of the widespread ownership of land and the growing prosperity of the province. The assimilative concept of loyalty was based on the constitutional rights of British subjects, especially if those subjects were respectable men of property; there were no democrats among the effective participants in the debate on the nature of loyalty.

Perhaps the shift from an exclusive to an assimilative character was the greatest change made in the understanding of loyalty during the first half of the nineteenth century. It opened the political arena to groups which would hardly have acquiesced in their continued exclusion and which would otherwise have had to seek more radical justifictions for their admission. It transformed the idea of loyalty from an aristocratic apologia for a narrow oligarchy into the basic assumption of a developing middle-class political system. It also enabled the idea of loyalty to encompass a provincial feeling looking to the future rather than to the past and was expressed in nationalist rather than Loyalist rhetoric. That provincial feeling, in turn, was called upon in support of a desire for increased local autonomy, although the arguments for local autonomy were also legitimized by appeals to British constitutional principles.

The hottest debates involving the nature of loyalty were those over which British constitutional principles should be taken as models for Upper Canada. Here there was a progression both in the success and in the moderation of Reformers. First, they developed a justification for individual expressions of political dissent, based on the constitutional rights of British subjects and, by analogy to the House of Commons, on the independence of legislators; appeals to natural rights and natural law, or to American practice, were too open to counter-charges of disloyalty to be effective. Next came the justification of a formed opposition in the Assembly and then of ministerial responsibility and of party government. When these justifications were met, not only with moderate Tory acceptance but with imperial sanction, the new measure of agreement over the nature of loyalty was completed; and it had also achieved its definitive political expression.

The acceptance of a party system, with a legitimate opposition and a responsible ministry, was a victory for moderate Reform. Yet the evolution of parties in the 1850s reflected the conservatism of the ideological consensus which had been reached. Parties did not approach the question of the future political and social development of the province with the same ideological intensity as their predecessors because that issue had been resolved by the failure of the rebellion and confirmed by the attainment of responsible government.[3] Enduring success went only to those Reformers who became conservative enough to think that it was more important to preserve the new status quo than to keep the banner of Reform aloft. The reorganization of parties in 1854 provided further evidence of this consensus as the Hincksites – the remnants of Robert Baldwin's moderate Reformers – joined the moderate Tories, led by John A. Macdonald, to form the Liberal-Conservative party. Their opponents, the assorted Reformers and Grits for whom George Brown was sometimes able to speak, also admired British political institutions; they did not look to the example of the United States because local self-government had been achieved within the imperial system.

The development of political consensus was matched by the success of a new political elite. Unlike the old Tory Compact, which reflected the aspirations of a propertied professional oligarchy, the new elite reflected the concerns of an urban and commercial community. It represented the success of the "respectable" middle class in Upper Canada – prosperous professional men like John A. Macdonald, Francis Hincks, George Brown, and Egerton Ryerson.[4] They represented a class which felt increasingly optimistic about provincial development because of the progress and prosperity spurred by the commercial expansion associated with railway construction, increased investments of British and American capital, and, finally, reciprocity in natural products with the United States. Francis Hincks had articulated this view quite clearly in 1849 when he wrote to Sir Allan MacNab about the development of consensus politics in the province: "however great may be the present excitement, there yet are some points of agreemt among which I trust are loyalty to our Sovereign, attachmt to British connexion, a firm determination to maintain faith with the public creditor under all circumstances, and a desire to develope [sic] the resources of our country ..." He concluded that co-operation between Reformers and Tories "would yield such handsome remuneration to the capitalists"; besides, they "do not hate one another personally any more than party politicians ... in other countries."[5] The nature of Upper Canadian politics had changed dramatically since the 1820s and 1830s.

The prospect of closer economic relations with the Americans did not raise the spectre of disloyalty. With the reorientation of traditional trade patterns in the 1840s, provincial economic development replaced political development as the primary consideration of the administration. The pessimism which underpinned the loyalty debate before 1850 – the concern about the continued existence of Upper Canada as part of the empire – had dissipated. Both Tories and Reformers supported reciprocity because greater access to American markets would fuel continued economic growth.[6] The desire for reciprocity also reflected a shift in Upper Canadian perceptions about the United States. The threat of an aggressive and expansionist neighbour diminished and there were references to the United States sharing with the province the common position of being in North America. *The Globe* remarked, for instance: "It is a miserable affair at this time of day to build up the walls between people of the same origin and language, and inhabiting the same country."[7] For the new political elite, like the old Compact Tories, it was essential that the province continue to prosper if it was to survive as a viable community.

The confidence stimulated by provincial development was expressed in a growing sense of provincial nationalism. Clear Grits, defending themselves against the charge of disloyalty because of their sympathy for republican institutions, could assert their loyalty in provincial rather than in imperial terms: "We look with unutterable contempt upon every man ... who attempts to teach us loyalty ... A rough Canadian ... knows what loyalty to Canada means. He knows that in *Canada*, not in England, are his home, his possessions, his wife, his children ... Our loyalty commences and ends with our country."[8] The optimism about Canada's future, expressed in nationalist terms, was maintained as a consequence of the nation-building associated with Confederation and the expansionist movement into the North West.[9] Politicians like D'Arcy McGee and Edward Blake sought consciously to stimulate a sense of nationalism to complement Canadian development. Blake, a leader of the Liberal party, declared in his Aurora speech of 3 October 1874 that: "The future of Canada, I believe, depends upon the cultivation of a national spirit."[10]

This new sense of nationalism reintroduced a measure of the traditional Canadian distrust of the United States and American ideas because of the Civil War and the abrogation of reciprocity. Macdonald, for example, drew on old arguments about loyalty when he discussed the election of 1861 as a contest "which may determine the future of Canada – and whether it will be a limited Constitutional Monarchy or a Yankee democracy."[11] The *Globe* viewed American expansion with alarm: the Americans were "a people ... [who] have before now proved themselves aggressive – a people who believed in 'manifest destiny,' 'universal sovereignty,' and other ideas not very re-assuring to their neighbours."[12] As a counterbalance to the American threat, the imperial connection remained important. But there was increased emphasis upon Canadian autonomy; during the Confederation Debates, John A. Macdonald had said that: "Gradually a different colonial system is being developed – and it will become, year by year, less a case of dependence on our part, and of over-ruling protection on the part of the Mother Country, and more a case of healthy and cordial alliance."[13] While the controversy over the nature of loyalty had diminished, the idea itself still influenced Canadian responses.

Loyalty re-emerged as a contentious issue in the late 1880s. The optimism and confident nationalism of the Confederation period diminished in the face of growing uncertainty about Canada's future. The doubts reflected the heightened conflict between English and French Canadians as a result of the Riel controversy and the pessimism associated with the disappointing results of the National Policy. The responses were framed in terms of loyalty and the issue of racial conflict gave an opportunity for the resurrection of many of the old Tory ideas about the nature of the concept. The emergence of Canadian imperialism in this period, for instance, produced a defence of Canada which looked to British traditions as the predominant influences shaping national development. The emotional loyalty of the imperialists required adherence to the imperial connection without question because of its political and economic benefits; the idea of Canada as a specialist Loyalist bastion re-emerged;[14] and the spectre of annexation to the United States reinforced apprehensions of the expansionist republic to the south. Canadian imperialism, as Carl Berger has concluded, "was one variety of Canadian nationalism – a type of awareness of nationality which rested upon a certain understanding of history, the national character, and the national mission."[15]

The pessimism of the period also engendered significant hostility to the Canadian political system – hostility which was also expressed in old Tory terms. The growing criticism of the excessive partisanship and corruption associated with political parties was represented most forcefully in the observations of an outsider, Goldwin Smith. Smith, a former professor of history at Oxford and Cornell, saw himself as a liberal but articulated the traditional High Tory fears of party; during his association with Canada First in the 1870s, he asked: "What is there to preserve our parties from gradually becoming mere factions, and our country from becoming the unhappy scene of a perpetual struggle of factions for place ... For party without principles inevitably becomes a faction; and faction as inevitably supports itself by intrigue, demagogism and corruption."[16] Smith's equation of party government with faction meant that he would not join a political party because he supported the idea of a "national government" which could rise above partisan conflicts. By the 1890s, Smith was arguing that party government was not simply corrupt, it was disloyal; he stated that: "All but pure straightforward and honourable conduct in the management of public affairs is disloyalty."[17]

Smith's was not an isolated voice; as Berger suggests, the Canadian imperialists and the intellectual community in general expressed hostility to the party system.[18] J.C. Dent, the journalist and historian,[19] who also saw himself as a liberal, believed that there was little to distinguish between Canada's political parties; they had "outlived their usefulness." His newspaper, *Arcturus*, would support "no individual party or clique" because, quoting the Toronto *Mail*: "Party government has simply been a contest of factions, each side fighting for its own hand, and both agreeing to shirk those great moral and political questions which must be settled if the prosperity of the country is to endure."[20]

While Smith and Dent shared the disgust of the imperialists with the Canadian political system, they did not support the goal of closer imperial ties. Dent believed imperial federation was "totally impracticable"; he felt that the only alternatives facing the nation were "annexation or independence." As a nationalist he supported Canadian independence, although he noted that "loyalty to the British name and traditions is quite consistent with a severance of our political connection."[21] Goldwin Smith argued that closer imperial ties represented colonialism rather than nationalism, and were, therefore, disloyal: "To say that loyalty consists in keeping this community always in dependence on a community three thousand miles off, and condemning it to be without a life of its own, is to set loyalty at fatal odds not only with nature but with genuine sentiment."[22] This was an idiosyncratic conception of loyalty. It did not merely omit, it positively excluded the imperial connection; and yet Smith did not share Dent's commitment to national development. He simply believed that Canada – "a number of fishing rods tied together by the ends" – had no future. He advocated the unity of the Anglo-Saxon peoples and North America through a reunion with the United States and wrote: "On this continent, not in Europe; in the New World, not in the Old, the lot of Canada and of Canadians is cast. This fixes our general destiny ... This sets the mark of our aspirations and traces the line of our public duty. This determines for us what is genuinely loyal."[23]

Smith was especially appalled by the exploitation of the loyalty question during the election of 1891. The Liberals had adopted the policy of unrestricted reciprocity as a means to stimulate Canadian economic expansion. It was argued that closer economic links with the United States would, in fact, invigorate feelings of loyalty. W.R.

Lockhart Gordon wrote: "by improving the prosperity and increasing the wealth of the country we are strengthening the whole of the British Empire."[24] But they were opposed by the Macdonald-led Conservatives, who had been rebuffed in their attempts to attain a reciprocity agreement and were desperate for a political issue to revive their sagging fortunes. As a consequence, they fell back, once more, on the loyalty question. Sir John A. equated the Liberal policy with annexation and so attacked it as disloyal, in terms that might have been familiar in Tory rhetoric over the Alien Question. He declared that "the great contest that is now going on ... will determine whether Canada is to remain British or become part of the United States." J. Castell Hopkins, an imperialist, later wrote that the election involved "the principles of British unity, British commerce, and British sympathy as against Continental unity, Continental trade, and Continental sympathy."[25]

Although many factors contributed to the Tory victory in 1891, the loyalty issue was once again significant, as the Liberals themselves noted in their election post-mortems.[26] The popularity of the question was not lost on that master tactician, Macdonald, either; in a letter to George Stephen, the Prime Minister conveyed his willingness to exploit loyalty yet again for maximum political benefit: "I was surprised and grieved to find the hold unrestricted reciprocity had got of our farmers ... I have of course pointed out that unrestricted reciprocity meant annexation, and that movements of Cartwright, Farrer and Wiman enabled us to raise the loyalty cry, which had considerable effect."[27]

The idea of loyalty therefore had continued vitality in post-Confederation Canada; and with the resurgence of imperialism its rhetoric sometimes raised echoes of its early nineteenth-century form. It remained central to the debate about the country's future in the late nineteenth century; it also remained as a potent political weapon with which the Tories could assail their opponents. Loyalty had been modified and made more assimilative and nationalist by the political evolution of the nation but a majority of Canadians remained committed to the preservation of a British-Canadian society in North America.

Notes

1 G.W. Brown, "The Durham *Report* and the Upper Canadian Scene," *Canadian Historical Review*, 20 (1939), 145.

2 "Political culture" is a term first introduced by the American political scientist, Gabriel Almond, in 1956. It can be defined as the broad patterns of individual political values, attitudes, and beliefs within a particular society; it reveals the character and common objectives of a community and reflects important symbols and myths. Consequently it becomes a determinant of political behaviour. (See J.H. Pammett and M.S. Whittington, eds, *Foundations of Political Culture: Political Socialization in Canada* [Toronto: Macmillan of Canada 1976] 1–3; and David Bell and Lorne Tepperman, *The Roots of Disunity: A Look at Canadian Political Culture* [Toronto: McClelland & Stewart 1979], esp. 11–16.)

Gordon Stewart has outlined a provocative interpretation of the development of the Canadian political culture in *The Origins of Canadian Politics: A Comparative Approach* (Vancouver: University of British Columbia Press 1986). He employs the "court-country" duality as a means to understand British, American, and Canadian political ideologies; Stewart argues that in Canada "court" values were victorious and in the nineteenth century "developed into a statist outlook by which administrators of the day deployed patronage and influence to shore up their positions, stimulated and participated in economic growth, and tried to free themselves as much as possible from close legislative supervision ..." (p viii).

3 David V.J. Bell, "The Loyalist Tradition in Canada," *Journal of Canadian Studies*, 5 (May 1970), 30.

4 Merle Curti, *The Roots of American Loyalty* (New York: Columbia University Press 1946), 3, 19, 42–3, 52–3, viii.
5 Chester Martin, *The Foundations of Canadian Nationhood* (Toronto: University of Toronto Press 1958), 70.
6 S.F. Wise, "Upper Canada and the Conservative Tradition," in Ontario Historical Society, *Profiles of a Province: Studies in the History of Ontario* (Toronto: Ontario Historical Society 1967), 31; Wise, "Consensus or Ideological Battleground: Some Reflections on the Hartz Thesis," in Canadian Historical Association, *Historical Papers* (1974), 12. See also his "Conservatism and Political Development: The Canadian Case," in *South Atlantic Quarterly*, 69 (Spring 1970), 226–43 and Wise, "Colonial Attitudes from the Era of the War of 1812 to the Rebellion of 1837," in S.F. Wise and R.C. Brown, eds, *Canada Views the United States: Nineteenth Century Political Attitudes* (Toronto: Macmillan of Canada 1972), 42. More recently Ramsay Cook has developed the same theme in an essay about nationalist ideologies. He argued that nationalism in English Canada has not been based on ethnic or cultural unity, as in French Canada, but rather on loyalty to the state. It is a self-determined, not a predetermined, identity. (See his "Nationalist Ideologies in Canada," in Ramsay Cook, *Canada, Quebec, and the Uses of Nationalism.* [Toronto: McClelland & Stewart, 1986], 186–91.)
7 J.M. Bumsted has alerted historians to the problem of defining terms such as nationalism. (Cf. J.M. Bumsted, "Loyalists and Nationalists: An Essay on the Problem of Definition," *Canadian Review of Studies in Nationalism*, 6 [1979], 218–32.) Upper Canadians remained unanimous in endorsing British symbols to identify themselves and their polity in the nineteenth century. The use of nationalism might obscure this important reality, although the term "colonial nationalism", while more appropriate, may appear oxymoronic.
8 S.F. Wise, "Sermon Literature and Canadian Intellectual History," *The Bulletin of the Committee on Archives, the United Church of Canada* (1965), 4.
9 John Higham, "Intellectual History and Its Neighbors," *Journal of the History of Ideas*, 55 (June 1954), 341–2.
   Brian McKillop has pointed out that historians of ideas in Canada continue to be more concerned with "delineating the major contours of Canadian thought" than engaging in methodological introspection (A.B. McKillop, "So Little on the Mind," *Transactions of the Royal Society of Canada*, series IV, vol. (1981), 184). As a consequence, intellectual history has been overwhelmed by the new social history. Donald Akenson, for example, has noted that "the argument about the nature of ideological beliefs of early Upper Ca-

nadians does not provide an adequate basis for drawing hypo-
theses that can be operationally tested" (Akenson, *The Irish in Ontario: A Study in Rural History* [Kingston: McGill-Queen's University
Press 1984], 117). But local studies may be simply expressions of
historical empiricism, just as social histories of this period are too
often examples of economic determinism focusing upon the experiences of the radical urban artisan. They cannot provide models for
a broader understanding of regional or national character and consciousness that may be provided by a study of ideas, attitudes and
values. The directions to pursue in intellectual history have been
outlined in McKillop's "So Little on the Mind," 191–9.

10 Wise, "Sermon Literature and Canadian Intellectual History,"   4.

11 *Upper Canada Gazette*, 13 March 1800; in Edith Firth, ed., *The Town of
York, 1783–1815* (Toronto: University of Toronto Press 1962), 157.

12 Herbert Bloch, "The Concept of our Changing Loyalties," in G.N.D.
Evans, ed., *Allegiance in America: The Case of the Loyalists* (Reading:
Addison-Wesley Publishing Co. 1969), 172.

CHAPTER TWO

1 S.F. Wise, "Upper Canada and the Conservative Tradition," in Edith
Firth, ed., *Profiles of a Province: Studies in the History of Ontario* (Toronto: Ontario Historical Society 1967), 20.

2 There is little discussion of Loyalist political attitudes in, for example,
J.J. Talman, ed., *Loyalist Narratives from Upper Canada* (Toronto:
Champlain Society 1946).

3 Robert Hamilton, the Scottish merchant from Niagara, provides a
good example of a Loyalist leader who was more concerned with
translating his loyalty into tangible political and economic benefits
than articulating traditional preoccupations about loyalty. Cf. B.G.
Wilson, *The Enterprises of Robert Hamilton: A Study of Wealth and Influence in Early Upper Canada, 1776–1812* (Ottawa: Carleton University Press 1983), esp. 35–57 and 128–40.

4 Janice Potter, *The Liberty We Seek: Loyalist Ideology in Colonial New York
and Massachusetts* (Cambridge: Harvard University Press 1983), 12.

5 Letter from "J" [Jonathan Sewell] in the Boston *Evening Post*, 23 May
1763, Supplement; ibid., 14 May 1763. Quoted in Ann Gorman Condon, "Marching to a Different Drummer: The Political Philosophy
of the American Loyalists," in Esmond Wright, ed., *Red, White and
True Blue: The Loyalists in the Revolution* (New York: AMS Press
1976), 9, 10. Janice Potter has argued that the concept of deference
was central to Loyalist attitudes. It was shaped by two assumptions: first, that "there was a natural aristocracy of men of superior

merit whose role it was to guide the community ..." and second, "deference involved *voluntary* acceptance by the majority of the minority's ... superior merit to ... govern." See Potter, *The Liberty We Seek*, 26; see also her chapter on "The Loyalists: Conservatism," 39–61.

6 Bernard Bailyn, *The Ideological Origins of the American Revolution* (Cambridge: Harvard University Press 1967), 319. The victory of the "country" position in American politics is also described by Gordon Stewart in *The Origins of Canadian Politics: A Comparative Approach* (Vancouver: University of British Columbia Press 1986), 16–20. For the Loyalist perception of "democratic tyranny," see Potter, *The Liberty We Seek*, 15–38.

7 Anthony Stokes to Evan Nepean, 7 February 1785; cited in Mary Beth Norton, *The British-Americans: The Loyalist Exiles in England, 1774–1789* (Boston: Little, Brown & Co. 1972), 128. See also Wallace Brown, *The Good Americans: The Loyalists in the American Revolution* (New York: William Morrow & Co. 1969).

8 William H. Nelson, *The American Tory* (Boston: Beacon Press 1971), 88–90, 91. Economic factors were also very important. The Loyalists came from the frontier areas from Georgia in the south through the Middle Colonies to Vermont, plus the maritime regions of Long Island, the lower Hudson Valley in New York, southern New Jersey, the Philadelphia area, and the tidal basin of Delaware. Nelson argued that these regions had "suffered or were threatened with economic and political subjugation by richer adjoining areas. The geographical concentration of the Tories was in peripheral areas, regions already in decline, or not yet risen to importance." As a result, they looked to Britain for support for their interests (ibid., 87).

9 A good outline of these attitudes is contained in Jane Errington's "Loyalists in Upper Canada: A British American Community," in S.F. Wise et al., eds, *"None was ever better ...": The Loyalist Settlement of Ontario* (Cornwall: Stormont, Dundas and Glengarry Historical Society 1984), 57–71. The similarity of Loyalist attitudes across British North America can be seen in the conservative views of Loyalists in New Brunswick and Nova Scotia. See Ann Gorman Condon, *The Envy of the American States: The Loyalist Dream for New Brunswick* (Fredericton: New Ireland Press 1984), 39–71 and Neil MacKinnon, *This Unfriendly Shore: The Loyalist Experience in Nova Scotia, 1783–1791* (Kingston: McGill-Queen's University Press 1986), 67–88.

10 S.F. Wise, "Colonial Attitudes from the Era of the War of 1812 to the Rebellions of 1837," in S.F. Wise and R.C. Brown, eds, *Canada*

Views the United States: Nineteenth-Century Political Attitudes (Toronto: Macmillan of Canada 1972), 22.

11 Abridged from the Funeral Sermon of John Strachan (1815); in C.E. Cartwright, ed., *Life and Letters of the Late Honourable Richard Cartwright* (Toronto: Belford Brothers 1876), 20–1, 13. Richard Cartwright, "A Journey to Canada" (1977); cited in Donald C. MacDonald, "Honourable Richard Cartwright, 1759–1815," *Three History Theses* (Toronto: Ontario Department of Public Records and Archives 1961), 7–8.

12 Funeral Sermon of John Strachan, in Cartwright, *Life and Letters of ... Richard Cartwright*, 12. Jane Errington has pointed out that the Crown and the imperial connection were personified by George III. See *The Lion, the Eagle and Upper Canada: A Developing Colonial Ideology* (Kingston: McGill-Queen's University Press 1987), 24–7.

13 PAC Pamphlets, Anonymous [Richard Cartwright], *Letters from an American Loyalist in Upper-Canada, to his Friend in England* (Halifax 1810), 17. Richard Cartwright to General Peter Hunter, 23 August 1799, quoted in Cartwright, *Life and Letters of ... Richard Cartwright*, 95.

14 Cf. Bruce Wilson, "The Struggle for Wealth and Power at Fort Niagara, 1775–1783," *Ontario History*, 68 (1976), 137–54.

15 Reprinted in the York *Gazette*, 12 February 1812.

16 Richard Cartwright to Chief Justice John Elmsley, 7 January 1798; quoted in *Three History Theses*, 114. Anonymous [Richard Cartwright], *Letters from an American Loyalist in Upper-Canada, to His Friend in England*, 15.

17 Reprinted in the Niagara *Gleaner*, 1 November 1823.

18 Jane Errington and George Rawlyk, "The Loyalist-Federalist Alliance of Upper Canada," *The American Review of Canadian Studies*, 14 (Summer 1984), 158–9.

19 Errington, *The Lion, the Eagle and Upper Canada*, 6–7, 21.

20 Cf. R.R. Palmer, *The Age of the Democratic Revolution* (Princeton: Princeton University Press' 1974), 1, 23, 514–15. Gordon Stewart points out that late eighteenth-century Toryism had its roots in the "court ideology" which emerged out of the revolutionary settlement of 1688. The "court" view of politics emphasized the importance of an active administration centred on the King, or his representative, and his officials, plus the role of the established church to complement the government and ensure stability. See Stewart, *The Origins of Canadian Politics*, 10–15. See also J.C.D. Clark, *English Society, 1688–1832: Ideology, Social Structure and Political Practice during the Ancien Regime* (Cambridge: Cambridge University Press 1985), esp. 42–276; S.R. Mealing, "The Enthusiasms of

John Graves Simcoe," in J.K. Johnson, ed., *Historical Essays on Upper Canada* (Toronto: McClelland & Stewart 1975), 311–13.

21 Jane Errington argues that Loyalists like Hamilton who wished to shape British structures to North American circumstances resisted Simcoe's attempts to impose his principles. See Errington, *The Lion, the Eagle and Upper Canada*, 30–3. The reasons for Hamilton's opposition to Simcoe's policies are outlined in Wilson, *The Enterprises of Robert Hamilton*, 106–27.

22 John Graves Simcoe to Henry Dundas, 16 September 1793; in E.A. Cruikshank, ed., *The Correspondence of Lieutenant-Governor John Graves Simcoe* (Toronto: Ontario Historical Society 1925), II, 54–5.

23 Ontario Archives (OA), *Sixth Report, 1909* (Toronto: King's Printer 1909), p. 18; Simcoe's speech proroguing Parliament, 15 October 1792.

24 PAC Pamphlets, John Strachan, *A Discourse on the Character of King George the Third. Addressed to the Inhabitants of British America* (Montreal: Nahum Mower 1810), 43; see also 18, 21.

25 York *Gazette*, 30 April 1808; in Edith C. Firth, ed., *The Town of York, 1793–1815: A Collection of Documents of Early Toronto* (Toronto: Champlain Society 1962), 189.

26 Strachan, *A Discourse* ..., 39–40. Strachan to James Brown, 21 October 1809; in J.L.H. Henderson, ed., *John Strachan: Documents and Opinions* (Toronto: McClelland & Stewart 1969), 26. See also Wise, "Colonial Attitudes from the Era of the War of 1812 to the Rebellions of 1837," 19–21, 26–8; and Errington, *The Lion, the Eagle and Upper Canada*, 40–7.

27 Strachan, *A Discourse* ..., 39–40, 43, 42.

28 Cf. Graeme Patterson, "Whiggery, Nationality and the Upper Canadian Reform Tradition," *Canadian Historical Review*, 56 (1975), 25–44.

29 Simcoe to Dundas, 16 September 1793; in Cruikshank, ed., *The Simcoe Papers*, II, 53.

30 Cartwright to Isaac Todd, 1 October 1794; quoted in Cruikshank, ed., *Life and Letters of ... Richard Cartwright*, 56. See also Errington, *The Lion, the Eagle and Upper Canada*, 47–8.

31 The Thorpe controversy is not the only example, of course. John Mills Jackson, an Englishman, became allied with Thorpe against the Lieutenant-Governor, Sir Francis Gore, because he was denied a grant of land. See CO42/350, pp. 12–19, which provides Gore's despatch of 1 February 1810 commenting on Jackson's pamphlet, *A View of the Political Situation of Upper Canada* (London: W. Earle 1809).

32 PAC CO42/347, p. 151; Sir Francis Gore to George Watson, 29 July 1807. See also CO42/342, p. 108; Robert Thorpe to Edward Cooke, 24 January 1806.

33 PAC CO42/342, p. 108; Thorpe to Cooke, 24 January 1806.
34 York *Gazette*, 31 October 1807. See also Errington, *The Lion, the Eagle and Upper Canada* 48–51.
35 PAC CO42/342, p. 74, Gore to William Windham, 29 October 1806.
36 Enclosed in CO42/343, p. 59; Gore to Windham, 13 March 1807. Gore saw Thorpe as the product of the agitation aroused by William Weekes. Weekes, from Ireland by way of the United States, had been elected to the Assembly in 1805, where he was a critic of the administration until he was killed in a duel a year later. The Lieutenant-Governor also linked Thorpe to two republican causes – the United Ireland Movement and the American Revolution.
37 R.C. Harris and John Warkentin, *Canada before Confederation* (Toronto: Oxford University Press 1974), 116–17.
38 See Cruikshank, ed., *The Simcoe Papers* I, 108–9 and 112–15 for a copy of the Proclamation and a discussion of its intentions.
39 Harris and Warkentin, *Canada before Confederation*, 116–17.
40 Cartwright to General Peter Hunter, 23 August 1799; in Cartwright, ed., *Life and Letters of ... Richard Cartwright*, 96–7. A year later the Assembly did pass legislation which required a seven-year residence, plus an oath of allegiance, before the American settlers were allowed to vote.

   PAC, Upper Canada State Papers, XXIII, 21; Major Graham to D.W. Smith, 29 March 1802. See also Gore's address to "the magistrates, clergy and principal inhabitants of the Eastern District" (March 1811); quoted in E.A. Cruikshank, "A Study of Disaffection in Upper Canada in 1812–15," in *Proceedings and Transactions of the Royal Society of Canada*, series III, 6 (1912), 15.

   Gore to Sir James Craig, 5 January 1808; quoted in S.D. Clark, *Movements of Political Protest in Canada, 1640–1840* (Toronto: University of Toronto Press 1959), 229.
41 Wilson, *The Enterprises of Robert Hamilton*, 102 and Errington, *The Lion, the Eagle and Upper Canada*, 47–8.
42 *Niagara Herald* 21 February 1801. Norfolk Historical Society: Thomas Welch Papers, Welch to William Halton, 11 November 1807. Quoted in Graeme H. Patterson, "Studies in Elections and Public Opinion in Upper Canada" (PhD dissertation, University of Toronto 1968), 20.
43 PAC CO42/343, p. 59; Gore to Windham, 13 March 1807.
44 PAC CO42/342, p. 208; Thorpe to George Shee, 1 December 1806. The political perspective of these early oppositionists was based in eighteenth-century Irish political thought and their arguments were based on the parallels drawn between contemporary Ireland and Upper Canada. Cf. W.L. Morton, "The Local Executive in the British Empire, 1763–1828," *English Historical Review*, 78 (1963), 436–57;

D. Kennedy, "The Irish Whigs, Administrative Reform, and Responsible Government, 1782–1800," *Eire-Ireland*, 8 (1973), 55–69.

45 Affidavit of John Richardson of York, Farmer and Bailiff, 14 February 1807; quoted in W.R. Riddell, "Joseph Willcocks, Sheriff, Member of Parliament and Traitor," *Ontario Historical Society Papers and Records*, 24 (1927), 475–99.

46 PAC CO42/350, p. 212; Gore to Lord Liverpool, 9 August 1810.

47 Simcoe to the Lords of Trade, 1 September 1794; in Cruikshank, ed., *The Simcoe Papers*, III, 67–68. *The Upper Canadian Guardian*, 6 August 1807: enclosed in CO42/350, p. 212; Gore to Liverpool, 9 August 1810.

48 OA, Rogers Papers, Memo re School Bill (1808); quoted in Patterson, "Studies in Elections and Public Opinion," 310–11. Errington also emphasizes the Americanness of the Loyalists in "The Loyalists of Upper Canada," 61–6.

49 *The Upper Canadian Guardian*, 6 August 1807 and 3 September 1807.

50 CO42/347, p. 54; in Firth, ed., *The Town of York*, I, 182.

51 *The Upper Canadian Guardian*, 6 August 1807; letter from "A Loyalist" and 27 August 1807.

52 Jane Errington argues that the Kingston elite was ambivalent about the outbreak of war in 1812; while they remained loyal to Britain, they continued to see themselves as American. Errington does show that social, economic, and ideological ties with the United States were maintained in the early nineteenth century but overstates the federalist influence on Upper Canadian conservatives. There may have been an awareness of and sympathy for the federalist position, but American political values were continually rejected.

Cf. Jane Errington, "Friends and Foes: The Kingston Elite and the War of 1812: A Case Study in Ambivalence," *Journal of Canadian Studies*, 20 (Spring 1985), 58–79; and *The Lion, the Eagle and Upper Canada*, 70–7. See also Jane Errington and George Rawlyk, "The Loyalist-Federalist Alliance of Upper Canada," *American Review of Canadian Studies*, 14 (Summer 1984), 157–76.

53 Powell Papers, 1252; John Powell's address to "Volunteers, Men of the Flank Companies and Embodied Militia" (1812). A.N. Bethune, *Memoir of the Right Reverend John Strachan, First Bishop of Toronto* (Toronto: Henry Rowsell 1870), 42.

54 PAC, Powell Papers, 1252; Bethune, *Memoir...*, 42–3.

55 PAC, Powell Papers, 1258; letter to the King's Printer, undated.

56 *Upper Canada Sundries*, Brock to General George Prevost, 12 July 1812; quoted in Clark, *Movements of Political Protest*, 220.

57 Edward Baynes to General Prevost, 18 June 1814; quoted in Cruikshank, "A Study of Disaffection in Upper Canada in 1812–15," 44.

58 John Strachan to Col. John Harvey, 23 June 1818; in G.W. Spragge, ed., *The John Strachan Letter Book, 1812–1834* (Toronto: Ontario Historical Society 1946), 166. See also Cruikshank, "A Study of Disaffection ...," 30–1, 35–7, and D.H. Akenson, *The Irish in Ontario: A Study in Rural History* (Kingston: McGill-Queen's University Press 1984), 120–5.

59 James Strachan, *A Visit to the Province of Upper Canada, 1819* (reprinted New York: Johnson Reprint Corp. 1968), 35. This pamphlet was written by John Strachan but published in Britain under his brother's name. See S.F. Wise, "God's Peculiar Peoples," in W.L. Morton, ed., *The Shield of Achilles: Aspects of Canada in the Victorian Age* (Toronto: McClelland & Stewart 1968), 54.

60 PAC, *Powell Papers, 1244; Proclamation dated 22 July 1812. Upper Canada Gazette,* 16 February 1817; "Address to the Electors of Halton County." See also *Upper Canada Gazette,* 8 May 1816, address by Peter Robinson; and PAC, Charles Jones Papers, electoral address (1816?).

61 PAC, Powell Papers, 1258; letter to the King's Printer, undated. Kingston *Gazette,* 7 April 1818.

62 John Strachan, sermon delivered at York, 2 August 1812; in Bethune, *Memoir...,* p. 43. Strachan believed that the oppositionists were immoral, as well as factious and designing: He wrote: "the principal members in opposition were often unworthy in private life; and, however eminent in talents, could not claim the confidence of the country, by the noble firmness and purity of their conduct" (James Strachan, *A Visit ...,* 22).

63 Toronto Public Library, W.D. Powell Papers, Gore to Powell; dated only "Sunday morning"; quoted in G.M. Craig, *Upper Canada, 1784–1841: The Formative Years* (Toronto: McClelland & Stewart 1963), 91.

64 Niagara *Spectator,* 14 February 1817; "Address to the Independent Electors in the County of Wentworth." *Journals of the Legislative Assembly* (1818), in Ontario Archives, *Ninth Report* (Toronto: King's Printer 1912), 348.

65 Robert Gourlay, *Statistical Account of Upper Canada* (London: Simpkin & Marshall 1822), II, 422. For a full discussion of the Gourlay controversy see W.R. Riddell, "Robert (Fleming) Gourlay," *Ontario Historical Society Papers and Records,* 14 (1916), 5–133; L.F. Gates, *Land Policies of Upper Canada* (Toronto: University of Toronto Press 1974), 99–119; and Errington, *The Lion, the Eagle and Upper Canada,* 107–11.

66 Quoted in E.A. Cruikshank, "The Government of Upper Canada and Robert Gourlay," *Ontario Historical Society Papers and Records*, 23 (1926), 78. Niagara *Spectator*, 5 and 12 February 1818; Gourlay's Second Address "To the Resident Landowners of Upper Canada."

67 For a more complete assessment of these ideas see S.R. Mealing's introduction to Gourlay's *Statistical Account of Upper Canada* (reprinted Toronto: McClelland & Stewart 1974), 1–13.

68 Robert Gourlay, *The Banished Briton and Neptunian: Being a Record of the Life, Writings, Principles, and Projects of Robert Gourlay....* (Boston 1843–5), no. 18, p. 188; no. 33, p. 468. Gourlay's position was outlined in the Niagara *Spectator*, 23 April 1818. See Asa Briggs, *The Age of Improvement, 1783–1867* (London: Longman, Green & Co. 1966), 88–100; and John Cannon, *Parliamentary Reform, 1640–1832* (Cambridge: Cambridge University Press 1973), 98–115 on this point.

69 Maitland's response was contained in a despatch to the Colonial Office, PAC CO42/361, p. 115; Maitland to the Earl of Bathurst, 19 August 1818. See also his address to the Assembly in the *Journals of the Legislative Assembly* (1818); quoted in Cruikshank, "The Government of Upper Canada and Robert Gourlay," 91.

70 *Upper Canada Sundries*, vol. 40; Robinson to Col. Samuel Smith, 29 June 1818; quoted in Lois D. Milani, *Robert Gourlay, Gadfly: Forerunner of the Rebellion in Upper Canada, 1837* (Thornhill: Ampersand Press 1971), 163; S.F. Wise, "John Macaulay: Tory for All Seasons," in G. Tulchinsky, ed., *To Preserve and Defend: Essays on Kingston in the Nineteenth Century* (Montreal: McGill-Queen's University Press 1976), 189.

71 Kingston *Gazette*, 7 April 1818. Strachan to Rev. James Brown, 1 December 1818; in Spragge, ed., *Strachan Letter Book*, 185. See, for example, PAC Pamphlets, John Simpson, *Essay on Modern Reformers, Addressed to the People of Upper Canada. To Which is added a Letter, to Mr. Robert Gourlay* (Kingston: Stephen Miles 1818). Simpson, a Loyalist and a friend of Strachan, developed the same theme in a letter to the Kingston *Gazette*, 12 May 1818.

72 See the Niagara *Spectator*, 12 March 1818 and 4 February 1819 for the responses of Clark and Durand. See also a letter by C. Stuart in the *Canadian Argus and Niagara Spectator*, 20 April 1820.

73 TPL, W.D. Powell Papers, William Dickson to the Gaoler of the Niagara District, 1 January 1819. See also PAO, Macaulay Papers, Strachan to Macaulay, 30 January 1819.

74 Gourlay, *Statistical Account*, 1, 458.

75 Robert Gourlay, *General Introduction to the Statistical Account of Upper Canada, compiled with a view to a Grand System of Emigration, in con-*

nexion with a Reform of the Poor Laws (London: Simpson & Marshall 1822), d, di. Niagara *Spectator*, 14 May 1818.

76 Edward Allan Talbot, *Five Years' Residence in the Canada* (London: Longman, Hunt, Rees, Orme, Brown & Green 1824), I, 418–19. See also the following letters in the Kingston *Gazette* for proofs of loyalty – from "Agricola" (30 June 1818); "Spectator" (25 August 1818); and "A British Born Subject" (15 December 1818).

77 *Upper Canada Gazette*, 6 April 1820.

78 Kingston *Chronicle*, 1 November 1822.

79 *Upper Canada Gazette*, 6 April 1820.

CHAPTER THREE

1 *Colonial Advocate*, 23 January 1827; an open letter from Jacob Gander to Robert Randall.

2 The Alien Question also illustrated the changing nature of politics in Upper Canada. During the 1820s the personal and local nature of politics began to disappear; cf. G. Patterson, "Studies in Elections and Public Opinion in Upper Canada" Ph D dissertation for the University of Toronto 1969) and H. Bowsfield, "Upper Canada in the 1820's: The Development of a Political Consciousness" Ph D dissertation, University of Toronto 1976). Yet personal and local quarrels often spilled over into provincial politics; cf. S.F. Wise, "Tory Factionalism: Kingston Elections and Upper Canadian Politics, 1820–1836," *Ontario History*, 57 (1965), 205–25 and Paul Romney, "The Spanish Freeholder Imbroglio of 1824: Inter-Elite and Intra-Elite Rivalry in Upper Canada," *Ontario History*, 76 (1984), 32–47.

3 John Strachan to Col. John Harvey, 23 June 1818; in G.W. Spragge, ed., *The John Strachan Letter Book, 1812–1834* (Toronto: Ontario Historical Society 1946), 166. See also Kingston *Gazette*, 17 March 1818; letter from Richard Leonard and Kingston *Chronicle*, 4 June, 9 July 1819.

4 PAC, *Upper Canada Sundries* (RG 1 E3); W.D. Powell to Lieutenant Governor Sir Francis Gore, 23 January 1817. CO42/344, pp. 90–7; Opinion of the Attorney General, John Beverley Robinson, York, 1818; in A.G. Doughty and N. Story, eds, *Documents Relating to the Constitutional History of Canada, 1819–1828* (Ottawa: King's Printer 1935), 7–9. For a more detailed discussion of Robinson's role in defining the legal issues of, the Alien Question, see Patrick Brode, *Sir John Beverley Robinson: Bone and Sinew of the Compact* (Toronto: University of Toronto Press 1984), esp. 118–41.

5 Upper Canada Assembly, *Journals* (1821), 11–13; in Doughty and Story, eds, *Documents* ..., 82–3. See also W.R. Riddell, "The Bidwell Elec-

tions: A Political Episode in Upper Canada a Century Ago," in *Ontario Historical Society Papers and Records*, 21 (1924), 236–44.

6 OA, Macaulay Papers; Strachan to John Macaulay, 6 June 1820; ibid. 18 November 1821.

7 Kingston *Chronicle*, 11 January 1822.

8 Kingston *Chronicle*, 22 February 1822. A third by-election, which M.S. Bidwell lost, was voided in December 1823 because of electoral irregularities.

9 Kingston *Chronicle*, 18 April 1823.

10 Cf. John Garner, *The Franchise and Politics in British North America, 1755–1867* (Toronto: University of Toronto Press 1969), 164. See also Jane Errington, *The Lion, the Eagle and Upper Canada: A Developing Colonial Ideology* (Kingston: McGill-Queen's University Press 1987), 170–5.

11 See York *Observer*, 3 December 1821; reported in the Kingston *Chronicle*, 14 December 1821 and 22 February 1822.

12 *Colonial Advocate*, 4 January 1826.

13 Kingston *Chronicle*, 14 December 1821.

14 Kingston *Chronicle*, 23 February 1823.

15 *Upper Canada Herald*, 12 March 1822.

16 Kingston *Chronicle*, 14 December 1821 and, 22 April 1822. See also the York *Weekly Register*, 22 March 1823; "Bidwell's Case." Cf. speeches by Jonas Jones in the Kingston *Chronicle*, 14 December 1821 and 23 April 1823; also a speech by Christopher Hagerman in the Kingston *Chronicle*, 2 May 1823.

17 Q337-2, pp. 386–401, and Q337, p. 45; in "The Case of Mr. Bidwell," *Report on Archives (1899)* (Ottawa: Queen's Printer 1899), 37–8. Cf. Garner, *The Franchise and Politics ...*, 169.

18 CO42/365; Sir Peregrine Maitland to Lord Dalhousie, 2 October 1820; enclosed in Maitland to Lord Bathurst, 15 December 1820.

19 Bathurst to Maitland, 22 July 1825; in PAC Pamphlets, *Report ... of the Hon. Legislative Council on the Civil Rights of Certain Inhabitants (1825–26)* (np, nd), 6.

20 Q331, pp. 90–4; Maitland to Bathurst, 15 April 1822; in Doughty and Story, *Documents ...*, 93–4. Cf. PAC, Dalhousie Papers, Maitland to Lord Dalhousie, 13 October 1820; CO42, vol. 337, pp. 9–11; Maitland to Bathurst, 7 March 1826.

21 *Upper Canada Herald*, 24 February 1826; letter from Thomas Coleman to Reuben White. Paul Romney has argued that Charles Fothergill, an English Quaker and the King's Printer who was dismissed by Maitland in 1826 for attacking the government, played an important role in giving "the emergent reform movement a much needed respectability." As a "loyal English Whig" Fothergill justified his op-

position to the Family Compact "on impeccably 'constitutional' grounds" (Paul Romney, "A Conservative Reformer in Upper Canada: Charles Fothergill, Responsible Government and the 'British Party,' 1824–1840," Canadian Historical Association *Historical Papers* [1984], 45). Fothergill supported the opposition during the Alien Question and was discontented "with the colony's lack of sovereignty in internal affairs and the constitutional irresponsibility of its administration ..." (pp 48–9). While he saw himself as a reformer, he rejected the idea of responsible government in favour of impeachment as a means of changing the administration. Yet it more often seemed as if his stance was shaped by the opportunity to obtain official patronage than by political principles. (See ibid. 42–62.)

22 *Canadian Freeman*, 1 December 1825.

23 *Upper Canada Herald*, 24 February 1826; letter from "A Freeholder."

24 Aileen Dunham, *Political Unrest in Upper Canada, 1815–1836* (Toronto: McClelland & Stewart 1971), 78.

25 CO42/380; John Rolph to Robert Wilmot Horton, 18 May 1826; quoted in Dunham, *Political Unrest...*, 78.

26 Cf. Bernard Bailyn, *The Ideological Origins of the American Revolution* (Cambridge: Harvard University Press 1967), 22–54. Richard Hofstadter, *The Idea of a Party System: The Rise of Legitimate Opposition in the United States 1780–1840* (Berkeley: Stanford University Press 1970), 1–39; see also Gordon Stewart, *The Origins of Canadian Politics: A Comparative Approach* (Vancouver: University of British Columbia Press 1986), esp. 16–20, 28–30.

27 PAC Pamphlets, Francis Collins, *An Abridged View of the Alien Question Unmasked* (York: Canadian Freeman 1826), 16.

28 *Colonial Advocate*, 19 August 1824.

29 *Gore Gazette*, 30 August 1828.

30 Quoted in Collins, *An Abridged View ...*, 15. See, for example, TPL, Powell Papers, S.P. Jarvis to W.D. Powell, 3 March 1827.

31 *Gore Gazette*, 3 March 1827. See also ibid. 24 May 1828, letter from "Brush"; Kingston *Chronicle*, 6 April 1827 and Niagara *Gleaner*, 8 September 1828.

32 *Colonial Advocate*, 10 June 1824.

33 *Colonial Advocate*, 1 February 1827.

34 *Upper Canada Herald*, 20 February 1827.

35 *Canadian Freeman*, 8 February 1827.

36 *Upper Canada Herald*, 20 February 1827.

37 Collins, *The Alien Question Unmasked*, 16.

38 *Colonial Advocate*, 1 February 1827. The Tory nativism described by Matthews was also criticized in the *Gore Gazette* (24 May 1827). The Alien Bill was drawn up, it was suggested, by "certain individ-

uals of *European* birth, [who] looked down upon the American emigrants, not only with an eye of jealousy upon their professed *loyalty*, but also as upon an inferior order of beings!"

39 *Colonial Advocate*, 2 February 1826; *Canadian Freeman*, 8 February 1827.
40 Doughty and Story, *Documents ... 1819–1828*, 363–6. See also Phillip A. Buckner, *The Transition to Responsible Government: British Policy in British North America, 1815–1850* (Westport: Greenwood Press 1985), 105–7.
41 CO42/381, pp. 370–7; Maitland to Lord Goderich, 2 October 1827; in Doughty and Story, *Documents ...*, 428–431.
42 *U.E. Loyalist*, 17 March 1827; letter from "Vindex." Jane Errington has analyzed the views of the Compact Tories about the mother country quite well. The king was the focus of loyalty and their support of the British Constitution and pride in the empire remained strong. She also points out that the Tory interpretation of events in Britain reinforced claims about the necessity of a strong executive (*The Lion, the Eagle and Upper Canada*, 98–105). See also Buckner, *The Transition to Responsible Government*, 72–8 and 99–101.
43 Cf. R.J. Burns, "God's Chosen People: The Origins of Toronto Society, 1793–1818," Canadian Historical Association, *Historical Papers* (1973), 213–28; M.S. Cross, "The Age of Gentility: The Formation of an Aristocracy in the Ottawa Valley," Canadian Historical Association, *Historical Papers* (1967), 105–17; H.V. Nelles, "Loyalism and Local Power: The District of Niagara, 1792–1837," *Ontario History*, 58 (1966), 99–116; E.M. Richards, "The Joneses of Brockville and the Family Compact," *Ontario History*, 60 (1968), 169–84.
44 *The Farmers Journal and Welland Canal Intelligencer*, 12 November 1828. See also *Niagara Gleaner*, 1 November 1823.
45 Kingston *Chronicle*, 22 April 1822.
46 Kingston *Chronicle*, 1 February 1822; "John Barleycorn's Address to the Freeholders of the Incorporated Counties of Lenox [*sic*] and Addington." See also Kingston *Chronicle*, 11 May 1827; letter from "A True Born-Canadian."
47 Quoted in Collins, *The Alien Question Unmasked*, 8. See also *U.E. Loyalist*, 17 November 1827; "Idea of a Patriot."
48 Kingston *Chronicle*, 11 May 1827.
49 John Strachan, "A letter to the Right Honourable Thomas Frankland Lewis, M.P.," York, 1 February 1830; in J.L.H. Henderson, ed., *John Strachan: Documents and Opinions* (Toronto: University of Toronto Press 1969), 102–3. See also Kingston *Chronicle*, 26 January 1827; letter from "Argus."
50 *Colonial Advocate*, 5 January 1826.

51 *The Farmers Journal*, 12 November 1828. See also Kingston *Chronicle*, 3 January 1823 and *Gore Gazette*, 30 August 1828.

52 *U.E. Loyalist*, 3 February 1827.

53 See, for example, Kingston *Chronicle*, 1 February 1822; letter from "John Barleycorn."

54 S.F. Wise, "Upper Canada and the Conservative Tradition," in Ontario Historical Society, *Profiles of a Province: Studies in the History of Ontario* (Toronto: Ontario Historical Society 1967), 30–1. Errington also argues that in this period Tory defensiveness was intensified by the actions of the imperial government. British policies towards the United States and the British North American colonies were viewed more critically when they affected the Tories; for example, the idea of uniting Upper and Lower Canada in 1822 was forcefully opposed by Strachan and Robinson, among others. The colonial authorities were also condemned for sustaining the radicals both in Britain and in Upper Canada, as the Alien Question had illustrated. See Errington, *The Lion, the Eagle and Upper Canada*, 144–6 and 105–7.

55 TPL, W.W. Baldwin Papers, Rolph to Baldwin, 9 October 1828. Paul Romney has argued that Charles Fothergill was a leader in initiating such concerted activity as his letter of 26 August 1828 to Baldwin indicates: "It seems to me necessary we should endeavour to hold a meeting of a few of the leading *Independent* Members *before* the assembling of Parliament ... *to arrange our measures* ..." (cited in Paul Romney, "A Man Out of Place: The Life of Charles Fothergill: Naturalist, Businessman, Journalist, Politician, 1782–1840" Ph D dissertation, University of Toronto 1981], 405). See also Errington, *The Lion, the Eagle and Upper Canada*, 113–15 for the debate over the independence of legislators.

56 *Upper Canada Herald*, 13 March 1823. See also *Colonial Advocate*, 19 January 1826 and *Kingston Chronicle*, 9 February 1827. Robert Goulay had developed the same arguments a decade earlier in response to the attempts to limit further American settlement in the province. In his "Address to the Resident Landowners of Upper Canada," *Niagara Spectator*, 11 February 1818 and *Kingston Gazette*, 18 February 1818. Some Reformers also sought to turn the Loyalist myth back on their opponents; William Lyon Mackenzie pointed out: "There is, as we all know, a certain feeling among many of the native and immigrant United Empire Loyalists of this day, which teaches them to consider themselves much better subjects, nay even a superior race to their American brethren who by their later immigration cannot lay claim to the same rights. Nay even

British settlers are ... looked upon by these sub-aboriginals as in-
truders" (*Colonial Advocate*, 4 May 1826).
57 Kingston *Chronicle*, 25 February 1825; Supplement.
58 PAC Pamphlets, *Mr Bidwell's Speech on the Intestate Estate Bill in the
Provincial Assembly of Upper Canada, 14 January 1831* (York: np
1831), 3. See also *Niagara Gleaner*, 17 April 1824, letter from "An
Elector."
59 *Colonial Advocate*, 19 August 1824.
60 *U.E. Loyalist*, 27 January 1827. See also *Upper Canada Herald*, 20 February 1827 and *Canadian Freeman*, 8 February 1827. Tory spokesmen had a different view of the American farmers; they were
"men who are fattening on the best of the land, living under the
protection of our laws and partaking of all the blessings we enjoy
but who are ready to betray us to an enemy who would make fair
terms with them" (*Farmers Journal*, 21 February 1827; see also
United Empire Loyalist, 21 April 1827). The Americans and their supporters had no "spark of British feeling" and sought to sever the
imperial connection (Kingston *Chronicle*, 4 May 1827).
61 *Colonial Advocate*, 19 August 1824.
62 *Colonial Advocate*, 2 February 1826. See also *The Farmers Journal*, 25
March 1829.
63 *Colonial Advocate*, 12 January 1826. The Reformers also exhibited less
fear of the United States than did the Tories. John Rolph said:
"Who is associated most intimately with England for the great and
glorious purpose of improving the condition of the human race –
America ..." (ibid., 2 February 1826).
   Many Upper Canadians looked to the United States as a model
for economic development. While American political structures continued to be rejected, innovations in agriculture or transportation
could be adapted to Upper Canada. Errington emphasizes this ambivalence towards the United States in *The Lion, the Eagle and
Upper Canada*, 120–36 and 175–82.
64 *Gore Gazette*, 24 March 1827.
65 *Colonial Advocate*, 24 January 1826. The Tories, of course, challenged
these assumptions. In an open letter "To the Inhabitants of the District of Johnstown," Charles and Solomon Jones of Brockville asked:
"If they have not [been naturalized], can they be legally regarded
as British Subjects? The obvious reply is, No! But it is said we
have done all that has been required of us; we fought for the
country during the last war and is it now to be said we are not
Subjects? Your conduct during the war was praiseworthy, and in
conformity with your duty; but such conduct is not a compliance

with legal provisions by which done you could have become naturalized..." (*Upper Canada Herald*, 27 March 1827).

66 *Canadian Freeman*, 1 March 1827. See also *Upper Canada Herald*,
24 February 1824; letter from "A Freeholder" and *Canadian Freeman*,
1 December 1825.

67 *Colonial Advocate*, 2 February 1826. The attempt to use the schools to
inculcate loyalty has been outlined in G.W. Spragge, "The Upper
Canada Central School," *Ontario History*, 32 (1937), 171–91; R.D. Gidney, "Centralization and Education: The Origins of an Ontario Tradition," *Journal of Canadian Studies*, 7 (1972), 33–48; and Bruce Curtis,
"Schoolbooks and the Myth of Curricular Republicanism: The State
and the Curriculum in Canada West, 1820–1850," *Histoire sociale/So-
cial History*, 16 (1983), 305–30.

68 *Colonial Advocate*, 2 February 1826.

69 *Colonial Advocate*, 19 August 1824.

70 *Upper Canada Herald*, 20 February 1827.

71 *The Farmers Journal*, 26 November 1828.

72 Rolph asked: "Where will be the balance of power, if the crown can
not only refuse the royal assent to a measure submitted at the constitutional stages, but inform us before our deliberations begin that
deliberation is of no avail – argument of no use – for the bill shall
receive the royal assent only upon certain terms ... Our proceedings would thus become a mere matter of form ... an assembly
without a will of its own" (*Canadian Freeman*, 8 February 1827).
Rolph was, of course, perfectly happy with imperial instructions
which conformed to the Reformers' point of view.
There were even some Tories who expressed the same sentiments. S.P. Jarvis, a member of the York elite, believed that the imperial government exacerbated the controversy by ignoring the
advice of the provincial administration. (Cf. TPL, Powell Papers, S.P.
Jarvis to W.D. Powell, 12 September 1827).

CHAPTER FOUR

1 J.S. Moir, *The Church in the British Era: From the British Conquest to
Confederation* (Toronto: McGraw-Hill Ryerson 1972), 113. The popularity of the sect was the result of the mobility of itinerant preachers who could reach the scattered pioneer population and the
strong emotional appeal of its evangelical message; other denominations, notably the Church of England, lacked both ministers and
strong institutional frameworks and so faced immediate disadvantages. See S.D. Clark, *Church and Sect in Canada* (Toronto: Univer-

sity of Toronto Press, reprinted 1971), 108 and Moir, *The Church in the British Era*, 87.

2 Goldwin French, *Parsons and Politics: The Role of the Wesleyan Methodists in Upper Canada and the Maritimes from 1780 to 1855* (Toronto: Ryerson Press 1962), 279.

3 See S.F. Wise, "Upper Canada and the Conservative Tradition," Edith Firth, ed., *Profiles of a Province: Studies in the History of Ontario* (Toronto: Ontario Historical Society 1967), 20–32 for a more complete discussion of the distinctions between High and moderate Toryism.

Paul Romney has also stressed the importance of what he calls "conservative" Reformers like Ryerson and Charles Fothergill in the development of moderate Toryism. He saw this group as composed primarily of British immigrants who believed that the British Constitution as applied in Upper Canada was fundamentally sound; they simply sought to reform the apparent abuses as opposed to the "advanced" reformers who wished to revise the constitution, "even at the risk of political separation from the Empire." This second group was labelled American and included the Baldwins and the Bidwells among others (Paul Romney, "A Man Out of Place: The Life of Charles Fothergill: Naturalist, Businessman, Journalist, Politician, 1782–1840" [Ph D dissertation, University of Toronto 1981], 474–507). Yet Romney concedes that Fothergill did not have a significant political following; Ryerson spoke for a larger constituency in the province and therefore had more impact on political attitudes.

4 Egerton Ryerson, *Canadian Methodism: Its Epochs and Characteristics* (Toronto: William Briggs 1882), 1.

5 For a biography of Ryerson see C.B. Sissons, *Egerton Ryerson: His Life and Letters*, 2 vols (Toronto: Oxford University Press 1937, 1947); see also Neil McDonald and Alf Chaiton, eds, *Egerton Ryerson and His Times* (Toronto: Macmillan of Canada 1978), and R.D. Gidney, "Egerton Ryerson," *Dictionary of Canadian Biography*, XI (1881–90) (Toronto: University of Toronto Press 1982), 783–95.

6 *Christian Guardian*, 21 November 1829.

7 Perceptive observations about the importance of religion in this society may be found in William Westfall's "Order and Experience: Patterns of Religious Metaphor in Early Nineteenth Century Upper Canada," *Journal of Canadian Studies*, 20 (Spring 1985), 5–24.

8 For a biography of Strachan, see J.L.H. Henderson, *John Strachan 1778–1867* (Toronto: University of Toronto Press 1969) and G.M. Craig, "John Strachan," *Dictionary of Canadian Biography*, IX (1861–70) (Toronto: University of Toronto Press 1982), 751–66. Strachan's influence over the provincial elite has been noted in G.M. Craig, *Upper Canada: The Formative Years, 1784–1841* (Toronto: McClelland

& Stewart 1963), 106–13, 169ff.; F.M. Quealey, "The Administration of Sir Peregrine Maitland, Lieutenant Governor of Upper Canada, 1818–1828" (Ph D dissertation, University of Toronto 1968), 113–31, 438–64; and R.J. Burns, "The First Elite of Toronto: An Examination of the Genesis, Consolidation and Duration of Power in an Emerging Colonial Society" (Ph D dissertation, University of Western Ontario 1974), 114–20, and Chapter 8.

9 See Wise, "Upper Canada and the Conservative Tradition"; see also his articles "God's Peculiar Peoples" in W.L. Morton, ed., *The Shield of Achilles* (Toronto: McClelland & Stewart 1968), 36–62; "Sermon Literature and Canadian Intellectual History," *The Bulletin of the Committee on Archives, the United Church of Canada* (1965), 3–18. See also J.J. Talman, "The Position of the Church of England in Upper Canada, 1791–1840," *Canadian Historical Review*, 15 (1934), 361–75 and Curtis Fahey, "A Troubled Zion: The Anglican Experience in Upper Canada, 1791–1854" (Ph D dissertation, Carleton University 1981).

10 PAC, *The Seventh Report from the Select Committee … on Grievances* (Toronto: Correspondent & Advocate 1835), 86; Strachan's testimony. For a detailed examination of orthodox Anglican political theology in late eighteenth century Britain which analyzes more fully the concept of "the constitution in church and state," see J.C.D. Clark's *English Society, 1688–1832: Ideology, Social Structure and Political Practice during the Ancien Régime.* (Cambridge: Cambridge University Press 1985), 222–35.

11 PAC Pamphlets, John Strachan, *Claims of the Churchmen and Dissenters of Upper Canada Brought to the Test in a Controversy Between Several Members of the Church of England and a Methodist Preacher* (Kingston 1828), 20–1; see also Strachan, *A Sermon Preached at York, Upper Canada, Third of July 1825, on the Death of the Late Lord Bishop of Quebec* (Kingston 1826); in J.L.H. Henderson, ed., *John Strachan: Documents and Opinions* (Toronto: McClelland & Stewart 1969), 90–1.

12 See G.W. Spragge, "The Upper Canada Central School," *Ontario History*, 32 (1937), 171–91; J.D. Purdy, "John Strachan's Educational Policies, 1815–1841," *Ontario History*, 64 (1972), 45–64; and R.D. Gidney "Centralization and Education: The Origins of an Ontario Tradition," *Journal of Canadian Studies*, 7 (1972), 33–48.

13 PAO, *Strachan Letter Book, 1812–1834*, Report on Education, 26 February 1815, pp. 7–8; see also Strachan's Convocation Address to his Cornwall students (1807), in A.N. Bethune, *Memoir of the Right Reverend John Strachan* (Toronto: Henry Rowsell 1870), 26–9.

Chief Justice John Beverley Robinson also believed that selection into the Upper Canadian elite should be based upon merit and respectability. A man must be "the most worthy, intelligent, loyal, and opulent inhabitant ... a gentleman of high character, of large property, and of superior information" (J.B. Robinson, *Canada and the Canada Bill: Being an Examination of the Proposed Measure for the Future Government of Canada* ... [London: J. Harchard & Son 1840], 144–5).

14 Kingston *Gazette*, 3 September 1811; Strachan's address.

15 PAO, *Strachan Letter Book, 1812–1834*. Report on Education, 26 February 1815.

16 *Canada Church Establishment*; copy of a letter addressed to R.J. Wilmot Horton, Esq. by the Rev. Dr Strachan, Archdeacon of York, Upper Canada, dated 16 May 1827; respecting the State of the Church in that Province. Quoted in A.G. Doughty and N. Story, eds, *Documents Relating to the Constitutional History of Canada, 1819–1828* (Ottawa: King's Printer 1935), 304–5.

17 PAO Pamphlets, John Strachan, *An Appeal to the Friends of Religion and Literature on Behalf of the University of Upper Canada* (London: R. Gilbert 1827), 20.

18 Cf. G.W. Spragge, ed. *The John Strachan Letter Books, 1812–1834* (Toronto: Ontario Historical Society 1945), xiv–xv; see also Strachan's *Notes*, 222–3.

19 Quoted in R.A. Preston, ed., *Kingston before the War of 1812* (Toronto: University of Toronto Press 1959), 292.

20 PAC, CO42/355, p. 70; Sir Gordon Drummond to Lord Bathurst, 30 April 1814.

21 S.D. Clark, *Movements of Political Protest in Canada 1640–1840* (Toronto: University of Toronto Press 1959), 232–3. Fred Landon has noted, though, that: "there is nothing to indicate that Methodists were less ardent in their support of the war than other religious group ..." (in his *Western Ontario and the American Frontier* [Toronto: McClelland & Stewart reprinted 1967], 77).

22 G.F. Playter, *The History of Methodism in Canada* (Toronto: Wesleyan Printing Establishment 1862), 144.

23 Other High Tories were not as inflexible as Strachan. John Beverley Robinson believed that in a pioneer society like Upper Canada it was important that the principles of the Christian faith be inculcated into the population, even by dissenting preachers: "Frequently, in the most lonely parts of the wilderness, in townships where a clergyman of the Church of England had never been heard, and probably never seen, I have found the population assembled in some log building, earnestly engaged in acts of devotion, and listening to those doctrines and truths which are inculcated in common by most Christian denominations, but which, if it had not been for the ministrations of dissenting preachers, would for thirty years

have been but little known, if at all, to the greater part of the inhabitants of the interior of Upper Canada." Robinson believed that
all dissenters would eventually return to the Church of England
(cited in C.W. Robinson, *Life of Sir John Beverley Robinson, Bart.,
C.B., D.C.L., Chief Justice of Upper Canada* [Toronto: Morang & Co.
1904], 178–9).

24 Curtis Fahey, "A Troubled Zion," 125. The discussion of Strachan's
views is drawn from this analysis, 125–54.

25 Strachan, "History and the Present State of Religion in Upper
Canada," *Christian Recorder* (March 1819), 14–16.

26 PAO, *Strachan Papers*, Strachan to James Brown, 13 July 1806.

27 Kingston *Gazette*, 19 May 1819.

28 PAO, *Strachan Sermons*, "Another parable he spake unto them ...";
preached on 1 February 1835.

29 Fahey, "A Troubled Zion," 129. Strachan made this belief explicit in
a sermon delivered in 1847: "Faith ... is not a temporary or impetu-
ous emotion, but a habit, a state of mind, lasting and emotional ...
Faith is the yielding up of ourselves to the obedience of Christ –
but to obey Christ is to live the life under which Christ lived[,] a
life pre-eminently of good works" (PAO, *Strachan Sermons*, "If thou
will enter into life ...," preached on 21 November 1847). Good
works, then, were as important as faith as a means to attain salvation: the Methodist emphasis upon salvation "by grace" alone was
inadequate (PAO, Strachan Papers, Strachan to Brown, 27 October
1803).

30 PAC Pamphlets, *A Speech of the Venerable John Strachan, D.D., Archdeacon of York, in the Legislative Council, Thursday, Sixth March, 1828:
on the Subject of the Clergy Reserves* (York 1828), 27–8.

31 John Strachan, *A Sermon ... on the Death of the Late Lord Bishop of
Quebec*, in Henderson, *John Strachan: Documents and Opinions*, 93.

32 PAC CO42/399, p. 3; Sir Peregrine Maitland to Lord Bathurst,
4 January 1821.
   Tory distrust of American elements in the province shaped reactions to the Episcopal Methodists into the 1830s. (Cf. *The Patriot
and Farmers Monitor*, 10 May 1833 and the petition from Donald Bethune, an Anglican minister from Kingston, contained in the *Christian Guardian*, 9 February 1831.)

33 Ryerson, *Canadian Methodism*, 18.

34 In J.Telford, ed., *The Letters of John Wesley* (London 1931), VII, 305; IV,
271–2, in L. Tyerman, *The Life and Times of the Rev. John Wesley,
AM, Founder of the Methodists* (New York 1872), I, 441; quoted in
French, "Egerton Ryerson and the Methodist Model for Upper Canada," in McDonald and Chaiton, eds, *Egerton Ryerson and His Times*,

50. For a more detailed discussion of the political theology of the Methodists in England, see David Hempton, *Methodism and Politics in British Society, 1750–1850* (London: Hutchinson 1984) and especially, *Clark, English Society, 1688–1832*, 235–47.

35 Egerton Ryerson, *The Story of My Life: Being Reminiscences of Sixty Years' Public Service in Canada*, edited by J.G. Hodgins (Toronto: William Briggs 1883), 27.

36 *Christian Guardian*, 3 July 1830.

37 *Christian Guardian*, 8 October 1830.

38 *Christian Guardian*, 27 March 1830.

39 *Christian Guardian*, 27 March 1830.

40 *Christian Guardian*, 11 July 1838.

41 Ryerson to Lord Glenelg, 27 May 1836; quoted in R.G. Riddell, "Egerton Ryerson's Views on the Government of Upper Canada in 1836," *Canadian Historical Review*, 19 (1938), 405–6.

42 Ryerson, *Canadian Methodism*, 1.

43 *Christian Guardian*, 3 July 1830.

44 *Minutes* of the Conference, 1836, pp. 135–6; quoted in French, *Parsons and Politics*, 154–5.

45 Ryerson to J.M. Higginson, 8 March 1845; quoted in Susan E. Houston, "Politics, Schools, and Social Change in Upper Canada," *Canadian Historical Review*, 53 (1972), 263.

   After he became Superintendent of Education in 1844, Ryerson attacked American textbooks, which were "Anti-British in every sense of the word"; they were "one element of powerful influence against the established Government of the Country" (E. Ryerson, "Special Report on Measures which have been Adopted for the Establishment of a Normal School and for Carrying into Effect Generally the Common School Act" [Montreal 1847], 14–15; quoted *ibid*.). See also Neil McDonald, "Egerton Ryerson and the School as an Agent of Political Socialization," in McDonald and Chaiton, eds, *Egerton Ryerson and His Times*, 81–104; James H. Love, "Cultural Survival and Social Control: The Development of a Curriculum for Upper Canada's Common Schools in 1846," *Histoire sociale/Social History*, 15 (1982), 357–82; and Bruce Curtis, "Schoolbooks and the Myth of Curricular Republicanism: The State and the Curriculum in Canada West, 1820–1850," *Histoire sociale/Social History*, 16 (1983), 305–30.

46 *Colonial Advocate*, 11 May 1826.

47 Ryerson, *Canadian Methodism*, 133.

48 *Christian Guardian*, 3 July 1830.

49 Ryerson, *Canadian Methodism*, 138.

50 *Christian Guardian*, 3 July 1830.

51 PAC Pamphlets, *Letters from the Reverend Egerton Ryerson to the Hon. and Reverend Doctor Strachan.* Published originally in the *Upper Canada Herald* (Kingston 1828), Letter 2, p. 9.

52 Upper Canada, House of Assembly *Journal* (1828); "Report of the Select Committee, to which was referred ... the petition of Christians of all denominations in Upper Canada ...," 3–5.

53 *Christian Guardian,* 3 July 1830.

54 *Christian Guardian,* 21 August 1833.

55 Ryerson, *Canadian Methodism,* 61.

56 *Christian Guardian,* 15 May 1833.

57 *Christian Guardian,* 3 July 1830. Ryerson attacked the assumption that religious dissenters were disloyal in his response to Strachan in 1826; cf. *Colonial Advocate,* 11 May 1826. The same theme is developed in the *Christian Guardian* of 7 May 1831; 8 October 1831; 18 January 1832; 22 February 1832; 1 March 1832; 4 April 1832; 1 March 1837; 6 January 1838; 10 January 1838.

58 Ryerson, *Canadian Methodism,* pp. 157–158. See also *Christian Guardian,* 9 July 1831.

59 *Christian Guardian,* 3 July 1830.

60 *Christian Guardian,* 9 May 1838. See also editorials of 18 January 1832; 2 October and 27 November 1833.

61 *Christian Guardian,* 6 June 1832.

62 *Christian Guardian,* 11 November 1840.

63 See Douglas Owram, "Strachan & Ryerson: Guardians of the Future," *Canadian Literature,* 83 (Winter 1979), 21–9.

64 *Christian Guardian,* 30 October 1833.

65 Quoted in John Carroll, *Case and His Cotemporaries* (Toronto: Samuel Rose 1867–77), II, 213. See also United Church Archives, *Wesleyan Methodist Missionary Correspondence, 1829–1840.* Letter from John Fenton and Richard Coates, 3 June 1829.

66 See Clark, *Church and Sect,* 262–71.

67 Ryerson, *The Story of My Life,* 52.

68 United Church Archives, *The Journal of Benjamin Slight,* I, 55–6 (26 October 1834); quoted in Clark, *Church and Sect,* 267.

69 *Christian Guardian,* 17 July 1835.

70 *Christian Guardian,* 17 July 1835. United Church Archives, *Wesleyan Records;* H. Ryan to A. Clarke, 9 October 1815; quoted in French, *Parsons and Politics,* 71.

71 *Colonial Advocate,* 11 May 1826.

72 It has been estimated that the numbers of Methodists in Upper Canada increased from about 38,000 in 1830 to 61,000 by 1839 (*Christian Guardian,* 6 February 1830 and John Strachan to Dr Burns, 13 February 1839, in *Glasgow Colonial Society Correspondence;* cited in P.A.

Russell, "Church of Scotland Clergy in Upper Canada: Culture
Shock and Conservatism on the Frontier," *Ontario History*, 73 [June
1981], 90]).

73 United Church Archives, *Journal of the Rev. George Ferguson, a Minister
of the Wesleyan Methodist Church in Canada*, 93–4; cited in Clark,
Church and Sect, 200.

74 United Church Archives, *Wesleyan Records*. Peter Brown, Daniel Cum-
mins et al., Yonge Street and Ancaster circuits, to the London Methodist Missionary Society, 4 December 1816; quoted in French,
Parsons and Politics, 73.

75 Cf. Playter, *The History of Methodism*, 240–1, 315–30. The creation of a
separate Canadian Methodist Church did not silence all the critics.
Henry Ryan, who had been pushed to the periphery of the Methodist movement, broke with the main body and created his own
small sect, the Canadian Wesleyan Methodist Church. Ryan's flock
was concentrated in the Bay of Quinte area and numbered about
200; some were of Loyalist background and others were Irish Methodists (Moir, *The Church in the British Era*, 113). Ryan, while angry
at the main body for excluding him, also articulated the tensions
between his supporters and the "American" Episcopals. The Reverend George Ferguson wrote: "My removal to Hallowell [in 1828]
was still more distressing to me. Mr. Ryan had commenced his
career. He was zealous, and talented withal. Loyalty was his catch-
word, and he constantly denounced the ministers of the Canada
Conference as disloyal" (quoted in Moir, *The Church in the British
Era*, 202).

The Primitive Methodists also perceived the Episcopals to be disloyal because of their American ties: "The Methodists in this Province are very numerous and influential but are supposed
(especially by the highest authorities) to be disaffected, a great proportion of them being Emigrants from the United States, are supposed to retain much of the Republican feeling of that country,
and many of their Preachers coming from the United States are expected to exert an influence over their minds prejudicial to our
Government. ... If any Emigrants from England[,] Ireland or Scotland joins their Society he is made very uncomfortable by being assailed with political subjects, and unless he consent to join them in
their defamation of the Government or at least listen to it with
silence he is considered unsound in the faith" (United Church
Archives, *Primitive Methodist Minute Book*. Wm Lawson, John Fenton, Francis Swann to the Rev. Hugh Bourne; 1 October 1830; cited
in Edith Firth, ed., *The Town of York, 1815–1834* [Toronto: University
of Toronto Press 1966], 205–6).

76 Upper Canada, House of Assembly, *Journal* (1828); "Report of the Select Committee, to which was referred ... the petition of Christians of all denominations of Upper Canada; and other petitions on the same subject ...," 3–5. See also Ryerson, *The Story of My Life*, 104.

77 *Christian Guardian*, 15 May 1833. Methodist immigrants from Great Britain did distrust the Episcopals and viewed both their religious and political views with distaste. The British Wesleyan Society stated in a petition that: "We look forward to the time when thousands of Emigrants from Europe will make this Province their home and when true and genuine Methodism might be universally diffused throughout the country" (United Church Archives, *Wesleyan Methodist Correspondence 1829–1840*. Petition from the British Wesleyan Society of York, in a letter from Egerton Ryerson, dated 19 October 1831).

78 The union is discussed in more depth in French, *Parsons and Politics*, 138–42. Not all Episcopals saw the benefits of closer relations with the Wesleyans. George Ryerson, one of Egerton's older brothers, viewed the Toryism of the Wesleyans with distaste: "Perhaps I do not use too strong terms when I say that I detest their blind veneration for the writings of Mr. Wesley (excellent in themselves, but not inspired, and containing much of human infirmity and the prejudices of a High Church education); their exalted opinion of themselves and their system, their servile reverence for great men and great names and their servile clinging to the skirts of a corrupt, secularized anti-Christian Church. They are generally either anti-Reformers or half-hearted, lukewarm, hesitating reformers ... altogether I fear that the Wesleyan Conference is an obstacle to the extension of civil and religious liberty" (*Christian Guardian*, 6 August 1831).

79 *Kingston Chronicle*, 12 October 1833.

80 *Kingston Chronicle*, 10 March 1832.

81 *The Antidote*, 15 January 1833; see also *ibid.*, 1 January and 9 April 1833.

82 *Canadian Freeman*, 19 August 1830.

83 *Christian Guardian*, 15 May 1833.

84 *Christian Guardian*, 28 March 1832.

85 *Christian Guardian*, 30 October 1833.

86 *Christian Guardian*, 4 June 1834.

87 *Christian Guardian*, 7 November 1833.

88 David Wright, et al. to Ryerson, 21 November 1833; quoted in Sissons, *Egerton Ryerson ...*, I, 214–16. William Lyon Mackenzie was more succinct, and abusive, in his condemnation of Ryerson: "Another

Deserter" had gone "over to the enemy, press, types, & all, & hoisted the colours of a cruel, vindictive tory priesthood" (*Colonial Advocate*, 26 October 1833).

89 *Christian Guardian*, 13 November 1833.
90 United Church Archives, *Wesleyan Methodist Missionary Correspondence, 1829–1840*. Stinson to Robert Alder, 24 April 1834; quoted in French, *Parsons and Politics*, 148.
91 *Upper Canada Herald*, 9 August 1836. They were J. Cook and P. Shaver from Dundas County; D. Duncombe from Norfolk; C. Duncombe from Oxford; T.D. Morrison from York; A. Norton from Grenville; and T. Parke from Middlesex.
92 *Christian Guardian*, 15 June 1836.
93 *Christian Guardian*, 8 June 1836.
94 Sir Francis Hincks, *Reminiscences of His Public Life* (Montreal: William Drysdale 1882). 17.
95 See *Upper Canada Herald*, 9 August 1836. They were M. Aikman from Wentworth County, J.R. Armstrong from Prince Edward and G.H. Detlor from Lennox and Addington. (Cf. Sissons, *Egerton Ryerson*, 1,356; French, *Parsons and Politics*, 15–156; Craig, *Upper Canada*, 238.)
96 In the following session of the Assembly, the moderate Tories attempted to consolidate their growing Methodist support. A committee headed by William Henry Draper, the member from Toronto and future spokesmen for moderate conservatism in the 1840s, was established to examine means of settling the contentious Clergy Reserves question. Its report steered between Reform demands for the secularization of the Reserves and the High Tory defence of the exclusive claims of the Church of England. The committee recommended that the Reserves were to be sold and the revenues invested; the interest would be divided among the various denominations on the basis of the number of adherents of each church (*Journal of the Legislative Assembly of Upper Canada*, 11 January 1837). The committee's report was shelved because of the opposition of the High Tories.
97 Egerton Ryerson, *The Loyalists of America and Their Times* (Toronto: William Briggs 1880), II, 447–8, 449.

CHAPTER FIVE

1 *Kingston Chronicle*, 17 January 1829.
2 *Upper Canada Herald*, 1 December 1835.
3 *Upper Canada Herald*, 1 December 1835. See also *The Antidote*, 19 February 1833.

Letters and editorials in the Kingston *Chronicle and Gazette* reflected the same attitudes. For example, a letter from "Pitt" criticizing the idea of an elective council reflected a marked distrust of the people. The concept of equality was rejected more explicitly in an editorical of the same issue, 13 June 1835.

For a more detailed discussion of Upper Canadian conservatism see S.F. Wise, "Conservatism and Political Development: The Canadian Case," *South Atlantic Quarterly*, 69 (Spring 1970), 226–7 and Terry Cook, "John Beverley Robinson and the Conservative Blueprint for the Upper Canadian Community," *Ontario History*, 64 (1972), 79–94.

4 PAC Pamphlets, *Declarations of the Views and Objects of the British Constitutional Society, on its Reorganization* (Toronto 1836), 3. See also the "Declaration of the British Constitutional Society," 10 May 1836 in C. Read and R.J. Stagg, eds, *The Rebellion of 1837 in Upper Canada* (Ottawa: Carleton University Press 1985), 13–14.

5 *The Patriot*, 24 October 1834.

6 *The Upper Canada Herald*, 28 June 1836.

7 Hamilton *Gazette*, 8 June 1836. See also *Niagara Gleaner*, 8 September 1828. Although loyalty was defined in terms of the material benefits of the imperial connection, there were occasional conflicts between loyalty and economic self-interest. John Baldwin, a York merchant, found that he could buy cheaper and better quality goods in the United States than from England. "He then faced the dilemma of being either politically disloyal or economically immoral." Baldwin continued to do business in the United States (T.W. Acheson, "John Baldwin: Portrait of a Colonial Entrepreneur," *Ontario History*, 62 [1969], 165. Cf. Baldwin to Jules Quesnel, 5 June 1827, cited *ibid.*).

8 *The Patriot*, 3 June 1836.

9 *Upper Canada Herald*, 5 April 1836; see also 19 April 1836. In an editorial written two years earlier, the *Kingston Chronicle and Gazette* (15 April 1834) had expressed the same sentiments. The central question was: "can a colony be *independent*?"; the Tory journal answered explicitly that the mother country would always have an interest in Upper Canada. See also *Niagara Gleaner*, 5 April 1832; "Address to King William IV from the Inhabitants of Niagara," and PAC Pamphlets, *Speech of C.A. Hagerman … against the adoption of the Select Committee on the subject of the differences between His Excellency and the Executive Council* (18 April, 1836) (Toronto: Christian Guardian 1836).

10 *The Patriot* 23 October 1832.

11 *The Antidote*, 19 February 1833.

12 *The Patriot*, 6 March 1832.

13 *Upper Canada Herald*, 19 April 1836. See also ibid., 27 November 1833 and Kingston *Chronicle and Gazette*, 29 June 1833.

14 PAC Pamphlets, *Declaration of the Views and Objects of the British Constitutional Society, on its Reorganization* (Toronto 1836), 4.

15 Kingston *Chronicle and Gazette*, 9 April 1835. See also *Gore Gazette*, 3 March 1827.

16 John Beverley Robinson, *Canada and the Canada Bill* ... (London: J. Harchard & Son 1840), 19.

17 *The Patriot*, 7 June 1836; W.H. Draper's address "To the Electors of the City of Toronto." See also St Catharines *Journal*, 2 June 1836; address of William Rykert.

18 PAC, Adiel Sherwood Papers, "Address of the Electors of the Johnstown District" to the Lieutenant Governor (24 May 1836).

19 S.F. Wise, "Upper Canada and the Conservative Tradition," Edith Firth, ed., *Profiles of a Province: Studies in the History of Ontario* (Toronto: Ontario Historical Society 1967), 31. Wise suggests that "the seeds of a separate nationalism were implicit in the Upper Canadian Tory's approach to the economic problems involved in public improvements, trade and banking ..." Support for the Welland Canal, as "a *national* concern," reflected the belief that such projects had not only an economic impact, but "political, social and cultural contexts as well" (ibid., 30). He has also shown that the Tories were able to erect a provincial political system "based upon the alliance of the central bureaucracy with regional power groups." The responsiveness of this coalition to local needs ensured its "considerable electoral success. As a result it was able to break down the particularism of its supporters and ultimately to generate a provincial mentality" (Wise, "Conservatism and Political Development," 241; see also his "Upper Canada and the Conservative Tradition," 23–8).

20 *Courier of Upper Canada*, 1 May 1833.

21 CO42, Vol. 454, *Address to her Majesty, on the State of the Province*; J. Robinson, Speaker for Legislative Council, 28 February 1838. John Strachan also occasionally questioned the actions of the mother country. In 1828, he believed that Britain had been taken over by a "false liberality"; a House of Commons report on British North American affairs would "do great mischief in all Colonies – its tendency is to prostrate everything British – to nourish discontent – to depress the Friends of Good Government and to strengthen levellers and Democrats" (OA, John Strachan Letter Book, 1827–39, p. 27; Strachan to W.H. Hale, 29 December 1828).

22 *The Patriot*, 13 March 1832.

23 *Upper Canada Herald*, 13 June 1837.

24 *Upper Canada Herald*, 20 June 1837. John Beverley Robinson, in his *Canada and the Canada Bill* (1840), expressed the same sentiments. The feelings of the Loyalists, he wrote, "sprang from a pure source. Their loyalty was sincere for it led to the sacrifice of property, of country, of kindred, and friends." Cited in C.W. Robinson, *Life of Sir John Beverley Robinson* (Toronto: Morang & Co. 1904), 193.

This loyalty was confirmed during the War of 1812 when Upper Canadians defended the province "fighting under the immortal Brock" (*Niagara Gleaner*, 7 April 1832; see also *The Patriot*, 25 November 1836). Some Tories not only stressed the Loyalist tradition but argued that the Loyalists and their descendents were the natural leaders of the society. Christopher Hagerman said: "we have a priority of right as the earliest settlers of the country" (in Kingston *Chronicle and Gazette*, 3 February 1836).

25 Wise, "Conservatism and Political Development," 240.

26 PAC, Adiel Sherwood Papers, "Address of the Electors of the Johnstown District" to the Lieutenant Governor (24 May 1836).

27 *Christian Guardian*, 4 April 1838. See also *Gore Gazette*, 30 August 1828; Kingston *Chronicle*, 17 March 1832, letter from "Hibernicus"; and Kingston *Chronicle and Gazette*, 3 March 1838 for similar sentiments.

28 Kingston *Chronicle and Gazette*, 9 April 1836.

29 *Upper Canada Herald*, 20 June 1837. See also Kingston *Chronicle*, 30 July 1831 and 17 March 1832; letter from "O.P.Q."; Kingston *Chronicle and Gazette* 29 July 1833; and *The Patriot*, 24 October 1834. George Gurnett believed that in Upper Canada there were "a few desparate political adventurers, who are playing a deep game for the promotion of their own ambitious projects – by exciting a prejudice against the Government and by representing the persons composing the Government in as odious a light as possible" (*Gore Gazette*, 30 August 1828).

30 For a more detailed discussion of political organization, see G.H. Patterson, "Studies in Elections and Public Opinion in Upper Canada" (Ph D dissertation, University of Toronto 1969); see also Eric Jackson, "The Organization of Upper Canadian Reformers, 1818–1867," in *Ontario History*, 53 (1961), 95–115.

31 Richard Hofstadter, *The Idea of a Party System: The Rise of Legitimate Opposition in the United States, 1780–1840* (Berkeley: Stanford University Press 1970), 12.

32 *The Patriot*, 23 October 1832; see other examples, Kingston *Chronicle*, 10 March and 31 March 1832, and letters from "An Anglo-Canadian" (24 March 1832), and "Hibernicus" (31 March 1832); *Niagara Gleaner*, 17 November 1832, letter on "Party Spirit." In an address

to the electors of Frontenac, Robert Drummond stated: "I am not a party man; I deprecate [sic] party spirit; and should you do me the favor to elect me, I shall regard your interests and the interests of the Province, as the sole end and aim of my political career" (Kingston *Chronicle and Gazette*, 26 July 1834).

33 *Gore Gazette*, 13 December 1828; see also *U.E. Loyalist*, 17 November, 1, 29 December 1827; and a letter from "An Elector" in the Cornwall *Observer*, 18 April 1834; *The Patriot*, 21 February 1832, and Kingston *Chronicle*, 3 March 1832; "An Address of the inhabitants of Cobourg to the King," and a Petition from the inhabitants of Kingston.

34 *The Patriot*, 19 September 1834; Charles Fothergill's electoral address.

35 Hamilton *Gazette*, 18 May 1833. See also the expression of similar sentiments in the *Niagara Gleaner*, 7 April 1832; the *Courier of Upper Canada*, 22 January 1835; and *The Patriot*, 14 June 1836; the electoral address of William Dunlop.

36 *Bathurst Courier*, 3 June 1836; see also PAO, Robinson Papers, J.B. Robinson to R. Wilmot Horton, 14 December 1828.

37 Sir John Colborne to the Secretary of State, 7 May 1832, quoted in S.D. Clark, *Movements of Political Protest in Canada* (Toronto: University of Toronto Press 1959), 415. Tory attitudes were also reflected by Duncan Cameron, a retired British military officer who had settled in York Mills in 1836. He wrote to Joseph Gordon in Edinburgh: "the improvement throughout the country is going on as fast as possible, but radical Yankees and other evil-disposed people have been very busy endeavouring to agitate and poison the mind of the people against the Government, and against everything which tend to the welfare and prosperity of the country, but I think those evil agitators have gone the length of their tether" (Cameron to Gordon, 20 May 1836; in T.W.L. MacDermot, "Some Opinions of a Tory in the 1830's," *Canadian Historical Review*, 11 [1930], 233).

38 *Gore Gazette*, 13 December 1828.

39 R.C. Coyne, "The Talbot Papers," in *Transactions of the Royal Society of Canada*, series III, vol. 3 (1909), 121–2; quoted in S.D. Clark, *Movements of Political Protest in Canada*, 472.

40 Kingston *Chronicle and Gazette*, 20 September 1834. See also ibid., 13 June 1835, and a letter from "A Good Subject" in *The Patriot*, 29 July 1934.

41 Sir Francis Bond Head, *A Narrative* (London 1839), 74–5; quoted in Clark, *Moments of Political Protest*, 472; ibid., 65; quoted in G.M. Craig, *Upper Canada: The Formative Years, 1784–1841* (Toronto: McClelland & Stewart 1963), 236.

42 Head to Lord Glenelg, 15 February 1836; quoted in Bruce Walton, "The 1836 Election in Lennox and Addington," *Ontario History,* 67 (September 1975), 157.

43 PAC, Adiel Sherwood Papers, Sir Francis Bond Head's "Reply to the Electors of the Home District" (28 May 1836); and Kingston *Chronicle and Gazette,* 27 April 1836.

44 *The Patriot,* 26 July 1833.

45 *Bathurst Courier,* 6 May 1836. See also PAC, Adiel Sherwood Papers, Jonas Jones "To the Electors of the County of Leeds" (14 June 1836). Similar sentiments about the symbolic role of the Governor were expressed in England; for example, Thomas Carlyle articulated the concept of the hero-governor as an alternative to democracy. (Cf. Walter E. Houghton, *The Victorian Frame of Mind, 1830–1870* [New Haven: Yale University Press 1967], 329.)

46 All editorials were printed in the Cornwall *Observer,* 23 August 1836.

47 *Correspondent and Advocate,* 8 June 1836.

48 Cf. Perth *Courier,* 24 June 1836; in Andrew Haydon, *Pioneer Sketches in the District of Bathurst* (Toronto: Ryerson Press 1925), 121.

49 For a more detailed discussion of the composition of this Tory coalition see Wise, "Upper Canada and the Conservative Tradition," 20–32. See also Phillip A. Buckner, *The Transition to Responsible Government: British Policy in British North America 1815–50* (Westport: Greenwood Press 1985), 213–16 and 233–4 for a short analysis of developments in the 1830s.

50 Kingston *Chronicle and Gazette,* 7 May 1836.

51 *The Patriot,* 10 December 1833. For a discussion of the lack of consensus among Tories at the local level, see S.F. Wise, "Tory Factionalism: Kingston Elections and Upper Canadian Politics, 1820–1836," *Ontario History,* 57 (1965), 205–25. See also Paul Romney, "The Spanish Freeholder Imbroglio of 1824: Inter-Elite and the Intra-Elite Rivalry in Upper Canada," *Ontario History,* 76 (1984), 32–47.

52 Cf. Upper Canada, House of Assembly, *Journal,* 1831, pp. 94–5 (12 March 1831).

53 Upper Canada House of Assembly, *Journal,* 1833–4, p. 126 (24 February 1834).

54 *Upper Canada Gazette,* 15 February 1821; see also ibid., 22 February 1821.

55 PAC Pamphlets, "J.K.," *Plain Reasons for Loyalty, Addressed to Plain People* (Cobourg 1838), 2, 3. See also Susanna Moodie, *Roughing It in the Bush* (reprinted Toronto: McClelland & Stewart 1970), 139–42.

56 *The Loyalist,* 7 June 1828.

57 *The Loyalist,* 7 June 1828. The idea about the superiority of the "Men of the North" has been analyzed most fully in Carl Berger, "The

True North Strong and Free," in Peter Russell, ed., *Nationalism in Canada* (Toronto: McGraw-Hill, Ryerson 1966), 3–26.

58 Kingston *Chronicle and Gazette*, 7 May 1836.

59 Patrick Shirreff, *A Tour through North America* ... (Edinburgh 1835); quoted in Clark, *Movements of Political Protest...*, 484. S.D. Clark has offered the most apt analysis of the factors which produced a strong loyal response among recent immigrants: "Settlement in a new land like Upper Canada involved, immediately at least, a real social – and, in many cases, even among the poorer immigrants, a cultural – loss. Concern thus tended to be with restoring the ties of the past rather than with seeking the improvement of that which was of the present. The effect thus was to make the overseas immigrant an ardent patriot. He became increasingly ready to spring to the defence of the British empire, the monarchy, the es-tablished church, a system of social privilege, and all those other institutions and systems of ideas upon which the society he had known appear to have rested" (Clark, *Movements of Political Protest*, 486).

60 See D.H. Akenson, *The Irish in Ontario: A Study in Rural History* (Kingston: McGill-Queen's University Press 1984), 3–47. For a detailed discussion of the patterns of Irish settlement and the growth of the Orange Order, see C.J. Houston and W.J. Smyth, *The Sash Canada Wore: A Historical Geography of the Orange Order in Canada* (Toronto: University of Toronto Press 1980), 21–34.

61 PAO Pamphlets, W.B. Kerr, "The Orange Order in Upper Canada in the 1820's," in *The Sentinel*, 19 January 1939; see also Hereward Senior, *Orangeism: The Canadian Phase* (Toronto: McGraw-Hill 1972).

62 W. Fraser to Sir Peregrine Maitland (1827); quoted in Kerr, "The Orange Order in Upper Canada ..."

63 Kingston *Chronicle*, 30 May 1823.

64 *Kingston Chronicle*, 30 May 1823. Colonel James Fitzgibbon, also of Irish origin, expressed concern about the reaction of the old inhabitants to the prospect of Irish violence in Upper Canada. He wrote: "When the Irish Emigrants began to arrive in Canada, the old inhabitants often expressed their fears that the evils so unhappily rooted in Ireland would be transplanted into these hitherto peaceful Provinces; and I could not help participating in those fears. I was also afraid that even if party strife were not revived, individual Irishmen would be found more prone to irregular habits than the other emigrants, and such also was the general opinion in this Province" (*Upper Canada Sundries*, Vol. 78; Col. James Fitzgibbon "To the Orangemen of Cavan and Perth, June 18, 1826"). For a good discussion of Fitzgibbon's career, see J.K. Johnson, "Col.

James Fitzgibbon and the Suppression of Irish Riots in Upper Canada," in *Ontario History*, 58 (1966), 139–56.

65 *Upper Canada Sundries*, J.W. Macaulay and others to Sir John Colborne, 8 February 1830.

66 Brockville *Gazette*, 29 August 1828.

67 More detailed information on Gowan and the Orange Order can be obtained from Hereward Senior, *Orangeism: The Canadian Phase*, 13–56 and Akenson, *The Irish in Ontario*, 169–201.

68 PAC Pamphlets, *Objects and Principles of the Society: Rules and Regulations of the Orange Institution of British North America* (Brockville: Thomas Tompkins 1830).

69 Brockville *Gazette*, 29 August 1828.

70 Extract from the Proceedings of the Annual Meeting of the Grand Orange Lodge ..., quoted in the Cobourg *Star*, 11 July 1832.

71 *The Antidote*, 12 February 1833.

72 *The Antidote*, 10 December 1832; see also ibid., 19 February 1833.

73 *The Antidote*, 15 January 1833; see also ibid., 1 January 1833.

74 *The Antidote*, 10 December 1832.

75 *The Antidote*, 22 January 1833; see also ibid., 15 January 1833.

76 For a useful discussion of the problems faced by the Irish immigrants in Upper Canada, and their political responses, see Patterson, "Studies in Elections and Public Opinions in Upper Canada," 190–228 and Hereward Senior, "Ogle Gowan, Orangeism and the Immigrant Question, 1830–33," *Ontario History*, 66 (1974), 193–210.

77 See the Brockville *Gazette*, 18 September, 2 October, and 30 October 1830 and the Brockville *Recorder*, 28 September and 12 October 1830 for details of the local election. Gowan was praised for his attempts to mould the "Europeans" into a solid political bloc and stimulate a sense of immigrant consciousness. "A Friend to Fair Play and An Enemy to canting hypocrisy" wrote: "It must be a subject truly gratifying to the feelings of every Englishman, Irishman and Scotchman, that a spirit of nationality has been aroused, and now pervades all classes of Emigrants in this Country. Thanks to Mr. Gowan, he has boldly stepped forward to point out the degradation that has been cast on the 'Old Country people', to become their unpurchased and unpurchaseable advocate, and to arouse them to a just sense of their situation, the insults they have received, the neglect with which they have been treated, and their power and duty to punish such insult, and prevent such neglect. Let Europeans shake off their apathy, and the cause of justice will be complete, – the long-drawn whimperings of '*Yankee Doodle*' will be exchanged for the good old National music of '*God save the*

King'" (Brockville *Gazette,* 2 October 1830). See also Akenson, *The Irish in Ontario,* 173–5.

78 *The Antidote,* 17 December 1832; see also ibid., 10 December 1832, 15 January and 19 February 1833 and Committee on Orange History, *One Man's Loyalty* (Toronto: University of Toronto Press 1980), 8–9.

79 *The Antidote,* 1 January 1833. See also ibid., 25 December 1832. The issue was raised again in 1836 and Gowan was joined by Colonel John Prince in his defence of British lawyers. See R. Alan Douglas, ed., *John Prince, 1796–1870: A Collection of Documents* (Toronto: University of Toronto Press 1980), 8–9.

80 *The Antidote,* 1 January 1833.

81 *The Antidote,* 22 January 1833.

82 *The Antidote,* 29 January 1933. Cf. a letter from "A Friend to Economy" criticizing the appointment of "a Yankee engineer" (23 April 1833); a letter from "Amicus Hibernicus" listed political appointments in Leeds County, noting the lack of English and Irish in local offices (30 April 1833).

83 *The Antidote,* 8 January 1833.

84 *The Antidote,* 8 January 1833; See also 19 March 1833.

85 Gowan had lost his election in 1830; in 1832, G.H. Reade, an Orangeman, was defeated in a by-election. See *The Antidote,* 17 December 1832; also Akenson, *The Irish in Ontario,* 174–9.

86 *The Antidote,* 15 January 1833; see also ibid., 16 April 1833.

87 See, for example, the resolutions of the Lennox and Addington Reformers on pauper immigrants printed in the Brockville *Recorder,* 29 March 1832. It was reported a year later that the Reformers promised to come to a political meeting in Brockville in March 1833 "no matter what might be the consequence; aye, and bring guns too and shot [sic] those rascally Irish!!" Dreadful reports were spread – "give me but twenty men," cried one "and I'll beat the Irish out of the country ..." (*The Antidote,* 19 March 1833). When the Orangemen broke up the meeting, "Hibernicus" declared that they "have gained a glorious victory ... A few years ago, I looked around and saw my fellow countrymen insulted, reviled, trampled upon, bearded from the Magisterial bench by an arrogant, puffed up Magistrate – commanded in the Militia by boys and minions. Yes, Sir, so far was the enmity carried towards the Irish, that, in an advertisement for a servant woman, it was intimated that no Irish woman need apply. 'The vote of any Irishman can be bought for a glass of whiskey,' was the cry of a parliamentary candidate ... We have now got our foot upon their necks, and they, in turn, must bite the dust" (ibid., 26 March 1833). See also Brockville *Recorder,* 14 March 1833, and Ian MacPherson, *Matters of Loyalty: The*

Buells of Brockville, 1830–1850 (Brockville: Mika Publishing 1981), 140–4.

88 *The Antidote,* 10 December 1832. Cf. an editorial on 1 January 1833, and Gowan's speech, 22 January 1833.

89 Samuel Thompson, *Reminiscences of a Canadian Pioneer for the Last Fifty Years: An Autobiography* (Toronto: Hunter, Rose, & Co. 1984), 155.

90 Letter from Ogle Gowan to Gunner Charles Ames, cited in Ian E. Wilson, "Ogle R. Gowan, Orangeman," in *Douglas Library Notes,* 17: 4 (1969), 18–20. The Orange Order did attract some "respectable" support; Colonel J. Covert, a justice of the peace, wrote: "[W]hen we consider, that our constitution was assailed, the lives and property of the King's subjects in danger, our religious establishments derided and threatened, and every man of virtue and worth insulted, we naturally looked around for the best means to counteract these evils – it was then to avert these awful evils, to maintain the integrity of the Empire – to rescue from the sword and insurrection the families of good men, and to assist in accomplishing these hallowed purposes, that I judged it right and wise to join the Orange Society, jointly with other Magistrates and gentlemen of this Country" (Cobourg *Star,* 21 August 1833). Cf. a letter from "Presbyterian" in the *Correspondent and Advocate,* 22 February 1837 citing reasons for Presbyterian support of the Orange Order.

91 Electoral violence initiated by Gowan's Orange Irish supporters was a factor in both elections. The election of 1834 was voided as a result of Orange intimidation of Reformers. Jameson and Gowan were re-elected in 1835, again as a result of electoral violence. For a more detailed analysis of the politics of the area, see Patterson, "Studies in Elections and Public Opinion in Upper Canada," 260–87; Akenson, *The Irish in Ontario,* 180–3 and 186–190 and MacPherson, *Matters of Loyalty,* 152–6.

92 Mealing's argument is discussed in Bruce Walton, "The 1836 Election in Lennox and Addington," 153; see also Patterson, "Studies in Elections and Public Opinions in Upper Canada," 284–7 and Akenson, *The Irish in Ontario,* 189–91.

93 Hamilton *Gazette,* 26 December 1837; see also *The Church,* 9 May 1840; and PAC Pamphlets, *Report of the Select Committee of the Legislative Council, on the State of the Province* (Toronto 1839), 10.

94 *Christian Guardian,* 4 April 1838. See also PAC Pamphlets, "J.K.," *Plain Reasons for Loyalty.*

95 Egerton Ryerson, *Canadian Methodism: Its Epochs and Characteristics* (Toronto: William Briggs 1883), 385. See also John Langton to Hugh Hornby, 20 February 1838; in H.H. Langton, ed., *A Gentlewoman in*

Upper Canada: The Journals of Anne Langton (Toronto: Clarke, Irwin & Co. 1950), 63–4. The loyalty of the population was affirmed by the administration; cf. PAC Pamphlets, *Report of the Select Committee of the Legislative Council*, 10–11. See also the Kingston *Chronicle and Gazette*, 10 January 1838 and the *Upper Canada Herald*, 19 December 1837.

Conservative groups in the province seemed to use every opportunity to assert their loyalty. During the loyalty election of 1836, Head was flooded with loyal addresses. See, for example, "Peterborough Resolutions" of 24 April 1836 and an "Address from Toronto" (1836); in G.M. Craig, ed., *Discontent in Upper Canada* (Toronto: Copp Clark Publishing 1974), 187–9. Also Kingston *Chronicle and Gazette*, 5 July 1837; "Address from 2nd Regiment of Glengarry Militia."

96 Montreal *Herald*, 20 December 1838; in *Mackenzie's Gazette*, 30 March 1839; quoted in Colin F. Read, "The Rising in Western Upper Canada, 1837–38: The Duncombe Revolt and After" (Ph D dissertation, University of Toronto 1974), 241. See also Langton to Hornby, 20 February 1838 in Langton, *A Gentlewoman in Upper Canada*, 64; and Kingston *Chronicle and Gazette*, 16 May 1838; letter from "An Sa."

Recent scholarship suggests that Tory perceptions about the nature of the rebels may have been correct. See Read, "The Rising in Western Upper Canada," 239; R.J. Stagg, "The Yonge Street Rebellion of 1837: An Examination of the Social Background and a Reassessment of the Events" (Ph D dissertation, University of Toronto 1976), 199–200, 422.

97 R.B. Sullivan, "Report on the State of the Province" (1 June 1838); in C.R. Sanderson, ed., *The Arthur Papers* (Toronto: University of Toronto Press 1957), I, 152–3. Sullivan's assessment reinforced Arthur's view. Cf. Arthur to the Archbishop of Canterbury, 11 August 1838; ibid., II, 254.

98 Kingston *Chronicle and Gazette* 10 January 1838. Sullivan, "Report …," in Sanderson, ed., *The Arthur Papers*, I, 133.

99 Sullivan, "Report …," in Sanderson, ed., *The Arthur Papers*, I, 183. The Report of a Select Committee of the Tory-dominated House of Assembly pointed to the benefits of the imperial connection. The people lived in "security and peace"; the province was prosperous because of the expansion of trade and commerce which produced the "accumulation of wealth and independence." Therefore, the people remained loyal during the rebellion. "They point to their descent – they point to their deeds in a former war – and they point to their attitude and bearing at this moment of threatened invasion and revolt" [PAC Pamphlets, *Report of a Select Committee of the House*

of Assembly, on the Political State of the Provinces of Upper and Lower Canada [Toronto: R. Stanton 1838], 38, 22).
100 *Kingston Chronicle and Gazette,* 3 March 1838.
101 *The Christian Guardian,* 14 April 1838.

CHAPTER SIX

1 In the *Colonial Advocate,* 30 April 1829; see also *Canadian Freeman,* 16 October 1828.
2 See, for example, the *Christian Guardian,* 8 January 1831; the *Colonial Advocate,* 13 January and 23 June 1831; and Cobourg *Reformer,* quoted in the St Thomas *Liberal,* 27 December 1832. For a more detailed discussion of these developments, see G.M. Craig, *Upper Canada: The Formative Years, 1784–1841* (Toronto: McClelland & Stewart 1963), 188–209.
3 *Colonial Advocate,* 25 March 1830.
4 *Colonial Advocate,* 27 May 1824.
5 Charles Duncombe to Lord Glenelg, 20 September 1836; British Parliamentary Papers, no. 118, pp. 54–5; in G.M. Craig, ed., *Discontent in Upper Canada* (Toronto: Copp Clark Publishing 1974), 176–7.
6 Mackenzie totally rejected Tory optimism about the rate of provincial development. While Upper Canada prospered, it did so in spite of the administration: "our ministerial wiseacres say that the general prosperity of the Province is convincing proof that we can have no grievances to complain of. Yes it prospers, and will continue to prosper. This Province is purely agricultural, and if the Devil himself governed ... [his] efforts might retard, but could not prevent its prosperity" (*Colonial Advocate,* 12 April 1832).
7 Hamilton *Free Press,* in the Brockville *Recorder,* 17 November 1831.
8 *Colonial Advocate,* 4 May 1826.
9 St Thomas *Liberal,* 25 July 1833. See also PAC Pamphlets, *State of the Province: Proceedings of Eighteen Township Meetings in the Home District* (York: James Baxter 1831), 1.
10 *Colonial Advocate,* 12 April 1832.
11 *Correspondent and Advocate,* 8 June 1836.
12 Hamilton *Free Press,* 8 November 1832. See also the *Correspondent and Advocate,* 18 December 1834. Mackenzie also lay the economic and political problems of the province at the feet of the Governor, who rewarded his political friends at the expense of development; see the *Colonial Advocate,* 4 May 1826 and 27 December 1827.
13 William Lyon Mackenzie, *Sketches of Canada and the United States* (London: Effingham Wilson 1833), 409; see also *Canadian Freeman,* 14 August 1828 and *Correspondent and Advocate,* 8 January 1835.

14 *Colonial Advocate*, 17 May 1832; see also the St Thomas *Liberal*, 18 July
   1833. The St Thomas *Liberal* was even more blunt about the disloyalty of the Tories: "Who ever heard of a tory who was not a
   pretended stickler for the constitution?" Moreover, it was pointed
   out with some glee that: "According to our best Lexicographers the
   word Tory is derived from an ancient Irish word, signifying a rob-
   ber: the term in English has always been applied to that party in
   politics, who have ever been distinguished, for their strict adherence to the arbitrary, despotic and illiberal principles ..." (2 November 1832).

15 *Canadian Freeman*, 28 October 1830. See also *Niagara Gleaner*, 17 November 1832; letter on "Party Spirit." T.T. Orton, a Reformer, stated in
   his address to the electors of Durham: "I cannot reconcile my
   mind to the appellation of either Whig, or Tory. I am substantially
   attached to the spirit of the British Constitution" (Kingston
   Chronicle and Gazette, 16 August 1834).

16 The Hamilton *Free Press*, in *The Patriot*, 10 June 1834.

17 *Colonial Advocate*, 1 December 1831.

18 *Christian Guardian*, 14 December 1831. The Solicitor General, Christopher Hagerman, believed that Mackenzie's goal was "to excite the
   feelings of the people in all parts of the country and alienate their
   minds from the Government ..." (*Colonial Advocate*, 5 January 1832).

19 *Christian Guardian*, 14 December 1831.

20 In the *Christian Guardian*, 11 January 1832. See also *Colonial Advocate*,
   29 December 1831; "Address to the Electors of the County of York."

21 *Christian Guardian*, 11 January 1832.

22 *Canadian Correspondent*, 26 July 1834. Hiram Leavenworth, publisher
   of the *British American Journal*, also believed that the greatest threat
   to the rights and liberties of the people was a corrupt administration: "They [the members of the government] have it completely
   within their power to encroach upon the rights, and trample the
   liberties of the people in the dust; to withhold the enactment of
   the most wholesome and salutary laws, and enforce others of the
   most tyrannical and despotick [*sic*] character" (28 January 1834; see
   also an editorial of 1 July 1834).

23 Brockville *Recorder*, 29 January 1836.

24 *Correspondent and Advocate*, 8 June 1836.

25 Brockville *Recorder*, 26 January 1830.

26 *British American Journal*, 2 September 1834.

27 The Cobourg *Reformer*, in the Brockville *Recorder*, 14 June 1832.

28 *British Colonial Argus*, 20 August 1833; see also ibid., 26 October 1833
   and the *Canadian Correspondent*, 26 July 1834.

29 *Canadian Correspondent*, 27 September 1834; electoral address of T.D. Morrison.
   Mackenzie had developed this theme earlier in the decade; see *Colonial Advocate*, 11 March 1830.

30 Brockville *Recorder*, 4 April 1834; see also *The Advocate*, 25 September 1834.

31 St Thomas *Liberal*, 25 October 1832; see also ibid., 1 August 1833.

32 *The Advocate*, 25 September 1834; see also Mackenzie, *Sketches of Canada and the United States*, 155.

33 Brockville *Recorder*, 1 August 1834.

34 Brockville *Recorder*, 1 August 1834.

35 Cf. Robert Baldwin to the Colonial Secretary, 18 July 1836. British Parliamentary Papers (1839), no. 118, pp. 32–9. An enclosure in Lord Glenelg's dispatch to Sir F.B. Head, 20 August 1836; reprinted in Craig, *Discontent in Upper Canada*, 70–6.

36 St Thomas *Liberal*, 18 July 1833. It should also be noted that John Strachan, too, believed that the lieutenant governors should be required to "consult on all occasions with the Executive Council," which should, in turn, "be like the King's Ministers responsible for their advice" (John Strachan Letter Book, 1827–39, 109–10; Strachan to James Stephen, 18 January 1831; quoted in Craig, *Upper Canada: The Formative Years*, 202).

37 Graeme Patterson, "An Enduring Canadian Myth: Responsible Government and the Family Compact," *Journal of Canadian Studies*, 12 (Spring 1977), 10.

38 W.L. Morton, "The Local Executive in the British Empire, 1763–1828," *English Historical Review*, 78 (1963), 441–5, 456–7. W.W. Baldwin's father had articulated doctrines of ministerial responsibility in Ireland in the 1780s; see extracts from Robert Baldwin's Cork *Volunteer Journal* in R.M. and J. Baldwin, *The Baldwins and the Great Experiment* (Toronto: Longmans 1969), 19–32. See also K.D. McRae, ed., "An Upper Canada Letter of 1829 on Responsible Government," *Canadian Historical Review*, 31 (1950), 288–96.

39 Baldwin to Glenelg, 18 July 1836; in Craig, *Discontent in Upper Canada*, 70, 74–5.

40 *Correspondent and Advocate*, 25 January 1836.

41 Baldwin to Lord Durham, 23 August 1838; in the *Report of the Canadian Archives*, 1923 (Ottawa: King's Printer 1924), 328. An address of the Upper Canadian Assembly in 1835 stated that if "persons of worth and talent, who enjoy the confidence of the people" were appointed to the government, loyalty would be strengthened. "We have not the slightest apprehension but the happy connexion

between this Province and the parent state may long continue to exist and be a blessing advantageous to both" (in *The Patriot*, 30 January 1835).

42 Brockville *Recorder*, 1 August 1834. See also Cornwall *Observer*, 11 April 1834; Donald Cameron's address "To the Reformers of the County of Glengarry."

43 *The Advocate*, 25 September 1834.

44 Cornwall *Observer*, 25 April 1834.

45 St Thomas *Liberal*, in the Brockville *Recorder*, 24 October 1834.

46 *The Advocate*, 12 March 1834.

47 CO42/425; enclosed in Sir John Colborne to the Colonial Secretary, 26 January 1835; in Aileen Dunham, *Political Unrest in Upper Canada, 1815–1836* (reprinted Toronto: McClelland & Stewart 1971), 147.

48 Brockville *Recorder*, 20 January 1835.

49 Brockville *Recorder*, 6 February 1835.

50 Brockville *Recorder*, 20 January 1835. See also the letter from "Algernon Sidney" in the St Thomas *Liberal*, 20 September 1832 and the editorial of 4 October 1832 in the same journal; *The Patriot*, 30 January 1835; speech of James Wilson. In an address to "Politicians in the County of York," a small religious sect, the Children of Peace, vowed not to support any man "that doth abuse the subjects of the Province" by calling them disloyal (*Colonial Advocate*, 4 November 1830).

51 *The Patriot*, 27 January 1835. Perry also deplored Tory attempts to generate "loyal support" for the "making of canals, roads and bridges!" (Kingston *Chronicle and Gazette*, 24 February, 1836).

52 *Correspondent and Advocate*, 8 June 1836. The Reformers never missed an opportunity to attack Tory loyalty; they were as willing to use this ideological weapon as their opponents. The Tories exploded in anger at the dismissal of Boulton and Hagerman for their roles in the Mackenzie expulsions, and seriously questioned the imperial connection. In response to Gurnett's "mind's eye" editorial, the *Colonial Advocate* (23 May 1833) wrote: "It has never been a practice with us to accuse our opponents of treason, because they happen to differ from us on political questions; for we have ever been of the opinion, that men may differ on many points of political economy, and still possess a strong attachment to the same government ... The jealous advocates for the prerogative of the Crown – the sticklers for the constitution and delegated rights – the noisy pretenders to loyalty – ready and willing to abandon the 'Empire of their sires,' for a new state of political existence for no other reason, than because the government of that country saw fit to dispense with the services of their public servants, who opposed the

line of policy marked out for them and who obstinately persist in an unconstitutional course of conduct in their legislative capacity."

53 *The Patriot*, 27 January 1835 and Brockville *Recorder*, 6 February 1835; debate on the Speech from the Throne.

54 PAC Pamphlets, W.B. Wells, *Canadiana: Containing Sketches of Upper Canada and the Crisis in Its Political Affairs* (London: C. & W. Reynell 1837), 72, 73-4; cf. 17, 24. In his electoral address in 1834, T.D. Morrison asserted: "We have defended the Constitution in a time of war against the assaults of an external enemy, and we will preserve it, in a time of peace, from the withering influence of corrupt administrations. We have the physical courage for the first struggle, and we have moral courage for the last" (*Canadian Correspondent*, 11 October 1834; see also *Correspondent and Advocate*, 15 May 1835).

55 An excellent discussion of how Tory-Reform conflicts were injected into local politics can be found in Paul Romney, "A Struggle for Authority: Toronto Society and Politics in 1834," in Victor L. Russell, ed. *Forging a Consensus: Historical Essays on Toronto* (Toronto: University of Toronto Press 1984), esp. 14-35.

56 Kingston *Chronicle and Gazette*, 20 September 1834; see also *Niagara Gleaner*, 28 January 1832.

57 *The Patriot*, 23 May 1834. Joseph Hume had written to Mackenzie (in a letter published in *The Advocate* of 22 May 1834) that Mackenzie's expulsions from the Assembly "must hasten that crisis which is fast approaching in the affairs of the Canadas, and which will terminate in independence and freedom from the Baneful Domination of the Mother Country, and the tyrannical conduct of a small and despicable faction in the colony ... The proceedings between 1772 and 1782 in America ought not to be forgotten."

58 *Canadian Correspondent*, 16 August 1834.

59 *Correspondent and Advocate*, 15 June 1836; see also ibid., 3 May 1837. For a more complete discussion of Mackenzie and the grievances of Upper Canada, see Craig, *Upper Canada: The Formative Years*, 210-25.

60 It would be misleading to suggest that William Lyon Mackenzie presented a coherent philosophy of opposition. He was a grievance-monger whose newspaper editor mentality caused him to draw ideas from many sources. He was, in the words of G.M. Craig, "entirely unsuited to the life of politics, unable to work with colleagues toward an agreed objective, and quite without perspective. But ... [with] complete disregard for personal gain or advancement, he put himself unreservedly at the disposal of the plain

people of Upper Canada" (in *Upper Canada: The Formative Years*, 210).

Mackenzie's political ideas have been explored in the following sources: R.A. MacKay, "The Political Ideas of William Lyon Mackenzie," *Canadian Journal of Economics and Political Science*, 3 (1937), 1–22; G.M. Craig, "The American Impact on the Upper Canadian Reform Movement before 1837," *Canadian Historical Review*, 29 (1945), 333–52; Lillian Gates, "The Decided Policy of William Lyon Mackenzie," *Canadian Historical Review*, 40 (1959), 185–208; William Kilbourn, *The Firebrand: William Lyon Mackenzie and the Rebellion in Upper Canada* (Toronto: Clarke, Irwin & Co. 1964); J.E. Rea, "William Lyon Mackenzie – Jacksonian?", in J.M. Bumsted, ed., *Canadian History before Confederation* (Georgetown: Irwin-Dorsey 1972), 331–42.

61 D.P. Crook, *American Democracy in English Politics, 1815–1850* (Oxford: Oxford University Press 1965), 1.

62 Cf. *Correspondent and Advocate*, 7 September 1836. See also ibid., 11 January 1837 and Charles Duncombe to Lord Glenelg, 20 September 1836. British Parliamentary Papers (1839), no. 118, pp. 54–5; in Craig, *Discontent in Upper Canada*, 176–7.

63 S.F. Wise, "Colonial Attitudes from 1812 to 1837," in Wise and R.C. Brown, *Canada Views the United States: Nineteenth-Century Political Attitudes* (Toronto: Macmillan 1972), 36. See, for instance, *Colonial Advocate*, 11 March 1830; and Mackenzie, *Sketches of Upper Canada and the United States*.

64 Kingston *Chronicle and Gazette*, 6 February 1836. See also *Correspondent and Advocate*, 15 June 1836; Mackenzie's "State of the Colony."

65 *Correspondent and Advocate*, 18 April 1836; Report of the Committee on the Executive Council.

66 Kingston *Chronicle and Gazette*, 6 February 1836; see also *Canadian Correspondent*, 23 August 1834.

67 PAC, Charles Duncombe Papers, "Address to the free and independent electors of the County of Oxford" (1836).

68 *British American Journal*, 2 September 1834.

69 St Thomas *Liberal*, 18 October 1832; see also *British American Journal*, 1 July 1834. Francis Collins had long before labelled Mackenzie as "one of the most degraded characters in the colony – without honor, consistency, or fixed principle" (*Canadian Freeman*, 31 July 1828).

70 Cornwall *Observer*, 25 July 1834.

71 *Grenville Gazette*, 25 July 1834.

72 *British Colonial Argus*, 23 October 1833. Appeals to traditional British methods of opposition are also to be found in the St Thomas *Libe-*

ral, 13–27 December 1832. The Tories, on the other hand, argued that "Whatever Unions may be in England, it must be remembered that in this country, with Republicans at their head, they are the next step to Rebellion" (reprinted in the St Thomas *Liberal*, 10 January 1833; quoted in Fred Landon, *Western Ontario and the American Frontier* [Toronto: McClelland & Stewart, reprinted 1967], 149).

73 Eric Jackson, "The Organization of Upper Canadian Reformers, 1818–1867," in J.K. Johnson, ed., *Historical Essays on Upper Canada* (Toronto: McClelland & Stewart 1975), 98–102. The moderate Reformers and the Tories also saw the necessity of organizing for the "loyalty election" in 1836. W.W. Baldwin, for instance, was the president of two Reform organizations – the Constitutional Reform Society of Upper Canada and the City of Toronto Political Union – created in 1836. These societies were a response to the British Constitutional Society, re-formed by the Tories in Toronto earlier in the same year.

74 Kingston *Chronicle and Gazette*, 11 May 1836.

75 TPL, Baldwin Papers, W.W. Baldwin to Robert Baldwin, 6 July 1836.

76 TPL, Baldwin Papers., M.S. Bidwell to Robert Baldwin, 29 July 1836.

77 PAO, Mackenzie-Lindsey Papers, Mackenzie to John Neilson, 28 December 1835.

78 TPL, Baldwin Papers, Duncombe to Robert Baldwin, 15 September 1836. The *Correspondent and Advocate* also attacked imperial interference in the local affairs of the colony: "we are constrained to say that this interference of the Colonial Secretary in our local affairs is both presumptuous and intolerable. Can it be endured that a Minister several thousand miles removed from us, shall be permitted to hold us forever in leading-strings, and though ignorant of our condition, prescribe for us, and dictate to us according to his pleasure" (4 January 1837; see also ibid., 5 April 1837).

79 *Correspondent and Advocate*, 3 August 1836; see also ibid., 11 January 1837, and PAC Pamphlets, *The Speech of the Hon. John Rolph, M.P.P., delivered on the occasion of the late Inquiry into Charges of High Misdemeanors at the late Elections, preferred against His Excellency Sir Francis Bond Head ...* (Toronto: Correspondent & Advocate 1837).

80 The *Correspondent and Advocate*, in the Brockville *Recorder*, 10 August 1837.

81 *The Constitution*, 2 August 1837. Mackenzie's growing radicalism can be followed in his newspaper, *The Constitution*, which began publication on 4 July 1836. See also Charles Lindsey, *The Life and Times of Wm. Lyon Mackenzie* (Toronto: P.R. Randall 1882), II, 354.

82 Lindsey, *Life and Times*, II, 53, 27. G.M. Craig provides a good narrative of the events leading to the rebellion; cf. *Upper Canada: The Formative Years*, 240–7. See also Colin Read and R.J. Stagg, eds, *The*

Rebellion of 1837 in Upper Canada (Ottawa: Carleton University Press 1985), xix–c.

83 *British Colonist*, 8 March 1838.
84 Cf. Ronald J. Stagg, "The Yonge Street Rebellion of 1837: An Examination of the Social Background and a Re-assessment of the Events" (Ph D dissertation, University of Toronto 1976); chapter entitled "The Aftermath." See also R.J. Eady, "Anti-American Sentiment in Essex County in the Wake of the Rebellions of 1837," *Ontario History*, 61 (1969), 1–8 and Read and Stagg, eds, *The Rebellion of 1837 in Upper Canada*, lxvii, xcii–xciii.
85 See, for instance, R.B. Sullivan's "Report on the State of the Province" (1838) which articulated the traditional Tory distrust of the American settlers in Upper Canada; in C.R. Sanderson, ed., *The Arthur Papers* (Toronto: University of Toronto Press, 1959), I, 132–83. See also Colin Read, *The Rising in Western Upper Canada, 1837–8: The Duncombe Revolt and After* (Toronto: University of Toronto Press 1982), 107–63.
86 Cf. Stagg; "The Yonge Street Rebellion: The Aftermath"; Egerton Ryerson, *The Story of My Life: Being Reminiscences of Sixty Years of Public Service in Canada* (edited by J.G. Hodgins) (Toronto: William Briggs 1883), 184; Francis Hincks, *Reminiscences of His Public Life* (Montreal: William Drysdale 1884), 21–2; and R.S. Longley, "Emigration and the Crisis of 1837 in Upper Canada," *Canadian Historical Review*, 17 (1936), 29–40.
87 Brockville *Recorder*, 14 December 1837.
88 Cf. G.M. Craig, *Upper Canada: The Formative Years*, 249–50; Stagg, "The Yonge Street Rebellion," 184–234, 422–3; and Read, *The Rising in Western Upper Canada*, 164–204.
89 The Niagara *Reporter*, in the St Catharines *Journal*, 27 February 1838.
90 In the St Catharines *Journal*, 27 February 1838.
91 S.F. Wise, "Upper Canada and the Conservative Tradition," Edith Firth, ed, *Profiles of a Province: Studies in the History of Ontario* (Toronto: Ontario Historical Society 1967), 31.
92 Graeme Patterson, "Whiggery, Nationality, and the Upper Canadian Reform Tradition," *Canadian Historical Review*, 56 (March 1975), 44.

CHAPTER SEVEN

1 Toronto *Patriot*, 22 December 1849; 19 January 1850; *The Examiner*, 3 & 12 June 1850. Quoted in S.F. Wise, "The Annexation Movement and Its Effect on Canadian Opinion," in S.F. Wise and R.C. Brown, *Canada Views the United States: Nineteenth-Century Political Attitudes* (Toronto: Macmillan 1972), 47–8, 52.

2 Wise, "The Annexation Movement ...," in Wise and Brown, *Canada Views the United States*, 45.

3 See, for example, Stephen Leacock, *Baldwin, LaFontaine, Hincks: Responsible Government* (Toronto: Morang & Co. 1910); Chester Martin, *Empire and Commonwealth: Studies in Governance and Self-Government in Canada* (Oxford: Clarendon Press 1929); George E. Wilson, *The Life of Robert Baldwin: A Study in the Struggle for Responsible Government* (Toronto: Ryerson Press 1933); R.S. Longley, *Sir Francis Hincks: A Study of Canadian Politics, Railways, and Finance in the Nineteenth Century* (Toronto: University of Toronto Press 1943).

4 Cf. S.F. Wise, "Upper Canada and the Conservative Tradition," Edith Firth, ed, *Profiles of a Province* (Toronto: Ontario Historical Society Press 1967), 20–33; his presidential address to the Canadian Historical Association, "Liberal Consensus or Ideological Battleground: Some Reflections on the Hartz thesis," *Canadian Historical Association Annual Report* (1974), 1–14; and "The Annexation Movement ...," in Wise and Brown, *Canada Views the United States*, 44–97.

   The class-based interpretation has been developed in J.M.S. Careless, ed., *The Pre-Confederation Premiers: Ontario Government Leaders, 1841–1867.* (Toronto: University of Toronto Press 1980), 24 and Alison Prentice, *The School Promoters: Education and Social Class in Nineteenth Century Upper Canada* (Toronto: McClelland & Stewart 1977), among others.

5 *The Patriot*, 8 & 11 December 1840. See J.S. Moir, ed., "Four Poems on the Rebellion of 1837... by Susanna Moodie," *Ontario History*, 57 (1965), 47–52. Also Colin Read and R.J. Stagg, eds, *The Rebellion of 1837 in Upper Canada* (Ottawa: Carleton University Press 1985), 274–5 and 287–92.

6 *The Patriot*, 3 July 1840; also 7 August 1840. Sir George Arthur noted that Upper Canadians "appear to have been cemented by the blood of Sir Isaac Brock whose memory they still ardently cherish" (Arthur to Lord Normanby, 8 June 1839; in C.R. Sanderson, ed., *The Arthur Papers* [Toronto: University of Toronto Press 1959], II, 165).

7 PAC Pamphlets, Ogle R. Gowan, *An Important Letter on Responsible Government* (Toronto: Examiner 1839), 10. Gowan proved his own loyalty during the rebellion, as he was quick to note: "It is vain to urge that through his whole life he has been a devoted loyalist; that through the partial insurrections and invasions of 1837, 1838, and 1839, he rushed to the post of danger, and volunteered to expose his body to every passing bullet; nay, even the wounds upon his own body, received in his country's defence, are not sufficient to screen him from the malignant opposition of antagonists, or to

hush to silence the calumny of the secret and irresponsible enemy ..." (ibid.). See also D.H. Akenson, *The Irish in Ontario: A Study in Rural History* (Kingston: McGill-Queen's University Press 1984), 193–6.

Gowan's attempts to broaden the Loyalist tradition in Upper Canada were largely unsuccessful in the immediate post-rebellion period. It was not until Upper Canadians became aware of the social problems posed by the massive immigration of poverty-stricken Irish Roman Catholics in the 1840s, and began to perceive the increasing "French domination" of the Union that the Orange Order gained some respectability.

(Cf. C.J. Houston and W.J. Smyth, *The Sash Canada Wore: An Historical Geography of the Orange Order in Canada* [Toronto: University of Toronto Press 1980], 142–3.)

8 PAC Pamphlets. Philalethes, *Reply to Lord Durham's Report on the British North American Colonies* ... (Cobourg: Cobourg Star 1839), 8.

9 G.M. Craig, ed., *Lord Durham's Report* (Toronto: McClelland & Stewart 1969), 79–80.

10 C.P. Lucas, ed., *Lord Durham's Report on the Affairs of British North America*, II (Oxford: Clarendon Press 1912), 277–8, 281–2. Ged Martin has argued that Durham did not fully understand the implications of his recommendations. Cf. Ged Martin, *The Durham Report and British Policy: A Critical Essay* (Cambridge: Cambridge University Press 1972), 63.

11 Robinson to Arthur, 19 February 1839; in Sanderson, *The Arthur Papers*, II, 47; Hagerman to Arthur, May 1839; ibid., II, 142. See also John Macaulay to Arthur, 15 September 1839; ibid., II, 258–9; PAC Pamphlets, Philalethes, *Reply to Lord Durham's Report* ..., 61–3. See also Toronto *Patriot*, 11 December 1840; speech of Sir Allan MacNab.

12 *The Church*, 13 April 1839; Philalethes, *Reply* ..., 52; and J.B. Robinson to the Marquis of Normanby, 23 February 1839; in Sanderson, ed., *The Arthur Papers*, II, 52–65.

13 See, for example, Robinson to the Marquis of Normanby, 23 February 1839; in Sanderson, ed., *The Arthur Papers*, II, 52–65. Robinson's criticisms of the Durham *Report* were outlined more fully in his *Canada and the Canada Bill* (London: J. Harchard & Son 1840).

14 Toronto *Examiner*, 24 July 1839; see also Brockville *Recorder*, 25 July 1839.

15 PAC, Durham Papers, Baldwin to Lord Glenelg, 13 July 1836; quoted in J.M.S. Careless, "Robert Baldwin," in his *The Pre-Confederation Premiers*, 109.

16 G.M. Craig, ed. *Lord Durham's Report*, 139.

17 *British Colonist*, 26 December 1843.

18 J.P. Merritt, *Biography of the Honourable W.H. Merritt*, MP (St Catharines: H.S. Leavenworth 1875), 199; see also St Catharines *Journal*, 5 January 1844.

19 See PAC, LaFontaine Papers. See also Chester Martin, *Empire and Commonwealth* (Oxford: Clarendon Press 1929); W.G. Ormsby, *The Emergence of the Federal Concept in Canada* (Toronto: University of Toronto Press 1969).

J.M.S. Careless has compared the political approach of Hincks to that of the Reform leader, Robert Baldwin:

Baldwin was conservative and aristocractic by temperament; a man of principle acutely, even self-righteously, proud of his integrity, drawn reluctantly into politics by a sense of *noblesse oblige* and an abiding belief in responsible government. Hincks was flexible and adaptable, at home in the rough-and-tumble colonial business world, an ambitious opportunist who saw realities of power in politics and was eager to use them to achieve effective, popular, entrepreneurial rule. Yet in their very differences they complemented each other.

Baldwin furnished the idea and the moral authority. Not only did he have position and prestige; he conveyed an air of unassailable rectitude that was worth whole regiments of hot Mackenzie radicals in this critical era after the rebellion – Hincks was the gifted strategist and tactician who provided the staff work for political action to carry Baldwin's idea into effect.

(J.M.S. Careless, *The Union of the Canadas: The Growth of Canadian Institutions, 1841–1857* [Toronto: McClelland & Stewart 1967], 11–12).

20 Quoted in *The Examiner*, 24 June 1840 and repeated 9 September 1840. Hincks was an admirer of British Whigs such as T.B. Macaulay who contributed to the *Edinburgh Review*.

21 *The Examiner*, 24 June 1840. Hincks's views on party development and party organization were further outlined in an editorial of 14 April 1841, when he stated the importance of a party being "represented by its organs in Parliament, and by the Press which advocates its views." See also PAC Pamphlets, *Address of the Honorable Francis Hincks to the Reformers of Frontenac* (Toronto: Reform Association of Canada 1844), 5.

22 Lord John Russell to Charles Poulett Thomson, 14 October 1839; in W.P.M. Kennedy, ed., *Statutes, Treaties and Documents of the Canadian Constitution*, 2nd ed. (Oxford: Clarendon Press 1930), 421–2.

23 Russell to Thomson, 14 October 1839; in Kennedy, ed., *Statutes...*, 423. For a more detailed discussion, see Ormsby, *The Emergence of the Federal Concept*, 43–66.

24 Thomson to Russell, 15 December 1839; in Sanderson, ed., *The Arthur Papers*, II, 351.

25 Legislative Assembly of Canada. *Journals*, 13 June 1841, 7. See also Thomson's views quoted in *The Examiner*, 28 October 1840.

26 G.P. Scrope, *Memoir of the Life of the Right Honourable Charles Lord Sydenham* (London: John Murray 1843), 198–200. Cf. ibid., 164–72; George Metcalf, "Samuel Bealey Harrison: Forgotten Reformer," *Ontario History*, 50 (1958), 120. Sydenham to Russell, 27 June 1841; quoted in Irving Abella, "The 'Sydenham Elections' of 1841," *Canadian Historical Review*, 47 (1966), 343.

27 Thomson to Russell, 13 February 1840; in Paul Knaplund, ed., *Letters from Lord Sydenham, Governor General of Canada, 1839–1841, to Lord John Russell* (Clifton: Augustus M. Kelley 1973), 48. Thomson believed that the "Constitutional Party is as bad or worse than the other, in spite of all their professions of loyalty" (in Scrope, ed., *Memoir ...*, 149).

28 PAO, Macaulay Papers, John to Ann Macaulay, 17 December 1839. Macaulay's letters to his wife revealed the full extent of his opposition to the proposals. Of the union he wrote, "I do not like the measure – We shall never agree with the French" (7 April 1839). Responsible Government, through its "democratic fulness [sic]," would destroy the Constitution (15 April 1839). Yet he had to acquiesce because "the measure was one deliberately adopted by the Queen's Ministers" (17 December 1839).

29 For a more detailed discussion of Draper and his career, see George Metcalf, "William Henry Draper," in Careless, ed., *The Pre-Confederation Premiers*, 32–88. Draper quickly became the political hope of many Tories; Arthur believed that he could unite "all moderate men" (Arthur to Thomson, 12 August 1840; in Sanderson, *The Arthur Papers*, III, 105).

30 QUA, J.S. Cartwright Papers, Draper to Cartwright, 18 November 1840. See also "Report of the Committee of the Legislative Council of Upper Canada on Lord Durham's Report," speech of Sheriff Allan Macdonell of the Midland District, 11 May 1839; in Kennedy, ed., *Statutes ...*, 377. An important contribution to our understanding of the evolution of moderate Tory views may be found in Carol Wilton-Siegel, "Administrative Reform: A Conservative Alternative to Responsible Government," *Ontario History*, 78 (1986), 105–25.

31 PAC RG5 B3, *Upper Canada: Petitions and Addresses*. Addresses to Sir Charles Poulett Thomson and replies to the Circular on Union, 1839–40, 1820–3. PAC, J.S. Macdonald Papers. Draper to Macdonald, 25 March 1841. Sir George Arthur also labelled the Reformers "the

American party, for such in fact [they] are ..." (Arthur to Sir John Colborne, 3 October 1839; in Sanderson, ed. *The Arthur Papers*, II, 275).

Some moderate Tories did take up the idea of responsible government. Ogle Gowan, who found that the administration still would not accept the Orange Order, despite its loyalty proven during the rebellion, became a sudden convert to the concept of legitimate opposition in 1839. He also hoped that the introduction of executive responsibility might open the door to government office for the Orange Irish, and himself in particular, in the face of Tory opposition. In an attempt to extend the limits of loyalty, Gowan wrote: "In England, we find the greatest jealousy of, and opposition to, the great contending parties; but *there*, is no treason against the state; but simply Whigs against Tories; Ministers against Oppositionists; or, in other words, the *Ins* against the *Outs* ... Here every man, no matter how loyal, who asks for the British principle of responsibility, in the administration of the colonial government, is denounced as a rebel and traitor to his country" (PAC Pamphlets, Gowan, *An Important Letter on Responsible Government*, 10). The Grand Master was repudiated by his followers who believed that Gowan's arguments were "repugnant to the principles of our glorious Constitution" and posed a threat to the "connexion with the British Empire" (*The Statesman*, 25 May 1839).

32 PAC *Upper Canada, Petitions and Addresses ...*, 1650–6. Charles Fothergill, ed. *Mackenzie's Own Narrative of the Rebellion, with illustrations and notes...* (Toronto 1838), iii; quoted in Paul Romney, "A Man Out of Place: The Life of Charles Fothergill: Naturalist, Businessman, Journalist, Politician, 1782–1840" (Ph D dissertation, University of Toronto 1981), 576.

Thomas Butler, Chairman of the Quarter Sessions for the Niagara District, also criticized the exclusiveness of High Tory patronage policy. See PAC, *Upper Canada: Petitions and Addresses*, 1849–67.

33 *British Colonist*, 23 and 30 September 1840; see also the Toronto *Patriot*, 7 September 1841.

34 *British Colonist*, 16 September 1840. See also Toronto *Patriot*, 14 February 1841; letter from "Roger Roscoe."

35 QUA, J.S. Cartwright Papers, Draper to Cartwright, 18 November 1840. He also sought to strengthen the instruments of a party: "we are doing nothing thro' the press to make our course as a party and our future principles of action known to the people" (ibid.).

36 *Journals of the Assembly* (1841), 480ff., 18 June and 3 September. See also J.M.S. Careless, *The Union of the Canadas ...*, 55.

37 *The Examiner*, 1 October 1840. See also PAC, LaFontaine Papers; Hincks to LaFontaine, 23 August 1840; PAC, LaFontaine Papers, Baldwin to LaFontaine, 4 December 1841.

38 *The Examiner*, 9 September 1840; Kingston *Herald*, in the *Examiner*, 30 September 1840. See also *The Examiner*, 21 April, 9 June 1841.

39 Specifically, he supported the Bank of Issue scheme; the creation of District Councils, and the Board of Works; the resolution of the alien question; the marriage bill; the Clergy Reserve question; modifications of the university charter; improvement of the judicial system and education; and abolition of primo-geniture; in sum, "measures of improvement" for the province, including a British loan of 1.5 million pounds sterling for canal construction and the reduction of colonial debts.

40 TPL, Baldwin Papers, Hincks to W.W. Baldwin, 7 July 1841. The Harrison amendments of 1841 represented the response of the administration to Baldwin's resolutions which were designed to make the legislature define its position on the question of ministerial responsibility. Harrison, acting as Sydenham's spokesman, omitted Baldwin's reference to the right of the Assembly to hold the executive responsible for every policy of the government; instead, he simply reaffirmed the need for harmony between the executive and the legislature. Both Baldwin and Hincks were compelled to support the Harrison Resolutions, rather than see the whole measure defeated. (Cf. *Journals of the Assembly of the United Provinces of Canada* [1841], 480ff.; cited in Careless, *The Union of the Canadas*, 55.) See also Chester Martin, *The Foundations of Canadian Nationhood* (Toronto: University of Toronto Press 1955), 174.

The Examiner, 8 & 15 September, 6 October 1841. Cf. PAC, LaFontaine Papers, Hincks to LaFontaine 15 August and 23 August 1840. Hincks was disgusted with the breakdown of the Reform party because of the intransigence of the ultras. A moderate Reform party would isolate the political extremes. When he joined Sydenham, though, he was accused of "having *ratted from his party*" [Quoted in Leacock, *Baldwin, LaFontaine, Hincks* ..., 105.]

41 PAC, LaFontaine Papers, especially the letters from Hincks between 1839 and 1841.

42 PAC, LaFontaine Papers, Hincks to LaFontaine, 12 April 1839. Both Hincks and Baldwin opposed co-operation with the French-Canadian Reformers if LaFontaine sought to pursue "national questions." Cf. ibid., Hincks to LaFontaine, 12 April 1839 and September 1839 (no day given); Baldwin to LaFontaine, 26 November 1840; ibid., Hincks to LaFontaine, September 1839; Hincks to LaFontaine, 14 February 1841.

43 PAC, LaFontaine Papers, Hincks to LaFontaine, 11 November 1840.

44 TPL, Baldwin Papers. Hincks to Robert Baldwin, 15 June 1843. See also Donald R. Beer, *Sir Allan Napier MacNab* (Hamilton: Dictionary of Hamilton Biography 1984), 208–37.

45 Cf. Bagot to Lord Stanley, the Colonial Secretary, on the great coalition; quoted in Chester Martin, *Foundations of Canadian Nationhood*, 177.

46 *The Examiner*, 8 December 1843; speech of Robert Baldwin.

47 See Careless, *The Union of the Canadas*, 64–5. Some Tories, like J.S. Cartwright of Kingston, who resigned when Hincks entered the ministry, refused to co-operate with the Reformers and thus lost influence in the party.

48 PAC, Bagot Papers, II, Harrison to Bagot, 11 July 1842, 417–18. Ibid., II, Draper to Bagot, 18 June 1842. See also Brockville, *Recorder*, 21 December 1843, "The Substitutes for a Ministry."

49 See, for example, *British Colonist*, 27 March 1839.

50 See, for example, Kingston *Chronicle and Gazette*, 24 April 1841. See also *Upper Canada Herald*, 31 December 1839, speech of John Powell; and 18 August 1840. In addition, Draper recognized the basic social conservatism of the French Canadians when he asserted that "there was in fact no difference in sentiment" between LaFontaine's supporters and the moderate Tories (Journals of the Assembly of the United Province of Canada, *Debates*, 13 September 1842).

51 Careless, *The Union of the Canadas*, 75–95.

52 Metcalf to Lord Stanley, 24 April 1843; quoted in Leacock, *Baldwin, LaFontaine, Hincks* ..., 160. One day later (25 April 1843), Metcalfe attacked the development of party sentiment: "The violence of party spirit forces itself on one's notice immediately on arrival in the colony; and threatens to be the source of all the difficulties which are likely to impede the successful administration of the government for the welfare and happiness of the country" (quoted, ibid., 167).

53 See Metcalfe to Stanley, 9 October 1843; in Metcalfe, "William Henry Draper," in Careless, ed., *Pre-Confederation Premiers*, 64. This sentiment was echoed by many Upper Canadians; in a letter to Peter Brown, Isaac Buchanan stated that the Governor had *"Responsibility to the people of the colony"* (*British Colonist*, 20 January 1844). See also *British Colonist*, 16 February 1844; Metcalfe's address "To the Warden and Councillors of the Gore District."

Metcalfe's biographer noted that: "Inevitability, to a man who had spent his life in India, patronage was all important ... Patronage was the spring and framework of government, it *was* government and surrendering it, you surrendered all" (Edward Thompson, *The Life of Charles, Lord Metcalfe* [London: Faber &

Faber 1937], 389). See also Metcalfe to Stanley, 26 September 1844; cited in Leacock, *Baldwin, LaFontaine, Hincks...*, 250. Gordon Stewart also provides a useful analysis of Metcalfe's position in *The Origins of Canadian Politics: A Comparative Approach* (Vancouver: University of British Columbia Press 1986), 46–9, 52–3.

54 See G. French, *Parsons & Politics: The Role of the Wesleyan Methodists in Upper Canada & The Maritimes from 1780 to 1855* (Toronto: Ryerson Press 1962), 227. It was a contest between the "royal prerogative as against partisanship in government." Ryerson mistrusted party spirit, which he saw as "the bane and curse of this country for many years. It has neither eyes nor ears – nor principle of reason" (*Christian Guardian*, 11 July 1838); see also C.B. Sissons, "Ryerson and the Election of 1844," in the *Canadian Historical Review*, 23 (1942), 167, 172. Ryerson saw party government as a "system of political and moral corruption" which was *"the essence of responsible government"* (PAC Pamphlets, Egerton Ryerson, *Sir Charles Metcalfe Defended Against the Attacks of His Late Councillors* [Toronto: *The British Colonist* 1844] 143). See also Egerton Ryerson, *The Story of My Life* (Toronto: William Briggs 1883), 179; Kingston *Chronicle and Gazette*, 6 December 1843. Thomas C. Street emphasized the same point in a letter to W.H. Merritt, a moderate who broke with Baldwin and supported the Governor over the question of patronage: "I am, of course, as every other inhabitant of the Province ought to be, a staunch supporter of the British Crown, an admirer of British laws and institutions, and naturally jealous of any attempt to lessen or weaken the authority of the Government – by unreasonable demands, or the following up a system of executive policy entirely at variance and inconsistent with what I understand to be Her Majesty's prerogative as exercised in this Province through her legal representative" (Street to Merritt, 22 January 1844; in J.P. Merritt, *Biography of the Honourable W.H. Merritt, M.P.*, 270). Among the other prominent Upper Canadians who rallied behind the Governor were "Tiger" Dunlop, John Prince, and John Langton.

Cf. W.H. Graham, *The Tiger of Canada West* (Toronto: Clarke, Irwin 1962), 266; R. Alan Douglas, ed., *John Prince, 1796–1870: A Collection of Documents* (Toronto: University of Toronto Press 1980), and H.H. Langton, ed., *A Gentlewoman in Upper Canada: The Journals of Anne Langton* (Toronto: Macmillan 1950); John Langton to William Langton, December 1843, 221–2.

55 *British Colonist*, 5 January 1844; see also Kingston *Chronicle and Gazette*, 10 January 1844. Buchanan attacked Robert Baldwin as "the colonial republican," and attempted to illustrate the Reform leader's disloyalty during the rebellion. Buchanan accepted the traditional Tory

argument that loyalty must be proven and said: "Let us say we shall consider a man loyal who would turn out to defend the Government, in case of a rebellion occurring tomorrow; and the proof of this we shall require, is his not having declined to turn out in 1837." Baldwin, he argued, preferred "*his party to his country*, at the late rebellion, declining to fight against the former, or turn out in defence of the latter ..." (*British Colonist*, 9 January 1844).

Even the Tory Kingston *Chronicle* believed that Buchanan took his charges too far and defended Baldwin's loyalty: "How absurd then is it for Mr. Buchanan to propound such doctrines at this time of day – that because a man has once been suspected of disloyalty, he is forever after to be proscribed although his public acts are not only unexceptionable in themselves but are found worthy of commendation by the great majority" (Kingston *Chronicle and Gazette*, 10 January 1844).

56 Quoted in the *British Colonist*, 20 April 1844; the same themes were developed in a letter from Thomas Parke, M.P.P. "on the Political State of the Country" to the St Thomas *Chronicle,* reprinted ibid., 10 May 1844.

57 "The Idea of the Patriot King," *Works of Lord Bolingbroke* (Philadelphia 1841), II, 402; quoted in Michael Wallace, "Changing Concepts of Party in the United States, New York, 1815–1828," *American Historical Review,* 74 (1968), 472.

58 Quoted in Donald Creighton, *John A. Macdonald: The Young Politician* (Toronto: Macmillan of Canada, 1968), 94. Draper to Ryerson, 26 January 1844; *Mirror of Parliament*, 14 June 1847; quoted from George Metcalf, "Draper Conservatism and Responsible Government in the Canadas, 1836–1847," *Canadian Historical Review,* 42 (1961), 309–20. See also the *Monthly Review,* quoted in *The Examiner,* 12 January 1841, and *The British Colonist,* 21 November 1843.

59 *The Patriot,* 7 May 1841; see also *The Church,* 3 and 24 August 1839, and *British Colonist,* 21 November 1843.

60 In the *British Coloniost,* 5 January 1844. See the *British Colonist* 23 January 1844. An electoral address by John W. Partridge, "To the Farmers of the First Riding of York," also outlined the belief that constitutional balance was threatened by the emergence of parties. It represented "the too great power of the Democratic principle" (*British Colonist,* 14 May 1844). See also PAC Pamphlets, Egerton Ryerson, *Sir Charles Metcalfe Defended Against the Attacks on His Late Councillors.*

61 See PAC Pamphlets, *To the People of Canada, by the Reform Association* (Toronto: Examiner 1844), 12; also PAC Pamphlets, *Address of the*

Honourable Francis Hincks to the Reformers of Frontenac (Toronto: Reform Association of Canada 1844), 6.

62 *The Examiner* 2 October 1844; see also St Catharines *Journal*, 31 May 1844. At a reform meeting in March 1844, William Hume Blake stated that Upper Canadians were involved in a struggle for British liberty and freedom: "I hesitate not to declare that, much as I glory in the power of Britain, much as I admire her unparalleled greatness, I had rather see them mouldering in the dust than supported by an infringement of those Constitutional principles of liberty upon which they are found." (PAC Pamphlets, *Proceedings at the First General Meeting of the Reform Association of Canada* [Toronto: The Globe 1844), 19–20). Kingston *Chronicle and Gazette*, 13 April 1844; the address of Read Burritt to the electors of Leeds and Grenville contained, the same message: "I am a Canadian and a British subject by birth and do not hesitate to balance my attachment to the Throne with any man. We ask no more than has been granted to the people of Great Britain" (Brockville *Recorder*, 11 July 1844).

63 Brockville *Recorder*, 30 November 1843; at the meeting of the Reform association a few months later, Baldwin stressed the same points before an enthusiastic audience. Stating that he "had proved himself the firm and uncompromising friend of that great and vital principle of British Constitutional Liberty," Baldwin attacked Metcalfe for casting the Reformers aside "as a menstruous rag" (PAC Pamphlets, *Proceedings ... of the Reform Association ...*, 5).

64 Brockville *Recorder*, 15 August 1844. It was argued that the concept of party was supported by such significant British politicians as Edmund Burke, Lord John Russell, and Lord Stanley. See also *The Pilot*, 15 August 1844. PAC Pamphlets, "Legion," *Letters on Responsible Government* (Toronto: The Examiner, 1844), 24–5; see also PAC Pamphlets, *Proceedings of the Reform Association*, 12–13; PAC Pamphlets, The Reform Association of Canada. *Address of the Honorable Francis Hincks, to the Reformers of Frontenac*, 4; Kingston *Herald*, 13 February 1844; "To the Reformers of the County of Frontenac"; and *The Pilot*, 13 May 1844.

65 Brockville *Recorder*, 13 June 1844; see also Kingston *Herald*, 7 May 1844 and *The Examiner*, 20 March 1844.

66 Kingston *Herald*, 10 September 1844; see also *The Globe*, 10 September 1844.

67 Kingston *Herald*, 14 May 1844. Kingston *Herald*, 22 October 1844; see also PAC Pamphlets, *Proceedings of the Reform Association*, R.B. Sullivan's speech; and Brockville *Recorder*, 21 December 1843.

The Reformers were drawing upon arguments that they had been using without noticeable success since the 1830s. They believed that the Tories were attempting "to arrogate to themselves" exclusive loyalty. A letter from Adam Fergusson to the inhabitants of the Township of Nichol, for example, affirmed Reform loyalty and attacked the Tories who wished to preserve "the ancient regime by which the administration of affairs was conducted without any regard for – and often in direct opposition to – the majority of the people's representatives" (Hamilton *Journal*, quoted by the St Catharines *Journal*, 9 February 1844).

The Kingston *Herald* had earlier argued that "the tory principle of government" was "to concentrate all power and profit in the hands of a few ..." Moreover, Tory loyalty meant "British rule as understood and administered by themselves ... The Tories closely connect the maintenance of British rule with the maintenance of themselves in power" (in *The Examiner*, 1 January 1840). The Reformers, of course, believed that they were less self-serving and more disinterested.

68 *The Examiner*, 20 November 1844. *Kingston Herald*, 12 November 1844. See also *The Pilot*, 8 March 1844.

69 *The Patriot*, 29 October 1844; Richey was quoted in French, *Parsons and Politics*, 233.

70 Cf. P.G. Cornell, "The Genesis of Ontario Politics in the Province of Canada, 1838–1871," Firth, ed., *Profiles of a Province*, 63. Other factors which led to the rejection of the Reformers in Upper Canada included the removal of the capital from Kingston; Hincks's Upper Canada Assessment Bill, which raised taxes; and Methodist hostility to Baldwin's education policy.

71 The Toronto *Patriot* outlined the goals of the "United Empire Association," which stressed Tory loyalty to the empire and the current political structures. Tories were exhorted to "Organize! organize! organize!" (in *The Pilot*, 10 May 1844). The Reformers also recognized this: *The Pilot* editorialized: "no Government was ever conducted on more exclusively party principles than the present" (19 March 1844).

72 Draper used patronage to hold his majority in the Assembly; his party was still just a Parliamentary organization, as George Metcalf has noted: "though ... [Draper] understood the importance of party organization at the grass roots level he did little to further this end himself. Indeed, he sometimes betrayed an aristocratic fastidiousness far beyond that felt by most Tories" (Metcalf, "William Henry Draper," in Careless, *The Pre-Confederation Premiers*, 78). See also Gordon Stewart, "John A. Macdonald's Greatest Triumph," *Canadian Historical Review*, 63 (March 1982), 3–33. Moreover, Draper offered the only leadership for the party, as LaFontaine recognized: "with-

out his talents, their party ... would be no party at all" (TPL, Baldwin Papers, LaFontaine to Baldwin, 2 December 1845).

73 Careless, *The Pre-Confederation Premiers*, 24. The British historian, Norman Gash, has described similar events taking place in Great Britain in the same period. He argued that the emergence of a party system "destroyed the aristocratic concept of 'the King's Government'." But in the period from 1830 to 1850, party development "was working under the leadership of men who did not subscribe to a doctrine of party supremacy, still less of party infallibility, and in a society where local interests and opinions were still tenacious" (N. Gash, *Politics in the Age of Peel: A Study in the Technique of Parliamentary Representation, 1830–1850* [New York: W.W. Norton 1971], xviii).

74 See, for example, Kingston *Herald*, 23 April 1844; speech of John A. Macdonald.

75 Kingston *Chronicle and Gazette*, 13 April 1844.

76 Although, as one English historian has remarked: "The style of British politics down to 1867 was about a generation behind that of American politics" (H.J. Hanham, *Elections and Party Management: Politics in the Time of Disraeli and Gladstone* [Sussex: Harvester Press 1978] x).

77 See J.M. Ward, *Colonial Self-Government: The British Experience, 1759–1856* (Toronto: University of Toronto Press 1976), 172–208. See also A.S. Foord, *His Majesty's Opposition, 1714–1830* (Oxford: Clarendon Press 1964); and Gash, *Politics in the Age of Peel*, 264, 278–9.

78 Gash, *Politics in the Age of Peel*, xi–xii.

79 Phillip A. Buckner, *The Transition to Responsible Government: British Policy in British North America, 1815–1850* (Westport: Greenwood Press 1985), 6. See esp. 294–5 and 310–16. See also Ward, *Colonial Self-Government*, 205–7 and 290. The arguments of the Upper Canadian Reformers paralleled those of the British Whigs and Hincks drew his ideas explicitly from Whig political theorists.

80 Buckner, *The Transition to Responsible Government*, 310–11, 338.

81 *Mirror of Parliament* (1846), 290, quoted in Careless, *The Union of the Canadas*, 110.

82 Cf. G.A. Hallowell, "The Reaction of Upper Canadian Tories to the Adversity of 1849," *Ontario History*, 62 (1970), 4–56.

83 Reported in *The Independent*, 25 October 1849; quoted in G.A. Hallowell, "The Reaction of the Upper Canadian Tories ...," 43. Other journals which supported the concept of annexation were the Toronto *Mirror*, Prescott *Telegraph*, and Kingston *Argus*. Several letters to the *British Colonist* developed the same themes; cf. 11 and 25 May

1849. See Merritt, *Biography of ... W.H. Merritt*, 365–7, for the Annexation Manifesto.

84 Reported in Brockville *Recorder*, 15 March 1849; repeated 24 May 1849. See also *The Globe*, 21 March, 14 April, 20 June, 3 and 28 July and 17 November 1849.

85 TPL Pamphlets, A.N. Bethune, *The Duty of Loyalty* (A Sermon Preached at Cobourg, October 21, 1849) (Cobourg: The Star 1849). See also *The British Colonist*, 12 October 1849, in (Rev. Walter McCleary), *One Man's Loyalty* (Toronto: Committee on Orange Loyalty 1953).

86 After its initial flirtation with annexation, the *Patriot* returned to its traditional Tory position which stressed, like Bethune, the superiority of Canadian institutions over those of the United States: "Stubborn facts prove that Canada, under British rule, with all the drawbacks of a miserable misgovernment, injudicious tarifs [*sic*], denial of protection in British and British colonial markets, *uninterlaced* with railroads, and with an enormous debt, is advancing in prosperity with greater rapidity, than any portion of the United States ..." (28 November 1849).

See the *Minutes of the Proceedings of a Convention of Delegates of the British American League* ... (Kingston 1849), 7–8; quoted in Creighton, *John A. Macdonald*, 144. See also *Debates of the Toronto Convention*, cited in Hallowell, "The Reaction of Upper Canadian Tories ...," 53; and Wise, "The Annexation Movement and its Effect on Canadian Opinion, 1837–1867," 44. The Reformers saw the British American League as just another expression of the Tory party. (Cf. *The Globe*, 31 July, 5 August 1849.)

87 PAO Strachan Papers, Macaulay to J.B. Robinson, 22 February 1850.

CHAPTER EIGHT

1 See Murray Barkley, "Prelude to Tradition: The Loyalist Revival in the Canadas, 1849–1867," in S.F. Wise et al., eds, *"None was ever better ..."*: *The Loyalist Settlement of Ontario* (Cornwall: Stormont, Dundas & Glengarry Historical Society 1984), 81–109.

2 See, among others, Alison Prentice, *The School Promoters* (Toronto: McClelland & Stewart 1977) and N. McDonald and A. Chaiton, eds, *Egerton Ryerson and His Times* (Toronto: Macmillan of Canada 1978), esp. 81–183.

3 Gordon Stewart has also described the years before 1850 as a "turbulent, formative period of Canadian politics" (Gordon Stewart, "The Origins of Canadian Politics and John A. Macdonald," in R. Kenneth Carty and W. Peter Ward, eds, *National Politics and Community*

in Canada [Vancouver: University of British Columbia Press 1986],
44). But he concluded that political instability continued into the
1860s because of "the inability of one party to achieve a dominant
position... Stability was only to be achieved when the restrictive
Union framework was abolished and Confederation created a much
broader context within which party-building could take place" (Gordon Stewart, *The Origins of Canadian Politics: A Comparative Approach* [Vancouver: University of British Columbia Press 1986], 59).

Stewart does concentrate on attempts to establish a working political relationship between Anglophone and Francophone leaders in
the Canadas. This concern became paramount for politicians in
Upper Canada once a large measure of ideological consensus had
been reached in their province in the 1840s. Stewart's analysis of
developments after 1864 reveals important components of the Canadian political culture which had their roots in the first half of
the nineteenth century. His analysis of John A. Macdonald's success
in building the Conservative party through the use of patronage is
superb. (Cf. Stewart, *The Origins of Canadian Politics*, 59–90.) Macdonald's exploitation of patronage to ensure loyalty and discipline
was one of the factors which prompted the disgust with political
parties which emerged in the 1880s.

4 An excellent analysis of this development – specifically how Francis
Hincks pushed Robert Baldwin out of the leadership of the Reform
party – is contained in an unpublished paper by Michael S. Cross,
"The First Victim: The Canadian Economic Revolution and the Fall
of Robert Baldwin, 1851." See also J.K. Johnson, "John A. Macdonald," in J.M.S. Careless, ed., *The Pre-Confederation Premiers* (Toronto: University of Toronto Press 1980), 197–245 and Gordon Stewart,
"John A. Macdonald's Greatest Triumph," *Canadian Historical Review*, 63 (March 1982), 3–33.

5 PAC, Hincks Papers, Hincks to MacNab, 8 June 1849.

6 See J.M.S. Careless, *The Union of the Canadas: The Growth of Canadian
Institutions, 1841–1857* (Toronto: McClelland & Stewart 1967),
132–49; and D.C. Masters, *The Reciprocity Treaty of 1854* (Toronto:
McClelland & Stewart 1963).

7 *The Globe*, 24 January 1849; quoted in G.N. Tucker, *The Canadian Commerical Revolution, 1845–1851* (Toronto: McClelland & Stewart 1964), 104.

8 *The North American*, 30 October 1850.

9 See, for example, Donald Creighton, *John A. Macdonald: The Young
Politician* (Toronto: Macmillan of Canada 1968), esp. 431–81; P.B.
Waite, *The Life and Times of Confederation, 1864–1867: Politics, Newspapers, and the Union of British North America* (Toronto: University of
Toronto Press 1971), 117–33. For the expansionist movement, see

Doug Owram, *Promise of Eden: The Canadian Expansionist Movement and the Idea of the West, 1856–1900* (Toronto: University of Toronto Press 1980), esp. 38–78, 101–67.

10 Quoted in Frank Underhill, "Political Ideas of the Upper Canadian Reformers, 1867–1878" in his *In Search of Canadian Liberalism* (Toronto: Macmillan of Canada 1975), 82.

11 Macdonald to Egerton Ryerson, 18 March 1861; in C.B. Sissons, ed., *Egerton Ryerson: His Life and Letters.* (Toronto: Oxford University Press 1947) II, 426.

12 *The Globe*, 1 June 1871, quoted in R.C. Brown, "Canadian Opinion after Confederation, 1867–1914," in S.F. Wise and R.C. Brown, *Canada Views the United States: Nineteenth-Century Political Attitudes* (Toronto: Macmillan of Canada 1972), 109. Brown also discusses the continued criticism of the political institutions of the American republic, especially "the lack of impartial responsible authority" (p. 119).

13 Quoted in Frank H. Underhill, *The Image of Confederation* (Toronto: CBC Publications 1970), 10. *The Globe* echoed the same sentiment in an editorial of 2 August 1864: "The day may come when we shall be in a position to offer to Great Britain the friendship of a powerful and independent ally ..."

14 The Loyalist tradition had lasting currency in Canada. As Carl Berger notes: "All appeals for loyalty [in the late nineteenth century] harked back to this spirit ..." Cf. Berger, *The Sense of Power: Studies in the Ideas of Canadian Imperialism, 1867–1914* (Toronto: University of Toronto Press 1971), 106. For example, John Davidson, a professor of philosophy and political economy at the University of New Brunswick in the late nineteenth century, wrote of the Loyalist tradition that "Canada is and always has been loyal; and the intensity of that loyalty is apt to almost startle people from the Old Country ... [T]he underlying fact of Canadian political life and history is a steady dislike of the United States, and a steady love of the British connection. One does not say loyalty to the Mother Country ... It is a loyalty to British institutions, to the British connection ..." (John Davidson, "The Loyalist Tradition in Canada," in L.F.S. Upton, ed., *The United Empire Loyalists: Men and Myths* [Toronto: Copp Clark Publishing 1967], 171).

15 Berger, *The Sense of Power*, 9.

16 *The Canadian Monthly and National Review* (April 1872), in Underhill, "Political Ideas of the Upper Canadian Reformers," in his *In Search of Canadian Liberalism*, 68.

17 Goldwin Smith, "Loyalty, Aristocracy, and Jingoism," a speech delivered before the Young Men's Liberal Club, Toronto, 2 February 1891; in B. Hodgins and R. Page, eds, *Canadian History since Confeder-*

ation: Essays and Interpretations (Georgetown: Irwin-Dorsey 1972), 228, 233.

18 Cf. Berger, *The Sense of Power*, 199–207.

19 For a more complete biography of Dent see Donald Swainson's introduction to J.C. Dent, *The Last Forty Years: The Union of 1841 to Confederation* (Toronto: McClelland & Stewart 1972), v–vi.

20 *Arcturus*, 19 February 1887; see also 15 January 1887.

21 *Arcturus*, 15 January 1887, 12 February 1887.

22 Smith, "Loyalty...," in Hodgins and Page, eds, *Canadian History ...,* 236. In commenting on the colonial nature of Canadian imperialism, Smith wrote: "In the British Empire loyalty seems to have the peculiarity of being eminently colonial. It is like the reverence for the Papacy, the intensity of which was always found to vary in direct proportion to the distance from Rome" (ibid., 229).

23 Goldwin Smith, *Canada and the Canadian Question* (reprinted Toronto: University of Toronto Press 1971), 152.

24 In the *Handbook of Commerical Union*, 186; quoted in R.C. Brown, *Canada's National Policy, 1883–1900: A Study in Canadian-American Relations* (Princeton: Princeton University Press 1964), 134.

25 Quoted in Brown, *Canada's National Policy*, 206; J. Castell Hopkins, *Life and Work of the Rt. Hon. Sir John Thompson* (Brantford 1895), 164; quoted in J.M. Beck, *Pendulum of Power: Canada's Federal Elections* (Scarborough: Prentice-Hall of Canada 1968), 52.

26 See, for example, J.V. Ellis, MP for Saint John, to Wilfrid Laurier, 7 March 1891; quoted in P.B. Waite, *Canada, 1874–1896: Arduous Destiny* (Toronto: McClelland & Stewart 1971), 225.

27 Macdonald to George Stephen, 31 March 1891; quoted in Donald Creighton, *John A. Macdonald: The Old Chieftain* (Toronto: Macmillan of Canada 1973), 558. Gordon Stewart has argued that: "To the end of his life, he [Macdonald] viewed opposition as factious and, even more seriously, as disloyal" (Stewart, "The Origins of Canadian Politics...," 40).

Bibliography

PRIMARY SOURCES

Government Collections

National Archives of Canada
Colonial Office Papers
Lieutenant Governors' Correspondence
Oaths of Allegiance | Oversize Petitions
Petitions and Addresses | Proclamations
Provincial Secretary's Office | State Books
Upper Canada, *Imperial Blue Books* | Upper Canada State Papers
on Affairs Relating to Canada | Upper Canada Sundries

Manuscript Sources

National Archives of Canada
Baldwin Papers | William Buell Papers
Charles Duncombe Papers | Francis Hincks Papers
W.B. Jarvis Papers | Charles Jones Papers
LaFontaine Papers | Macaulay Papers
W.L. Mackenzie Papers | Sir Allan MacNab Papers
William Morris Papers | Robert Nelles Papers
Powell Papers | Robinson Papers
John Rolph Papers | Adiel Sherwood Papers
John Strachan Papers

Provincial Archives of Ontario
"Journals and Proceedings of the House of Assembly of the Province of

Upper Canada," 1792-1804. *Sixth Report of the Bureau of Archives of the Province of Ontario*, ed. Alex Fraser (Toronto 1909)

– 1805–11 *Eighth Report* 1911
– 1812–18 *Ninth Report* 1912
– 1819–21 *Tenth Report* 1913
– 1822–4 *Eleventh Report* 1914
– 1825–8 *Twelfth Report* 1915

John Askin Papers
M.S. Bidwell Papers
A.N. Buell Papers
John Elmsley-J.S. Macaulay Papers
James R. Gowan-Ogle Gowan Papers
John George Hodgins Papers
Jessup Family Papers
Macaulay Papers
Ridout Papers
Rogers Family Papers
John Strachan Papers

Baldwin Papers
H.J. Boulton Papers
Cartwright Papers
F.J. French Collection

Jarvis-Powell Papers
Solomon Jones Papers
Rebellion of 1837 Papers
Sir John Beverley Robinson Papers
John Rolph Papers

Toronto Public Library
William Allan Papers
Henry John Boulton Papers
John Elmsley Papers
W.L. Mackenzie Correspondence
Joseph Willcocks Papers

Baldwin Papers
Election Broadside Collection, 1800-28
Jarvis Family Papers
W.D. Powell Papers

United Church Archives
Wesleyan Methodist Missionary Correspondence, 1829-40

Pamphlets (listed chronologically)

National Archives of Canada
Boulton, D'Arcy, *Sketch of His Majesty's Province of Upper Canada*. London: Nornaville & Fell 1805
Gourlay, Robert, *A Specific Plan for Organizing the People and for Obtaining Reform Independent of Parliament*. London: J.M. Richardson 1809
Jackson, John Mills, *A View of the Political Situation of the Province of Upper Canada in North America*. London: W. Earle 1809
Anonymous [Richard Cartwright], *Letters, from an American Loyalist in Upper-Canada to His Friend in England*. Halifax: np 1810
Strachan, John, *A Discourse on the Character of King George the Third. Addressed to the Inhabitants of British America*. Montreal: Nahum Mower 1810

Burns, Rev. John, *True Patriotism: A Sermon, Preached in the Presbyterian Church in Stanford, Upper Canada, on the 3rd day of June 1814.* Montreal: Nahum Mower 1814

Simpson, John, *Essay on Modern Reformers; Addressed to the People of Upper Canada. To which is added a Letter, to Mr. Robert Gourlay.* Kingston: Stephen Miles 1818

Gourlay, Robert, *General Introduction to a Statistical Account of Upper Canada.* London: Simpkin & Marshall 1822

– *Statistical Account of Upper Canada.* 2 vols. London: Simpkin & Marshall 1822 (reprinted New York: Johnson Reprint Corp 1966)

"A Constitutional Conversation with a Conscientious Colonist; or Truth as Error" (np, nd)

Provincial Parliament of Upper Canada. *Report ... of the Hon. Legislative Council on the Civil Rights of Certain Inhabitants* (1825-6). (Printed by John Corey nd)

Collins, Francis, *An Abridged View of the Alien Question Unmasked.* York: Canadian Freeman 1826

First Report of the Central Committee of the Inhabitants of Upper Canada. York: Wm Lyon Mackenzie 1827

Speech in the Assembly on the Alien Bill (1828)

Letters from the Reverend Egerton Ryerson to the Hon. and Reverend Doctor Strachan (Published originally in the *Upper Canada Herald*) Kingston: The Herald Office 1828

"Objects and Principles of the Society." Rules and Regulations of the Orange Institution, of British North America. Adopted by the Grand Lodge at its First Meeting, held in the Court House, Brockville, Upper Canada. Brockville: Thomas Tomkins, Printer to the Grand Lodge 1830

First Report on the State of the Representation of the People of Upper Canada in the Legislature of that Province. York: Colonial Advocate 1831

Mr. Bidwell's Speech on the Intestate Estate Bill in the Provincial Assembly of Upper Canada, Jan. 24, 1831 (np 1831)

State of the Province – Proceedings of the Eighteen Township Meetings in the Home District. York: James Baxter 1831

Mackenzie, W.L., *Sketches of Canada and the United States.* London: Effingham Wilson 1833

Seventh Report from the Select Committee of the House of Assembly of Upper Canada on Grievances. Toronto: The Correspondent and Advocate 1835

Declaration of the Views and Objects, of the British Constitutional Society, on its Re-organization. Addressed to their Fellow Subjects in Upper Canada. Toronto: np 1836

Proceedings ... in the ... House of Assembly, on the Subject of an Address to His Excellency Sir F.B. Head, ... on the Affairs of the Colony. Toronto: R. Stanton 1836

The Reform Alliance Society to their Brother Reformers in Upper Canada. Toronto: np 1836

Report of a Select Committee of the Legislative Council of Upper Canada, upon the Complaints contained in an address to the King from the House of Assembly, passed 15th April 1835 ... Toronto: R. Stanton 1836

Report of the Select committee ... relative to a Responsible Executive Council. Toronto: M. Reynolds 1836

Speech of C.A. Hagerman ... against the adoption of the report of the Select Committee on the subject of the differences between His Excellency and the Executive Council (18 April 1836). Toronto: Christian Guardian 1836

A Canadian, [Egerton Ryerson]. *"The Affairs of the Canadas (in a series of letters)."* London: J. King 1837

Ryerson, Egerton, *"Wesleyan Methodism in Upper Canada" (A Sermon preached before the Conference of Ministers of the Wesleyan-Methodist Church in Canada).* Toronto: The Conference Office 1837

Speech of the Hon. John Rolph, M.P.P., delivered on the occasion of the late Inquiry into Charges of High Misdemeanors at the late Elections, preferred against His Excellency, Sir Francis Bond Head ... Toronto: Correspondent & Advocate 1837

Speeches of Dr. John Rolph and Christop'r A. Hagerman, Esq. His Majesty's Solicitor General, on the Bill for Appropriating the Proceeds of the Clergy Reserves to the Purposes of General Education (1st session, 13th Parliament). Toronto: M. Reynolds, Correspondent & Advocate 1837

Wells, W.B., *Canadiana: Containing Sketches of Upper Canada, and the Crisis in its Political Affairs.* London: C. & W. Reynell 1837

"J.K." *Plain Reasons for Loyalty. Addressed to Plain People.* Cobourg: np 1838

Report of a Select Committee of the House of Assembly, on the Political State of the Provinces of Upper and Lower Canada. Toronto: R. Stanton 1838

Report of the Select Committee of the Legislative Council of Upper Canada, on the State of the Province. Toronto: R. Stanton 1838

Ryerson, Egerton, *Civil Government – the late Conspiracy. A Discourse, delivered in Kingston, U.C. December 31, 1837.* Toronto: Joseph H. Lawrence 1838

Trial of Dr. Morrison, M.P.P., for high treason, at Toronto, on ... April 24, 1838. Toronto: np 1838

A United Empire Loyalist, [Egerton Ryerson], *Sir F.B. Head and Mr. Bidwell. The Cause and Circumstances of Mr. Bidwell's Banishment ...* Kingston: T.H. Bentley 1838

Gowan, Lt. Col., MPP for the County of Leeds in Upper Canada, *An Important Letter on Responsible Government.* Toronto: The Examiner 1839

Philalethes, *Reply to Lord Durham's Report on the British North American Colonies ...* Cobourg: Cobourg Star 1839

Gourlay, Robert Fleming, *The Banished Briton and Neptunian ... The Life ... of Robert Gourlay*. Boston: S.N. Dickinson 1843-5

Ryerson, Egerton, *Some Remarks upon Sir Charles Bagot's Canadian Government*. Kingston: Desbarats & Derbishire 1843

Address of the Honorable Francis Hincks, to the Reformers of Frontenac. Toronto: Reform Association of Canada 1844

Addresses Presented to His Excellency ... Sir Chas. T. Metcalfe ... on the Occasion of the Resignation of His Late Advisers. Toronto: H. & W. Rowsell 1844

Buchanan, Isaac, *First Series of five letters against the Baldwin Faction by an Advocate of Responsible Government ...* Toronto: British Colonist 1844

Legion [R.B. Sullivan], *Letters on Responsible Government*. Toronto: The Examiner 1844

Proceedings of the First General Meeting of the Reform Association of Canada ... Toronto: The Globe 1844

The Reform Association, *To the People of Canada*. Toronto: The Examiner Office 1844

Ryerson, Egerton, *Hon. R.B. Sullivan's Attacks upon Sir Charles Metcalfe Refuted; being a reply to the letters of 'Legion.'* Toronto: The British Colonist 1844

– *Sir Charles Metcalfe Defended Against the Attacks of His Late Counsellors*. Toronto: The British Colonist 1844

A Canadian Loyalist, *The Question Answered: "Did the Ministry Intend to Pay the Rebels?"* Montreal: Armour & Ramsay 1849

Anon. [E. McGrath], *A Letter on Canada in 1806 and 1817 during the administration of Governor Gore*. London: Savill & Edwards 1853

Provincial Archives of Ontario

Strachan, John, *A Sermon Preached at York before the Legislative Council and House of Assembly, August 2nd, 1812*. York: John Cameron 1812

– *An Appeal to the Friends of Religion and Literature, on Behalf of the University of Upper Canada*. London: R. Gilbert 1827

– *Observations on the Provision made for the maintenance of a Protestant Clergy ...* London: R. Gilbert 1827

– *Address to the Clergy of the Archdeaconry of York ...* Toronto: np 1837

Robinson, John Beverley, *Canada and the Canada Bill; Being an Examination of the Proposed Measure for the Future Government of Canada; With an Introductory Chapter, Containing Some General Views Respecting the British Provinces in North America*. London: J. Harchard & Son 1840

Explanation of the Proceedings of the Loyal and Patriotic Society of Upper Canada. Toronto: R. Stanton 1841

Gowan, Ogle R., *Orangeism: Its Origins and History* (vols 2 & 3). Toronto: Lovell & Gibson 1859-60

Kerr, W.B., *The Orange Order in Upper Canada in the 1820s*. Toronto: The Sentinel 1939 (compiled from newspaper clippings from the newspaper of the Orange Order, *The Sentinel*, in 1939 – 19 January; 2 & 16 February; 2 March)

Kerr, W.B., *The Orange Order and W.L. Mackenzie in the 1830s*. Toronto: The Sentinel 1939 (16 March; 6 & 20 April; 4 & 18 May)

Toronto Public Library
Bethune, A.N., *The Duty of Loyalty* (sermon preached in Cobourg, 21 Oct. 1849). Cobourg: The Star 1849

University of Alberta
Hincks, Sir Francis, *The Political History of Canada between 1840 and 1855: A Lecture delivered on the 17th October, 1877*. Montreal: Dawson Brothers 1877

Newspapers

Ancaster
  Gore Gazette
Brockville
  The Antidote   Gazette
  Recorder   The Statesman
Cobourg
  Reformer   Star
Cornwall
  Observer
Hamilton
  The Church   Gazette
  The Journal
Kingston
  Canadian Watchman   Chronicle
  Chronicle & Gazette   Gazette
  The Patriot & Farmers Monitor   Spectator
  Upper Canada Herald
Niagara
  The Canada Constellation   Gleaner
  Herald   Reporter
  The Spectator

Perth
  Bathurst Courier & Ottawa General Advertiser
Picton
  Hallowell Free Press

St Catharines
Farmers Journal & Welland Canal Intelligencer
British Colonial Argus　　　　　*British American Journal*
St Catharines Journal
St Thomas
Journal　　　　　　　　　　　*Liberal*
Sandwich
Canadian Emigrant
York-Toronto
Arcturus　　　　　　　　　　*The British Colonist*
Canadian Correspondent　　　*Correspondent & Advocate*
Canadian Freeman　　　　　　*The Christian Guardian*
Colonial Advocate　　　　　　*Constitution*
Courier of Upper Canada　　　*The Examiner*
The Globe　　　　　　　　　　*The Mirror*
The North American　　　　　*Observer*
Patriot　　　　　　　　　　　*The U.E. Loyalist*
Upper Canada Gazette　　　　*York Weekly Post*
Weekly Register

SECONDARY SOURCES

Books

Akenson, Donald H. *The Irish in Ontario: A Study in Rural History.* Kingston: McGill-Queen's University Press 1984

Altick, Richard D. *Victorian People and Ideas.* New York: W.W. Norton & Co. 1973

Bailyn, Bernard. *The Ideological Origins of the American Revolution.* Cambridge: Harvard University Press 1967

Bailyn, Bernard. *The Ordeal of Thomas Hutchinson.* Cambridge: Belknap Press 1974

Bailyn, Bernard. *The Origins of American Politics.* New York: Vintage Books 1968

Baldwin, R.M. and J. Baldwin. *The Baldwins and the Great Experiment.* Toronto: Longmans of Canada 1969

Banning, Lance. *The Jeffersonian Persuasion: Evolution of a Party Ideology.* Ithaca: Cornell University Press 1978

Beck, J.M. *Pendulum of Power: Canada's Federal Elections.* Scarborough: Prentice-Hall of Canada 1968

Beer, Donald R. *Sir Allan Napier MacNab.* Hamilton: Dictionary of Hamilton Biography 1984

Bell, David G. *Early Loyalists: Saint John. The Origin of New Brunswick Politics*. Fredericton: New Ireland Press 1983

Bell, David and Lorne Tepperman. *The Roots of Disunity: A Look at Canadian Political Culture*. Toronto: McClelland & Stewart 1979

Benson, Lee. *The Concept of Jacksonian Democracy* . Princeton: Princeton University Press 1961

Benton, William A. *Whig-Loyalism: An Aspect of Political Ideology in the American Revolutionary Era*. Rutherford: Fairleigh Dickinson University Press 1969

Berger, Carl. *The Sense of Power: Studies in the Ideas of Canadian Imperialism, 1867-1914*. Toronto: University of Toronto Press 1971

Berkin, Carol, *Jonathan Sewell: Odyssey of an American Loyalist*. New York: Columbia University Press 1974

Bethune, A.N. *Memoir of the Right Reverend John Strachan, First Bishop of Toronto*. Toronto: Henry Rowsell 1870

Bodo, J.R., *The Protestant Clergy and Public Issues*. Princeton: Princeton University Press 1954 (Ann Arbor: University Microfilms 1973)

Bouchier, Jonathan, ed., *Reminiscences of an American Loyalist, 1738-1789: Being the Autobiography of the Revd. Jonathan Boucher*. (with a new introduction by R.A. Brown). Port Washington, NY: Kennikat Press 1967

Bradley, A.G., *The United Empire Loyalists: Founders of British Canada*. London: Thornton Butterworth 1932

Brewer, John, *Party Ideology and Popular Politics at the Accession of George* III. Cambridge: Cambridge University Press 1976

Briggs, Asa. *The Age of Improvement, 1763-1867*. London: Longmans, Green & Co. 1966

Brode, Patrick. *Sir John Beverley Robinson: Bone and Sinew of the Compact*. Toronto: University of Toronto Press 1984

Brown, Mary, ed. *The Wait Letters*. Erin: Porcépic Press 1976

Brown, Robert Craig. *Canada's National Policy, 1883-1900: A Study in Canadian-American Relations*. Princeton: Princeton University Press 1964

Brown, R.C., ed. *Upper Canadian Politics in the 1850's*. Toronto: University of Toronto Press 1967

Brown, Wallace. *The Good Americans: The Loyalists in the American Revolution*. New York: William Morrow & Co. 1969

– *The King's Friends: The Composition and Motives of the American Loyalist Claimants*. Providence: Brown University Press 1965

– and Hereward Senior. *Victorious in Defeat: The Loyalists in Canada*. Toronto: Methuen 1984

Buckner, Phillip A. *The Transition to Responsible Government: British Policy in British North America, 1815-1850*. Westport: Greenwood Press 1985

Buel, Richard. *Securing the Revolution: Ideology in American Politics, 1789-1815*. Ithaca: Cornell University Press 1972

Burn, W.L. *The Age of Equipoise: A Study of the Mid-Victorian Generation*. London: George Allen & Unwin 1964

Burnet, Jean R. *Ethnic Groups in Upper Canada*. Toronto: Ontario Historical Society 1972

Burroughs, Peter, ed. *British Attitudes Toward Canada, 1822-1849*. Scarborough: Prentice-Hall of Canada 1971

– ed. *The Colonial Reformers and Canada, 1830-1849*. Toronto: McClelland & Stewart 1969

Burwash, Nathaniel. *Egerton Ryerson* (edited by C.B. Sissons for The Makers of Canada Series) London: Oxford University Press 1926

Calhoon, Robert. *The Loyalists in Revolutionary America*. New York: Harcourt Brace 1973

Cameron, Richard M. *Methodism and Society in Historical Perspective*. New York: Abingdon Press 1961

Caniff, William. *The Settlement of Upper Canada* (with a new introduction by Donald Swainson). Belleville: Mika Silk Screening 1971 (originally published Toronto: Dudley & Burns 1869)

Cannon, John. *Parliamentary Reform, 1640-1832*. Cambridge: Cambridge University Press 1973

Careless, J.M.S. *Brown of the Globe: The Voice of Upper Canada, 1818-1859*. Toronto: Macmillan of Canada 1972

– ed. *The Pre-Confederation Premiers: Ontario Government Leaders, 1841-1867*. Toronto: University of Toronto Press 1980

– *The Union of the Canadas: The Growth of Canadian Institutions, 1841-1857*. Toronto: McClelland & Stewart 1967

Carroll, John. *Case and His Cotemporaries; or, The Canadian Itinerants' Memorial: Constituting a Biographical History of Methodism in Canada, from its Introduction into the Province, till the Death of the Reverend William Case in 1855*. 5 vols. Toronto: Samuel Rose 1867-77

Carruthers, John. *Retrospect of Thirty-Six Years' Residence in Canada West: Being a Christian Journal and Narrative*. Hamilton: T.L. M'Intosh 1861

Cartwright, C.E., ed. *Life and Letters of the Late Honorable Richard Cartwright*. Toronto: Belford Brothers 1876

Cell, J.W. *British Colonial Administration in the Mid-Nineteenth Century: The Policy-Making Process*. New Haven: Yale University Press 1970

Clark, J.C.D. *English Society, 1688-1832: Ideology, Social Structure and Political Practice during the Ancien Régime*. Cambridge: Cambridge University Press 1985

Clark, S.D. *Church and Sect in Canada*. Toronto: University of Toronto Press, reprinted 1971

– *Movements of Political Protest in Canada, 1640-1840*. Toronto: University of Toronto Press 1959

Cole, Donald B. *Martin Van Buren and the American Political System*. Princeton: Princeton University Press 1984

Committee on Orange History, *One Man's Loyalty*. Toronto: The Committee 1953

Condon, Ann Gorman. *The Envy of the American States: The Loyalist Dream for New Brunswick*. Fredericton: New Ireland Press 1984

Cook, Ramsay. *Canada, Quebec, and the Uses of Nationalism*. Toronto: McClelland & Stewart 1986

Corey, Albert B. *The Crisis of 1830-1842 in Canadian-American Relations*. New York: Russell & Russell, reprinted 1970

Cornell, P.G. *The Alignment of Political Groups in Canada, 1841-1867*. Toronto: University of Toronto Press 1962

Cowan, Helen I. *British Emigration to British North America: The First Hundred Years*. Toronto: University of Toronto Press 1961

Craig, Gerald, ed. *Discontent in Upper Canada*. Toronto: Copp Clark Publishing 1974

– *Early Travellers in the Canadas*. Toronto: Macmillan of Canada 1955

– ed. *Lord Durham's Report*. Toronto: McClelland & Stewart 1969

– *Upper Canada: The Formative Years, 1784-1841*. Toronto: McClelland & Stewart 1963

Crary, Catherine S. *The Price of Loyalty: Tory Writings from the Revolutionary Era*. New York: McGraw-Hill 1973

Creighton, Donald. *The Empire of the St Lawrence*. Toronto: Macmillan of Canada 1972

– *John A. Macdonald: The Young Politician*. Toronto: Macmillan 1968

– *John A. Macdonald: The Old Chieftain*. Toronto: Macmillan 1973

Crook, David Paul. *American Democracy in English Politics, 1815-1850*. Oxford: Clarendon Press 1965

Cruikshank, E.A., ed. *The Correspondence of Lieutenant Governor John Graves Simcoe*. 5 vols. Toronto: Ontario Historical Society 1923-31

– ed. *The Settlement of the United Empire Loyalists on the Upper St. Lawrence and Bay of Quinte in 1784: A Documentary Record*. Toronto: Ontario Historical Society 1934 (Reprinted 1966)

– and A.F. Hunter, eds. *The Correspondence of the Honourable Peter Russell*. 3 vols. Toronto: Ontario Historical Society 1932-6

Curti, Merle. *The Roots of American Loyalty*. New York: Columbia University Press 1946

Dangerfield, George. *The Era of Good Feelings*. New York: Harcourt, Brace & World 1963

– *The Awakening of American Nationalism, 1815-1828*. New York: Harper & Row 1965

Dawe, Brian. *Old Oxford Is Wide Awake! Pioneer Settlers and Politicians in Oxford County, 1793-1853*. Toronto: Wm Brian Dawe 1980

Dent, J.C. *The Story of the Upper Canadian Rebellion.* 2 vols. Toronto: C. Blackett Robinson 1885

Doughty, A.G. and N. Story, eds. *Documents Relating to the Constitutional History of Canada, 1819-1828.* Ottawa: King's Printer 1935

Douglas, R. Alan, ed. *John Prince, 1796-1870: A Collection of Documents.* Toronto: Champlain Society (University of Toronto Press) 1980

Doyle, James, ed. *Yankees in Canada.* Downsview: ECW Press 1980

Duffy, Dennis. *Gardens, Covenants, Exiles: Loyalism in the Literature of Upper Canada/Ontario.* Toronto: University of Toronto Press 1982

Dunae, Patrick. *Gentleman Emigrants: From the British Public Schools to the Canadian Frontier.* Vancouver: Douglas & McIntyre 1981

Dunham, Aileen. *Political Unrest in Upper Canada, 1815-1836.* Toronto: McClelland & Stewart 1971

Earl, D.W.L., ed. *The Family Compact: Aristocracy or Oligarchy?* Toronto: Copp Clark Publishing Co. 1967

Edgar, Matilda. *Ten Years of Upper Canada in Peace and War, 1805-1815; being the Ridout Letters.* Toronto: William Briggs 1890

Elgee, W.H. *The Social Teachings of the Canadian Churches: Protestant. The Early Period, before 1850.* Toronto: Ryerson Press 1964

Errington, Jane. *The Lion, the Eagle and Upper Canada: A Developing Colonial Ideology.* Kingston: McGill-Queen's University Press 1987

Evans, G.N.D. *Allegiance in America: The Case of the Loyalists.* Reading: Addison-Wesley 1969

Fairley, Margaret, ed. *The Selected Writings of William Lyon Mackenzie, 1824-1837.* Toronto: Oxford University Press 1960

Firth, Edith. *Early Toronto Newspapers, 1793-1867.* Toronto: McClelland & Stewart 1961

– ed. *The Town of York, 1793-1815.* Toronto: Champlain Society (University of Toronto Press) 1962

– ed. *The Town of York, 1815-1834.* Toronto: University of Toronto Press 1966

Fischer, David Hackett. *The Revolution of American Conservatism.* New York: Harper & Row 1965

Flick, Alexander, ed. *History of the State of New York.* New York: Columbia University Press 1934

Foord, A.S. *His Majesty's Opposition, 1714-1830.* Oxford: Clarendon Press 1964

Fowler, Marian. *The Embroidered Tent: Five Gentlewomen in Early Canada.* Toronto: Anansi 1982

Fox, Dixon Ryan. *The Decline of Aristocracy in the Politics of New York, 1801-1840* (ed. by Robert V. Remini.) New York: Harper & Row 1965

Fraser, Alexander, ed. *Report of the Bureau of Archives for the Province of Ontario (1914).* Toronto: King's Printer 1915

French, Goldwin. *Parsons and Politics: The Role of the Wesleyan Methodists in Upper Canada and the Maritimes from 1780 to 1855*. Toronto: Ryerson Press 1962

Gagan, David, *Hopeful Travellers: Families, Land, and Social Change in Mid-Victorian Peel County, Canada West*. Toronto: University of Toronto Press, 1981.

Garner, John. *The Franchise and Politics in British North America, 1755-1867*. Toronto: University of Toronto Press 1969

Gash, Norman. *Politics in the Age of Peel: A Study in the Technique of Parliamentary Representation, 1830-1850*. New York: W.W. Norton & Co. 1971

– *Reaction and Reconstruction in English Politics, 1832-1852*. Oxford: Clarendon Press 1965

Gates, Lillian. *Land Policies of Upper Canada*. Toronto: University of Toronto Press 1968

General Conference of the Methodist Church of Canada. *Centennial of Canadian Methodism*. Montreal: C.W. Coates 1891

Gipson, Lawrence Henry. *American Loyalist: Jared Ingersoll*. New Haven: Yale University Press, reprinted 1971

Glazebrook, G.P. de T. *Life in Ontario: A Social History*. Toronto: University of Toronto Press 1971

– *Sir Charles Bagot in Canada*. Oxford: Clarendon Press 1929

Graham, W.H. *The Tiger of Canada West*. Toronto: Clarke, Irwin & Co. 1962

Green, Anson. *The Life and Times of the Reverend Anson Green, D.D.* Toronto: Methodist Book Room 1877

Halevy, Elie. *The Growth of Philosophic Radicalism*. London: Faber & Faber 1928

Hamil, F.C. *Lake Erie Baron: The Story of Colonel Thomas Talbot*. Toronto: Macmillan 1955

Hammond, Jabez D. *The History of Political Parties in the State of New York*. 2 vols. Albany: C. Van Benthuysen 1842

Hanham, H.J. *Elections and Party Management: Politics in the Time of Disraeli and Gladstone*. Sussex: Harvester Press 1978

Hansen, Marcus Lee and J.B. Brebner. *The Mingling of the Canadian and American Peoples*. New York: Russell & Russell 1970

Harris, R.C. and J. Warkentin, *Canada before Confederation*. Toronto: Oxford University Press 1974

Harvey, A.D. *Britain in the Early Nineteenth Century*. London: B.T. Batsford 1978

Hathaway, E.J. *Jesse Ketchum and His Times: Being a Chronicle of the Social Life and Public Affairs of the Province of Upper Canada during the First Half Century*. Toronto: McClelland & Stewart 1929

Haydon, Andrew. *Pioneer Sketches in the District of Bathurst.* Toronto: Ryerson Press 1925

Hempton, David. *Methodism and Politics in British Society, 1750-1850.* Stanford: Stanford University Press 1984

Henderson, J.L.H. *John Strachan, 1778-1867.* Toronto: University of Toronto Press 1969

– ed. *John Strachan: Documents and Opinions.* Toronto: McClelland & Stewart 1969

Higham, John and P.K. Conkin, eds. *New Directions in American Intellectual History.* Baltimore: Johns Hopkins University Press 1979

Hincks, Sir Francis. *Reminiscences of his Public Life.* Montreal: William Drysdale 1884

Hodgins, Bruce W. *John Sandfield Macdonald.* Toronto: University of Toronto Press 1971

Hofstadter, Richard. *The Idea of a Party System: The Rise of Legitimate Opposition in the United States, 1780-1840.* Berkeley: Stanford University Press 1969

Houghton, Walter E. *The Victorian Frame of Mind, 1830-1870.* New Haven: Yale University Press 1967

Houston, C. and W.J. Smyth. *The Orange Order in Nineteenth Century Ontario: A Study of Institutional Cultural Transfer.* Toronto: Department of Geography, University of Toronto Press 1977

– *The Sash Canada Wore: A Historical Geography of the Orange Order in Canada.* Toronto: University of Toronto Press 1980

Howe, Daniel Walker. *The Political Culture of the American Whigs.* Chicago: University of Chicago Press 1979

Jackman, S.W.A. *Galloping Head: The Life of the Right Honourable Sir Francis Bond Head, Bart., P.C., 1793-1875, Late Lieutenant-Governor of Upper Canada.* London: Phoenix House 1958

Jameson, Anna Brownell. *Winter Studies and Summer Rambles in Canada.* Reprinted Toronto: McClelland & Stewart 1965

Johnson, J.K., ed. *Historical Essays on Upper Canada.* Toronto: McClelland & Stewart 1975

– ed. *The Letters of John A. Macdonald.* I: 1836-57. Ottawa: Public Archives of Canada 1968

Johnson, Leo A. *History of the County of Ontario, 1615-1875.* Whitby: Corporation of the County of Ontario 1973

Kammen, Michael. *A Machine that Would Go of Itself: The Constitution in American Culture.* New York: Alfred A. Knopf 1986

Kass, Alvin. *Politics in the State of New York, 1800-1830.* Syracuse: Syracuse University Press 1965

Kaye, J.W. *The Life and Correspondence of Charles, Lord Metcalfe.* 2 vols. London: R. Bentley 1854

Kennedy, W.P.M., ed. *Documents of the Canadian Constitution, 1759-1915.* Toronto: Oxford University Press 1918

Kerber, Linda. *The Federalists in Dissent: Imagery and Ideology in Revolutionary America.* Ithaca: Cornell University Press 1970

Kilbourn, William. *The Firebrand: William Lyon Mackenzie and the Rebellion in Upper Canada.* Toronto: Clarke, Irwin 1964

Knaplund, Paul, ed. *Letters from Lord Sydenham, Governor-General of Canada, 1839-1841, to Lord John Russell.* Clifton, NJ: Augustus M. Kelley 1973

Labaree, Leonard Woods. *Conservatism in Early American History.* Ithaca: Cornell University Press 1965

Landon, Fred. *Western Ontario and the American Frontier.* Toronto: McClelland & Stewart 1967

Langton, H.H., ed. *A Gentlewoman in Upper Canada: The Journals of Anne Langton.* Toronto: Clarke, Irwin 1950

Langton, W.A., ed. *Early Days in Upper Canada: Letters of John Langton from the Backwoods of Upper Canada and the Audit Office of the Province of Canada.* Toronto: Macmillan Co. of Canada 1926

Leacock, Stephen. *Baldwin, LaFontaine, Hincks: Responsible Government* (The Makers of Canada Series). Toronto: Morang & Co. 1910

Lindsey, Charles. *The Life and Times of Wm. Lyon Mackenzie and the Rebellion of 1837-38.* 2 vols. Toronto: P.R. Randall 1862

Livermore, Shaw. *The Twilight of Federalism: The Disintegration of the Federalist Party, 1815-1830.* Princeton: Princeton University Press 1962

Longley, R.S. *Sir Francis Hincks: A Study of Canadian Politics, Railways, and Finance in the Nineteenth Century.* Toronto: University of Toronto Press 1943

Lucas, Sir Charles P., ed. *Lord Durham's Report on the Affairs of British North America.* 3 vols. Oxford: Clarendon Press 1912

McCormick, R.P. *The Second American Party System: Party Formation in the Jacksonian Era.* Chapel Hill: University of North Carolina Press 1966

McDonald, Neil and A. Chaiton, eds. *Egerton Ryerson and His Times.* Toronto: Macmillan 1978

Macdonald, Norman. *Canada, 1763-1841: Immigration and Settlement.* London: Longmans, Green & Co. 1939

McGill, Jean S. *A Pioneer History of the County of Lanark.* Toronto: T.H. Best Printing Co. 1969

McKenzie, Ruth. *Leeds and Grenville: Their First Two Hundred Years.* Toronto: McClelland & Stewart 1967

McKillop, A.B., ed. *W.D. LeSueur's William Lyon Mackenzie: A Reinterpretation.* Toronto: Macmillan of Canada 1979

MacKinnon, Neil. *This Unfriendly Soil: The Loyalist Experience in Nova Scotia, 1783-1791*. Kingston: McGill-Queen's University Press 1986

MacPherson, Ian. *Matters of Loyalty: The Buells of Brockville, 1830-1850*. Belleville: Mika Publishing 1981

Maitland, F.W. *The Constitutional History of England* (edited by H.A.L. Fisher). Cambridge: Cambridge University Press 1974

Mannion, J. *Irish Settlements in Eastern Canada: A Study of Cultural Transfer and Adaption*. Toronto: University of Toronto Press 1974

Mansfield, Harvey C. *Statesmanship and Party Government: A Study of Burke and Bolingbroke*. Chicago: University of Chicago Press 1965

Martin, Chester. *Empire and Commonwealth: Studies in Governance and Self-Government in Canada*. Oxford: Clarendon Press 1929

– *Foundations of Canadian Nationhood*. Toronto: University of Toronto Press 1955

Martin, Ged. *The Durham Report and British Policy: A Critical Essay*. Cambridge: Cambridge University Press 1972

Masters, D.C. *The Reciprocity Treaty of 1854*. Toronto: McClelland & Stewart 1969

Matthews, Hazel C. *The Mark of Honour*. Toronto: University of Toronto Press 1967

Mealing, S.R., ed. *Robert Gourlay's Statistical Account of Upper Canada*. Toronto: McClelland & Stewart 1974

Merritt J.P. *Biography of the Honourable W.H. Merritt, MP*. St Catharines: H.S. Leavenworth 1875

Middleton, J.E. and Fred Landon. *The Province of Ontario: A History, 1615-1927*. 4 vols. Toronto: Dominion Publishing Co. 1927

Milani, Lois D. *Robert Gourlay: Gadfly*. Thornhill: Ampersand Press 1971

Miller, A.S. ed. *The Journals of Mary O'Brien, 1828-1838*. Toronto: Macmillan 1968

Miller, John C. *The Federalist Era, 1789-1801*. New York: Harper & Row 1960

Moir, John S., ed. *Church and State in Canada, 1627-1867*. Toronto: McClelland & Stewart 1967

– *The Church in the British Era: From the British Conquest to Confederation*. Toronto: McGraw-Hill Ryerson 1972

Moodie, Susanna. *Life in the Clearings* (edited by R.L. McDougall). Reprinted Toronto: Macmillan of Canada 1976

– *Roughing It in the Bush, or Forest Life in Canada*. Reprinted Toronto: McClelland & Stewart 1970

Moore, Christopher. *The Loyalists: Revolution, Exile, Settlement*. Toronto: Macmillan of Canada 1984

Nelson, W.H. *The American Tory*. Boston: Beacon Press 1971

New, Chester. *Lord Durham's Mission to Canada* (edited by H.W. McCready) Toronto: McClelland & Stewart 1968

Niven, John. *Martin Van Buren: The Romantic Age of American Politics.* New York: Oxford University Press 1983

Norton, Mary Beth. *The British Americans: The Loyalist Exiles in England, 1774-1789.* Boston: Little, Brown & Co. 1972

Ormsby, W.G., ed. *Crisis in the Canadas, 1838-1839: The Grey Journals and Letters.* Toronto: Macmillan 1964

– *The Emergence of the Federal Concept in Canada, 1839-1845.* Toronto: University of Toronto Press 1969

Owram, Douglas. *Building for Canadians: A History of the Department of Public Works, 1840-1960.* Ottawa: Public Works of Canada 1979

– *Promise of Eden: The Canadian Expansionist Movement and the Idea of the West, 1856-1900.* Toronto: University of Toronto Press 1980

Palmer, R.R. *The Age of the Democratic Revolution.* 2 vols. Princeton: Princeton University Press 1974

Pammett, Jon H. and M.S. Whittington, eds. *Foundations of Political Culture: Political Socialization in Canada.* Toronto: Macmillan of Canada 1976

Patterson, Gilbert C. *Land Settlement in Upper Canada* (Sixteenth Report of the Department of Archives for the Province of Ontario). Toronto: King's Printer 1921

Perkin, Harold. *The Origins of Modern English Society, 1780-1880.* Toronto: University of Toronto Press 1972

Playter, George F. *The History of Methodism in Canada.* Toronto: Wesleyan Printing Establishment 1862

Potter, Janice. *The Liberty We Seek: Loyalist Ideology in Colonial New York and Massachusetts.* Cambridge: Harvard University Press 1983

Prentice, Alison. *The School Promoters.* Toronto: McClelland & Stewart 1977

Prest, John. *Lord John Russell.* London: Macmillan 1972

Preston, R.A., ed. *Perspectives on Revolution and Evolution.* Durham: Duke University Press 1979

Preston, T.R. *Three Years' Residence in Canada from 1837 to 1839.* London: R. Bentley 1840

Rea, J.E. *Bishop Alexander Macdonell and the Politics of Upper Canada.* Toronto: Ontario Historical Society 1974

Read, Colin. *The Rising in Western Upper Canada.* Toronto: University of Toronto Press 1982

Read, Colin and R.J. Stagg, eds. *The Rebellion of 1837 in Upper Canada.* Ottawa: Champlain Society with Carleton University Press 1985

Read, D.B. *The Lieutenant-Governors of Upper Canada and Ontario, 1792-1899.* Toronto: William Briggs 1900

Read, D.B. *The Life and Times of Lieutenant Governor John Graves Simcoe.* Toronto: George Virtue 1890
– *The Lives of the Judges of Upper Canada and Ontario from 1791 to the Present Time.* Toronto: George Virtue 1888
Remini, R.V. *Martin Van Buren and the Making of the Democratic Party.* New York: W.W. Norton & Co. 1970
Riddell, W.R. *The Life of John Graves Simcoe.* Toronto: McClelland & Stewart 1926
– *The Life of William Dummer Powell, First Judge at Detroit and Fifth Chief Justice of Upper Canada.* Lansing: Michigan Historical Commission 1924
Robinson, C.W. *The Life of Sir John Beverley Robinson, Bart., C.B., D.C.L.: Chief Justice of Upper Canada.* Toronto: Morang & Co. 1904
Ryerson, Egerton. *Canadian Methodism: Its Epochs and Characteristics.* Toronto: William Briggs 1882
– *The Loyalists of America and Their Times: From 1620-1816.* 2 vols. Toronto: William Briggs 1880
– *The Story of My Life: Being Reminiscences of Sixty Years' Public Service in Canada.* (edited by J.G. Hodgins). Toronto: William Briggs 1883
Sabine, Lorenzo. *Loyalists of the American Revolution.* 2 vols. (1864). Port Washington: Kennikat Press, reprinted 1966
Sanderson, Charles R., ed. *The Arthur Papers.* 3 vols. Toronto: University of Toronto Press 1957
Sanderson, J.E. *The First Century of Methodism in Canada.* 2 vols. Toronto: William Briggs 1908-10
Saunders, L.H. *The Story of Orangeism.* 3rd ed. Toronto: Grand Orange Lodge of Ontario West 1960
Scrope, G. Poulett, ed. *Memoir of the Life of the Right Honourable Charles Lord Sydenham.* London: John Murray 1843
Semmel, Bernard. *The Methodist Revolution.* New York: Basic Books 1973
Senior, Hereward. *Orangeism in Ireland and Britain, 1795-1836.* Toronto: Ryerson Press 1966
– *Orangeism: The Canadian Phase.* Toronto: McGraw-Hill 1972
Shaw, A.G.L. *Sir George Arthur, Bart, 1784-1854.* Melbourne: Melbourne University Press 1980
Shortt, Adam. *Lord Sydenham* (The Makers of Canada series). Toronto: Morang & Co. 1909
Sissons, C.B. *Egerton Ryerson: His Life and Letters.* 2 vols. Toronto: Oxford University Press 1937
Smelser, Marshall. *The Democratic Republic, 1801-1815.* New York: Harper & Row 1968
Smith, Goldwin. *Canada and the Canadian Question* (introduction by Carl Berger). Reprinted, Toronto: University of Toronto Press 1971

Smith, Mary Larratt, ed. *Young Mr Smith in Upper Canada*. Toronto: University of Toronto Press 1980

Smith, Michael. *A Geographical View of the Province of Upper Canada; And Promiscuous Remarks on the Government* ... Philadelphia: J. Bioren 1813

Smith, William. *Political Leaders of Upper Canada*. Toronto: Thomas Nelson & Sons 1931

Spragge, G.W., ed. *The John Strachan Letter Book, 1812-1834*. Toronto: Ontario Historical Society 1946

Stewart, Gordon. *The Origins of Canadian Politics: A Comparative Approach*. Vancouver: University of British Columbia Press 1986

Stewart, W.S., ed. *Mackenzie's Narrative of the Rebellion with Notes*. Toronto: Rous & Mann 1937

Strachan, James. *A Visit to the Province of Upper Canada in 1819*. New York: Johnson Reprint Corp. 1968

Sutherland, Alexander. *Methodism in Canada: Its Work and Its Story*. Toronto: Methodist Mission Books 1904

Swainson, Donald, ed. *J.C. Dent's The Last Forty Years: The Union of 1841 to Confederation*. Toronto: McClelland & Stewart 1972

Sweet, W.W. *Religion in the Development of American Culture, 1765-1840*. New York: Charles Scribner's Sons 1952

Talbot, Edward Allan. *Five Years' Residence in the Canadas*. 2 vols. London: Longman, Hurst, Rees, Orme, Brown and Green 1824

Talman, J.J., ed. *Loyalist Narratives from Upper Canada*. Toronto: Champlain Society 1946

Taylor, E.R. *Methodism and Politics, 1791-1851*. Cambridge: Cambridge University Press 1935

Thomas, Clara. *Ryerson of Upper Canada*. Toronto: Ryerson Press 1969

Thompson, Edward. *The Life of Charles, Lord Metcalfe*. London: Faber and Faber 1937

Thompson, Samuel. *Reminiscences of a Canadian Pioneer for the Last Fifty Years: An Autobiography*. Toronto: Hunter, Rose & Co. 1884

Tucker, G.N. *The Canadian Commercial Revolution, 1845-1851* (edited by H.G.J. Aitken). Toronto: McClelland & Stewart 1964

Underhill, Frank. *The Image of Confederation*. Toronto: CBC Publications 1970

– *In Search of Canadian Liberalism*. Toronto: Macmillan of Canada, 1975

United Empire Loyalist Centennial Committee. *The Centennial of the Settlement of Upper Canada by the United Empire Loyalists, 1784-1884* (introduction by G.A. Billias). Boston: Gregg Press 1972

Upton, L.F.S. *The Loyal Whig: William Smith of New York and Quebec*. Toronto: University of Toronto Press 1969

– ed. *The United Empire Loyalists: Men and Myths*. Toronto: Copp Clark 1967

Van Buren, Martin. *The Autobiography of Martin Van Buren* (J.C. Fitzpatrick, ed.) New York: Augustus M. Kelley 1969

Waite, P.B. *Canada, 1874-1896: Arduous Destiny.* Toronto: McClelland & Stewart 1971

Wade, Mason. *The French Canadians,* I: 1760-1911. Toronto: Macmillan of Canada 1968

Wallace, W.S. *The Family Compact: A Chronicle of the Rebellion in Upper Canada.* Toronto: Glasgow, Brook & Co. 1915

– *The United Empire Loyalists: A Chronicle of the Great Migration.* Toronto: Glasgow, Brook & Co. 1914

Walsh, H.H. *The Christian Church in Canada.* Toronto: Ryerson Press 1956

Ward, John Manning. *Colonial Self-Government: The British Experience, 1759-1856.* Toronto: University of Toronto Press 1976

Ward, J.T. *Chartism.* London: B.T. Batsford 1973

Ward, W.R. *Religion and Society in England, 1790-1850.* London: B.T. Batsford 1972

Warner, Donald F. *The Idea of Continental Union: Agitation for the Annexation of Canada to the United States, 1849-1893.* Lexington: University of Kentucky Press 1960

Wearmouth, Robert F. *Methodism and the Common People of the Eighteenth Century.* London: Epworth Press 1957

Webster, Thomas. *History of the Methodist Episcopal Church in Canada.* Hamilton: Canadian Christian Advocate 1870

Welter, Rush. *The Mind of America, 1820-1860.* New York: Columbia University Press 1975

Wiebe, R.H. *The Opening of American Society: From the Adoption of the Constitution to the Eve of Disunion.* New York: Alfred A. Knopf 1984

Wilson, Alan. *The Clergy Reserves of Upper Canada: A Canadian Mortmain.* Toronto: University of Toronto Press 1968

Wilson, Bruce. *As She Began: An Illustrated Introduction to Loyalist Ontario.* Toronto: Dundurn Press 1981

– *The Enterprises of Robert Hamilton. A Study of Wealth and Influence in Early Upper Canada, 1776-1812.* Ottawa: Carleton University Press 1983

Wilson, George E. *The Life of Robert Baldwin: A Study in the Struggle for Responsible Government.* Toronto: Ryerson Press 1933

Wise, S.F., ed. *Sir Francis Bond Head: A Narrative.* Toronto: McClelland & Stewart 1969

– et al., eds, *"None was ever better ...": The Loyalist Settlement of Ontario.* Cornwall: Stormont, Dundas and Glengarry Historical Society 1984

– and R.C. Brown. *Canada Views the United States: Nineteenth-Century Political Attitudes.* Toronto: Macmillan 1972

Wood, Gordon. *The Creation of the American Republic, 1776-1787.* Chapel Hill: University of North Carolina Press 1969

Wright, Esmond, ed. *Red, White and True Blue: The Loyalists in the Revolution*. New York: AMS Press 1976

Wright, E.C. *The Loyalists of New Brunswick*. Fredericton: np 1955

Young, Alfred F. *The Democratic Republicans of New York*. Chapel Hill: University of North Carolina Press 1967

Zaslow, Morris, ed. *The Defended Border: Upper Canada and the War of 1812*. Toronto: Macmillan of Canada 1964

Zimmer, Anne Y. *Jonathan Boucher: Loyalist in Exile*. Detroit: Wayne State University Press 1978

Articles

Abella, Irving. "The 'Sydenham Elections' of 1841," *Canadian Historical Review*, 47 (1966), 326-43

Acheson, T.W. "John Baldwin: Portrait of a Colonial Entrepreneur," *Ontario History*, 61 (1969), 153-66

Appleby, Joyce. "The Social Origins of American Revolutionary Ideology," *Journal of American History*, 64 (March 1978), 935-58

Armstrong, F.H. "The Oligarchy of the Western District," Canadian Historical Association, *Historical Papers* (1977), 86-103

– "Reformer as Capitalist: William Lyon Mackenzie and the Printer's Strike of 1836," *Ontario History*, 59 (1967), 187-96

– "William Lyon Mackenzie, First Mayor of Toronto: A Study of a Critic in Power," *Canadian Historical Review*, 48 (1967), 309-31

– "The York Riots of March 23, 1832." *Ontario History*, 55 (1963), 61-72

Baker, G. Blaine. "The Juvenile Advocate Society, 1821-1826: Self-Proclaimed Schoolroom for Upper Canada's Governing Class," Canadian Historical Association, *Historical Papers* (1985), 74-101

Baldwin, Paul. "The Political Power of Colonel Thomas Talbot," *Ontario History*, 61 (1969), 9-18

Banks, John. "American Presbyterians in the Niagara Peninsula, 1800-1840," *Ontario History*, 57 (1965), 135-40.

Barnett, John. "Silas Fletcher, Instigator of the Upper Canadian Rebellion," *Ontario History*, 41 (1949), 7-35

Barkley, Murray. "The Loyalist Tradition in New Brunswick," *Acadiensis*, 4 (1975), 3-45

– "Prelude to Tradition: The Loyalist Revival in the Canadas, 1849-1867," S.F. Wise, D. Carter-Edwards, and J. Witham, eds. *"None Was Ever Better...": The Loyalist Settlement of Ontario*. Cornwall: Stormont, Dundas and Glengarry Historical Society 1984, 81-109

Baskerville, P.A. "Entrepreneurship and the Family Compact: York-Toronto, 1822-1855," *Urban History Review*, 9 (1981), 15-34

Beer, D.R. "Sir Allan MacNab and the Russell-Sydenham Regime," *Ontario History*, 66 (1974), 37-49

Bell, David V.J. "The Loyalist Tradition in Canada," in J.M. Bumsted, ed. *Canadian History before Confederation: Essays and Interpretations*. Georgetown: Irwin-Dorsey Ltd 1972, 211-29

Benn, Carl. "The Upper Canadian Press, 1793-1815," *Ontario History*, 70 (1978), 91-114

Bloch, Gerald. "Robert Gourlay's Vision of Agrarian Reform" in D.H. Akenson, ed. *Canadian Papers in Rural History*, III. Gananoque: Langdale Press 1982, 110-28

Brooke, John. "Party in the Eighteenth Century," in Alex Natan, ed. *Silver Renaissance: Essays in Eighteenth-Century English History*. London: Macmillan & Co. 1961, 20-37

Brown, George W. "The Durham Report and the Upper Canadian Scene," *Canadian Historical Review*, 20 (1939), 136-60

– "The Early Methodist Church and the Canadian Point of View," *Canadian Historical Association Annual Report* (1938), 79-96

Brown, Wallace. "The View at Two Hundred Years: The Loyalists of the American Revolution," *Proceedings of the American Antiquarian Society*, 80 (April 1970), 25-47

Bumsted, J.M. "Loyalists and Nationalists: An Essay on the Problem of Definitions," *Canadian Review of Studies in Nationalism*, 6 (Spring 1979), 218-32

Burns, R. "God's Chosen People: The Origins of Toronto Society, 1793-1818," Canadian Historical Association, *Historical Papers* (1973), 213-28

Calhoon, R.M. "The Loyalist Perception," *Acadiensis*, 2 (1973), 3-15

Cheal, David J. "Ontario Loyalism: A Socio-Religious Ideology in Decline," *Canadian Ethnic Studies*, 13 (1981), 40-51

Colley, Linda. "The Apotheosis of George III: Loyalty, Royalty and the British Nation, 1760-1820," *Past and Present*, 102 (February 1984), 94-129

Condon, Ann Gorman. "Marching to a Different Drummer: The Political Philosophy of the American Loyalists,"in Esmond Wright, ed. *Red, White & True Blue: The Loyalists in the Revolution*. New York: AMS Press 1976, 1-18

Cook, Terry. "John Beverley Robinson and the Conservative Blueprint for the Upper Canadian Community," *Ontario History*, 64 (1972), 79-94

Cornell, P.G. "The Genesis of Ontario Politics in the Province of Canada (1838-1871)," in Edith Firth, ed., *Profiles of a Province: Studies in the History of Ontario*. Toronto: Ontario Historical Society 1967, 59-72

Craig, G.M. "The American Impact on the Upper Canadian Reform Movement before 1837," *Canadian Historical Review*, 29 (1948), 333-52

- "Comments on Upper Canada in 1836 by Thomas Carr," *Ontario History*, 47 (1955), 171-9
- "Two Contrasting Upper Canadian Figures: John Rolph and John Strachan," *Transactions of the Royal Society of Canada*, series IV, vol. 12 (1974), 237-48

Creighton, Donald. "The Economic Background of the Rebellions of 1837," *Canadian Journal of Economics and Political Science*, 3 (1937), 322-34

Cross, M.S. "The Age of Gentility: The Formation of an Aristocracy in the Ottawa Valley," Canadian Historical Association, *Annual Report* (1967), 105-17
- "The Lumber Community of Upper Canada," *Ontario History*, 52 (1960), 213-33
- "The Shiners' War: Social Violence in the Ottawa Valley in the 1830's," *Canadian Historical Review*, 54 (1973), 1-26

Cross, M.S. "Stony Monday, 1849: The Rebellion Losses Riot in Bytown," in *Ontario History*, vol. 63 (1971), pp. 177-190.
- and R.L. Fraser. "'The Waste that Lies before Me': The Public and Private Worlds of Robert Baldwin," Canadian Historical Association, *Historical Papers* (1983), 164-83

Cruikshank, E.A. "Additional Correspondence of Robert Nichol," *Ontario Historical Society Papers and Records*, 26 (1930), 37-96
- "The Government of Upper Canada and Robert Gourlay," *Ontario Historical Society Papers and Records*, 23 (1926), 65-179
- "John Beverley Robinson and the Trials for Treason in 1814," *Ontario Historical Society Papers and Records*, 25 (1929), 191-217
- "Post-War Discontent at Niagara in 1818," *Ontario Historical Society Papers and Records*, 29 (1933), 14-46
- "Public Life and Services of Robert Nichol, a Member of the Legislative Assembly and Quartermaster-General of the Militia of Upper Canada," *Ontario Historical Society Papers and Records*, 19 (1922), 6-81
- "A Study of Disaffection in Upper Canada in 1812-15," *Proceedings and Transactions of the Royal Society of Canada*, series III, vol. 6 (1912), 11-65

Curtis, Bruce. "Schoolbooks and the Myth of Curricular Republicanism": The State and the Curriculum in Canada West, 1820-1850, *Histoire sociale/Social History*, 16 (November 1983), 305-30

Douglas, R.A. "The Battle of Windsor," *Ontario History*, 61 (1969), 137-52

Duncan, Kenneth. "Irish Famine Immigration and the Social Structure of Canada West," in M. Horn and R. Sabourin, eds. *Studies in Canadian Social History*. Toronto: McClelland & Stewart 1974, 140-63

Duffy, Dennis. "Upper Canadian Loyalism: What the textbooks tell," *Journal of Canadian Studies*, 12 (Spring 1977), 17-26

Eady, R.J. "Anti-American Sentiment in Essex County in the Wake of the Rebellions of 1837," *Ontario History*, 61 (1969), 1-8

Ells, Margaret. "Loyalist Attitudes," in G.A. Rawlyk, ed. *Historical Essays on the Atlantic Provinces*. Toronto: McClelland & Stewart 1971, 44-60

Errington, Jane. "Friends and Foes: the Kingston Elite and the War of 1812: A Case Study in Ambivalence," *Journal of Canadian Studies*, 20 (Spring 1985), 58-79

– "Loyalists in Upper Canada: A British American Community," in S.F. Wise et al., eds. *"None Was Ever Better...": The Loyalist Settlement of Ontario*. Cornwall: Stormont, Dundas and Glengarry Historical Society 1984, 57-72

– and George Rawlyk. "The Loyalist-Federalist Alliance of Upper Canada," *The American Review of Canadian Studies*, 14 (Summer 1984) 157-76

Fallis, Lawrence S. "The Idea of Progress in the Province of Canada: A Study in the History of Ideas," in W.L. Morton, ed. *The Shield of Achilles: Aspects of Canada in the Victorian Age*. Toronto: McClelland & Stewart 1968, 169-83

Farmer, Mrs. S. "Robert (Fleming) Gourlay: Reminiscences of His Last Days in Canada," *Ontario Historical Society Papers and Records*, 15 (1917), 28-35

Forbes, H.D. "Hartz-Horowitz at Twenty: Nationalism, Toryism and Socialism in Canada," in *Canadian Journal of Political Science*, 20 (June 1987) 287-315

French, Goldwin S. "Egerton Ryerson and the Methodist Model for Upper Canada," in Neil McDonald and Alf Chaiton, eds. *Egerton Ryerson and His Times*. Toronto: Macmillan of Canada 1978, 45-58

– "The People Called Methodists in Canada," in J.W. Grant, ed. *The Churches and the Canadian Experience*. Toronto: Ryerson Press 1963, 69-81

Gagan, David. "'Property and Interest': Some Preliminary Evidence of Land Speculation by the 'Family Compact' in Upper Canada, 1820-1840," *Ontario History*, 70 (1978), 63-70

Gates, L.F. "The Decided Policy of William Lyon Mackenzie," *Canadian Historical Review*, 40 (1959), 185-208

– "W.L. Mackenzie's 'Volunteer' and the First Parliament of United Canada," *Ontario History*, 59 (1967), 163-83

Gentilcore, R.L. "The Niagara District of Robert Gourlay," *Ontario History*, 54 (1962), 228-36

Gidney, R.D., "Centralization and Education: The Origins of an Ontario Tradition," *Journal of Canadian Studies*, 7 (1972), 33-48

Greene, Jack P. "Political Mimesis: A Consideration of the Historical and Cultural Roots of Legislative Behavior in the British Colonies in the Eighteenth Century," *American Historical Review*, 75 (December, 1969), 337-60

Guest, H.H. "Upper Canada's First Political Party," *Ontario History*, 54 (1962), 275-96

Hallowell, G.A. "The Reaction of Upper Canadian Tories to the Adversity of 1849," *Ontario History*, 62 (1970), 41-56

Hamil, F.C. "The Reform Movement in Upper Canada," in Edith Firth, ed., *Profiles of a Province: Studies in the History of Ontario*. Toronto: Ontario Historical Society 1967, 9-19

Hanyan, Craig R. "DeWitt Clinton and Partisanship: The Development of Clintonianism from 1811 to 1820," *New York Historical Quarterly*, 56 (1972), 109-31

Harris, Robin S. "Egerton Ryerson," in R.L. McDougall, ed. *Our Living Tradition*. 3rd series. Toronto: University of Toronto Press 1959, 244-67

Hett, Robert. "Judge Willis and the Court of King's Bench in Upper Canada," *Ontario History*, 65 (1973), 19-32

Higham, John. "Intellectual History and Its Neighbors," *Journal of the History of Ideas*, 55 (June 1954), 339-47

Horowitz, Gad. "Conservatism, Liberalism and Socialism in Canada: An Interpretation," *Canadian Journal of Economics and Political Science*, 32 (1966), 147-71

Houston, Susan E. "Politics, Schools, and Social Change in Upper Canada," *Canadian Historical Review*, 53 (1972), 249-71

Hunter, A.F. "The Ethnographical Elements of Ontario," *Ontario Historical Society Papers and Records*, 3 (1901), 180-99

Ireland, John. "Andrew Drew: The Man Who Burned the 'Caroline'," *Ontario History*, 59 (1967), 137-56

– "John H. Dunn and the Bankers," *Ontario History*, 62 (1970), 83-100

Jackson, Eric. "The Organization of Upper Canadian Reformers, 1818-1867," *Ontario History*, 53 (1961), 95-115

Jarvis, Eric. "Military Land Granting in Upper Canada Following the War of 1812," *Ontario History*, 67 (1975), 121-34

Johnson, J.K. "Col. James Fitzgibbon and the Suppression of Irish Riots in Upper Canada," *Ontario History*, 58 (1966), 139-56

– "The Upper Canada Club and the Upper Canadian Elite, 1837-1840," *Ontario History*, 69 (1977), 151-68

Johnson, Leo A. "Land Policy, Population Growth and Social Structure in the Home District, 1793-1851," *Ontario History*, 63 (1971), 41-60

Kealey, G. "Orangemen and the Corporation: The Politics of Class during the Union of the Canadas," in V.L. Russell, ed. *Forging a Consensus: Historical Essays on Toronto*. Toronto: University of Toronto Press 1984, 41-86

Kerr, W.B. "When Orange and Green United, 1832-39: The Alliance of

Macdonell and Gowan," *Ontario Historical Papers and Records*, 34 (1942), 34-42

Livermore, J.D. "The Orange Order and the Election of 1861 in Kingston," G. Tulchinsky, ed. *To Preserve and Defend: Essays on Kingston in the Nineteenth Century.* Montreal: McGill-Queen's University Press 1976, 245-59

Locke, G.H. "The Loyalists in Ontario," *Ontario Historical Society Papers and Records*, 30 (1934), 181-8

Longley, R.S. "Emigration and the Crisis of 1837 in Upper Canada," *Canadian Historical Review*, 17 (1936), 29-40

Love, James H. "Cultural Survival and Social Control: The Development of a Curriculum for Upper Canada's Common Schools in 1846," *Histoire sociale/Social History*, 15 (November 1982), 357-82

Lower, A.R.M. "Immigration and Settlement in Canada, 1812-20," *Canadian Historical Review*, 3 (1922), 37-47

– "Religion and Religious Institutions," in W.H. Heick, ed. *History and Myth: Arthur Lower and the Making of Canadian Nationalism.* Vancouver: University of British Columbia Press 1975, 75-96

McCalla, Douglas. "The Loyalist Economy of Upper Canada, 1784-1806," *Histoire sociale/Social History*, 32 (November 1983), 279-304

McCormick, R.P. "New Perspectives on Jacksonian Politics" in *American Historical Review*, 65 (1960), 288-301

MacDermot, T.W.L. "Some Opinions of a Tory in the 1830's," *Canadian Historical Review*, 11 (1930), 232-7

McDonald, Neil. "Egerton Ryerson and the School as an Agent of Political Socialization," in N. McDonald and A. Chaiton, eds. *Egerton Ryerson and His Times.* Toronto: Macmillan of Canada 1978, 81-106

Mackay, R.A. "The Political Ideas of William Lyon Mackenzie," *Canadian Journal of Economics and Political Science*, 3 (1937), 1-22

McKillop, A.B. "Nationalism, Identity and Canadian Intellectual History," *Queen's Quarterly*, 81 (Winter, 1974), 533-50

– "So Little on the Mind," *Transactions of the Royal Society of Canada*, series IV, vol. 19 (1981), 183-200

MacKinnon, Neil. "The Changing Attitudes of the Nova Scotian Loyalists to the United States, 1783-1791," *Acadiensis*, 2 (1973), 43-54

MacKirdy, K.A. "The Loyalty Issue in the 1891 Federal Election Campaign, and an Ironic Footnote," *Ontario History*, 55 (1963), 143-54

MacNutt, W.S. "The Loyalists: A Sympathetic View," *Acadiensis*, 6 (1976), 3-20

McRae, K.D. "The Structure of Canadian Society," in Louis Hartz, ed., *The Founding of New Societies* ... New York: Harcourt, Bruce & World 1964, 219-74

– ed. "An Upper Canada Letter of 1829 on Responsible Government," *Canadian Historical Review*, 31 (1950), 288-96

Manning, H.T. "The Colonial Policy of the Whig Ministers, 1830-1837," *Canadian Historical Review*, 33 (1952), 202-36

Martin, Ged. "Sir Francis Bond Head: The Private Side of a Lieutenant-Governor," *Ontario History*, 73 (1981), 145-70

Matthews, Robin. "Susanna Moodie, Pink Toryism, and Nineteenth Century Ideas of Canadian Identity," *Journal of Canadian Studies*, 10 (1975), 3-15

Mealing, S.R. "The Enthusiasms of John Graves Simcoe," *Canadian Historical Association Annual Report* (1958), 50-62

Metcalf, George. "Draper Conservatism and Responsible Government in the Canadas, 1836-1847," *Canadian Historical Review*, 42 (1961), 300-24

– "Samuel Bealey Harrison: Forgotten Reformer," *Ontario History*, 50 (1958), 112-31

Milani, L.D. "Robert Gourlay, Gadfly," *Ontario History*, 63 (1971), 233-42

Miller, A.S. "Yonge Street Politics, 1828 to 1832," *Ontario History*, 62 (1970), 101-18

Moir, J.S. "Early Methodism in the Niagara Peninsula," *Ontario History*, 43 (1951), 51-8

– ed. "Four Poems on the Rebellion of 1837 ... by Susanna Moodie," *Ontario History*, 57 (1965), 47-52

– "The Upper Canadian Roots of Church Disestablishment," *Ontario History*, 60 (1968), 247-58

Morton, W.L. "The Local Executive in the British Empire, 1763-1828," *English Historical Review*, 78 (1963), 436-57

Muggeridge, John. "John Rolph: A Reluctant Rebel," *Ontario History*, 51 (1959), 217-29

Murison, Barbara C. "'Enlightened Government': Sir George Arthur and the Upper Canadian Administration," *The Journal of Imperial and Commonwealth History*, 8 (May 1980), 161-80

Murrin, John. "The Great Inversion of Court versus Country," in J. Pocock, ed. *Three British Revolutions*. Princeton: Princeton University Press 1980, 368-453

"Naturalization Question, The," *Report on Canadian Archives* (1898). Ottawa: Queen's Printer 1899

Nelles, H.V. "Loyalism and Local Power: The District of Niagara, 1792-1837," *Ontario History*, 58 (1966), 99-114

New, Chester W. "Marshall Spring Bidwell," in R.G. Riddell, ed., *Canadian Portraits*. Toronto: Oxford University Press 1940, 29-37

"Oaths of Allegiance," *York Pioneer* (1961), 20-32

Owram, Douglas. "Strachan and Ryerson: Guardians of the Future," *Canadian Literature*, 83 (Winter 1979), 21-9

Patterson, Graeme. "An Enduring Canadian Myth: Responsible Government and the Family Compact," *Journal of Canadian Studies*, 12 (Spring 1977), 3-16
- "Whiggery, Nationality, and the Upper Canadian Reform Tradition," *Canadian Historical Review*, 56 (1975), 25-44

"Political State of Upper Canada in 1806-07," *Report on Canadian Archives* (1892). Ottawa: Queen's Printer 1893

Purdy, J.D. "John Strachan's Educational Policies, 1815-1841," *Ontario History*, 64 (1972), 45-64

Rawlyk, G.A. "The Reverend John Stuart: Mohawk Missionary and Reluctant Loyalist," in Esmond Wright, ed. *Red, White and True Blue: The Loyalists in the Revolution*. New York: AMS Press 1976, 55-71

Rea, James E. "Barnabas Bidwell: A Note on the American Years," *Ontario History*, 60 (1968), 31-37
- "William Lyon Mackenzie – Jacksonian?", in J.M. Bumsted, ed. *Canadian History before Confederation: Essays and Interpretations*. Georgetown: Irwin-Dorsey 1972, 331-42

Read, Colin. "The Duncombe Rising, the Aftermath, Anti-Americanism, and Sectarianism," in *Histoire sociale/Social History*, 9 (May, 1976), 47-69
- "The London District Oligarchy in the Rebellion Era," *Ontario History*, 72 (1980), 195-209
- "The Short Hills Raid of June, 1838, and Its Aftermath," *Ontario History*, 68 (1976), 93-109

Remini, R.V. "Thes Albany Regency," *New York History*, 39 (1958), 341-55

Richards, Elva M. "The Joneses of Brockville and the Family Compact," *Ontario History*, 60 (1969), 169-84

Riddell, R.G. "Egerton Ryerson's Views on the Government of Upper Canada in 1836," *Canadian Historical Review*, 19 (1938), 402-10

Riddell, W.R. "Benajah Mallory, Traitor," *Ontario Historical Society Papers and Records*, 26 (1930), 573-8
- "The Bidwell Elections: A Political Episode in Upper Canada a Century Ago," *Ontario Historical Society Papers and Records*, 21 (1924), 236-45
- "The Constitutional Debate in the Legislative Assembly of 1836," *Lennox & Addington Historical Society*, 7-8 (1916), 7-90
- "Joseph Willcocks, Sheriff, Member of Parliament and Traitor," *Ontario Historical Society Papers and Records*, 24 (1927), 479-99
- "Robert (Fleming) Gourlay," in *Ontario Historical Society Papers and Records*, 14 (1916), 5-133

Romney, Paul. "A Conservative Reformer in Upper Canada: Charles Fothergill, Responsible Government and the 'British Party,' 1824-1840," Canadian Historical Association *Historical Papers* (1984), 42-62
- "From Types Riot to Rebellion: Elite Ideology, Anti-legal Sentiment,

Political Violence, and the Rule of Law in Upper Canada," *Ontario History*, 79 (1987), 113-44

- "The Spanish Freeholder Imbroglio of 1824: Inter-Elite and Intra-Elite Rivalry in Upper Canada," *Ontario History*, 76 (1984), 32-47
- "A Struggle for Authority: Toronto Society and Politics in 1834," in V.L. Russell, ed. *Forging a Consensus: Historical Essays on Toronto.* Toronto: University of Toronto Press 1984, 9-40
- "William Lyon Mackenzie as Mayor of Toronto," *Canadian Historical Review*, 46 (1975), 416-36

Rosser, L.T. "Col. Thomas Talbot vs John Nixon," *Ontario Historical Society Papers and Records*, 38 (1946), 23-9

Russell, P.A. "Church of Scotland Clergy in Upper Canada: Culture Shock and Conservatism on the Frontier," *Ontario History*, 73 (1981), 88-111

Saunders, R.E. "What Was the Family Compact?", *Ontario History*, 49 (1957), 165-78

Savelle, Max. "Nationalism and Other Loyalties in the American Revolution," *American Historical Review*, 68 (July 1962), 901-23

Senior, Hereward. "The Character of Canadian Orangeism," *The Learned Societies of Canada: Thought 1961.* Toronto: W.J. Gage, 1961, 177-89

- "The Genesis of Canadian Orangeism," *Ontario History*, 60 (1968), 13-39
- "Ogle Gowan, Orangeism, and the Immigrant Question, 1830-33," *Ontario History*, 66 (1974), 193-210

Shelton, W.G. "The United Empire Loyalists: A Reconsideration," *Dalhousie Review*, 45 (1965-6), 5-16

Sissons, C.B., ed. "The Case of Bidwell," *Canadian Historical Review*, 27 (1946), 368-82

- "Canadian Methodism in 1828: A Note on an Early Ryerson Letter," *Douglas Library Notes*, 12 (Spring, 1963), 2-6
- "Letters of 1844 and 1846 from Scobie to Ryerson," *Canadian Historical Review*, 29 (1948), 393-411
- "Ryerson and the Elections of 1844," *Canadian Historical Review*, 23 (1942), 157-76

Skinner, Quentin. "The Principles and Practices of Opposition: The Case of Bolingbroke versus Walpole," in Neil McKendrick, ed. *Historical Perspectives: Studies in English Thought and Society.* London: Europa Publications 1974, 26-38

Smith, Goldwin. "Loyalty, Aristocracy and Jingoism," in B. Hodgins and R. Page, eds. *Canadian History since Confederation: Essays and Interpretations.* Georgetown: Irwin-Dorsey 1972, 228-43

Smith, W.E.L. "The Methodist Episcopal Church in Canada 1833-1883,"

The Bulletin of the Committee on Archives, United Church of Canada, 17 (1964), 3-14

Smyth, William J. "The Irish in Mid-Nineteenth Century Ontario," *Ulster Folklife*, 23 (1977), 97-105

Sorrell, R.S. "1828 Upper Canada Election Results Table," *Ontario History*, 63 (1971), 67-69

Spragge, G.W. "John Strachan's Contribution to Education, 1800-1823," *Canadian Historical Review*, 22 (1941), 147-58

– "The Upper Canada Central School," *Ontario History*, 32 (1937), 171-91

Stacey, C.P., ed. "The Crisis of 1837 in a Back Township of Upper Canada, Being the Diary of Joseph Richard Thompson," *Canadian Historical Review*, 11 (1930), 223-32

Stewart, Gordon. "John A. Macdonald's Greatest Triumph," *Canadian Historical Review*, 63 (1982), 3-33

– "The Origins of Canadian Politics and John A. Macdonald," R.K. Carty and W.P. Ward, eds. *National Politics and Community in Canada*. Vancouver: University of British Columbia Press 1986, 15-47

Stewart, I.A. "The 1841 Election of Dr. William Dunlop as Member of Parliament for Huron County," *Ontario History*, 39 (1947), 51-62

Stouck, David. "The Wardell Family and the Origins of Loyalism," *Canadian Historical Review*, 68 (1987), 63-82

Talman, J.J. "The Position of the Church of England in Upper Canada, 1791-1840," *Canadian Historical Review*, 15 (1934), 361-75

– "The United Empire Loyalists," in Edith Firth, ed., *Profiles of a Province: Studies in the History of Ontario*. Toronto: Ontario Historical Society 1967, 3-8

Tyler, Moses Coit. "The Party of the Loyalists in the American Revolution," *American Historical Review*, 1 (1895), 24-45

Wallace, Michael. "Changing Concepts of Party in the United States: New York, 1815-1828," *American Historical Review*, 74 (1968), 453-91

Walton, Bruce. "The 1836 Election in Lennox and Addington," *Ontario History*, 67 (1975), 153-67

Westfall, W.E. de Villiers. "The Dominion of the Lord: An Introduction to the Cultural History of Protestant Ontario in the Victorian Period," *Queen's Quarterly*, 83 (1976), 47-70

– "Order and Experience: Patterns of Religious Metaphor in Early Nineteenth Century Upper Canada," *Journal of Canadian Studies*, 20 (Spring 1985), 5-24

Wilson, Ian E. "Ogle R. Gowan, Orangeman," in *Douglas Library Notes*, 17 (1969), 18-20

Wilson, Major L. "The Concept of Time and the Political Dialogue in the United States, 1828-1848," *The American Quarterly*, 19 (1967), 617-44

Wilton-Siegel, Carol. "Administrative Reform: A Conservative Alternative to Responsible Government," *Ontario History*, 78 (1986), 105-26

Wise, S.F. "Conservatism and Political Development: The Canadian Case," *South Atlantic Quarterly*, 69 (Spring 1970), 226-43

– "God's Peculiar Peoples," in W.L. Morton, ed., *The Shield of Achilles: Aspects of Canada in the Victorian Age*. Toronto: McClelland & Stewart 1968, 36-61

– "John Macaulay: Tory for All Seasons," in G. Tulchinsky, ed., *To Preserve and Defend: Essays on Kingston in the Nineteenth Century*. Montreal: McGill-Queen's University Press 1976, 185-202

– "Liberal Consensus or Ideological Battleground: Some Reflections on the Hartz Thesis," Canadian Historical Association *Historical Papers* (1974), 1-14

– "The Rise of Christopher Hagerman," *Historic Kingston*, 14 (1965), 1-14

– "Sermon Literature and Canadian Intellectual History," in *The Bulletin* of the Committee on Archives, United Church of Canada (1965), 3-18

– "Tory Factionalism: Kingston Elections and Upper Canadian Politics, 1820-1836," *Ontario History*, 57 (1965), 205-25

– "Upper Canada and the Conservative Tradition," in Edith Firth, ed., *Profiles of a Province: Studies in the History of Ontario*. Toronto: Ontario Historical Society 1967, 20-33

Theses

Aitchison, J.H. "The Development of Local Government in Upper Canada, 1783-1850" (Ph D, University of Toronto 1953)

Armstrong, F.H. "Toronto in Transition: The Emergence of a City, 1828-1838" (Ph D, University of Toronto 1965)

Beaven, Brian, P.N. "A Last Hurrah: Studies in Liberal Party Development and Ideology in Ontario, 1878-1893" (Ph D, University of Toronto 1981)

Bowsfield, Hartwell. "Upper Canada in the 1820's: The Development of a Political Consciousness" (Ph D, University of Toronto 1976)

Burns, Robert J. "The First Elite in Toronto: An Examination of the Genesis, Consolidation and Duration of Power in an Emerging Colonial Society" (Ph D, University of Western Ontario 1974)

Conway, Sean G. "Upper Canadian Orangeism in the Nineteenth Century: Aspects of a Pattern of Disruption" (MA, Queen's University 1977)

Cross, M.S. "The Dark Druidical Groves: The Lumber Community and the Commercial Frontier in British North America to 1854" (Ph D, University of Toronto 1966)

Dyster, B.D. "Toronto, 1840-1860: Making It in a British Protestant Town" (Ph D, University of Toronto 1970)

Errington, Jane. "The 'Eagle,' the 'Lion' and Upper Canada: A Developing Colonial Ideology: The Colonial Elites' Views of the United States and Great Britain, 1784-1828" (Ph D, Queen's University 1984)

Fahey, Curtis. "A Troubled Zion: The Anglican Experience in Upper Canada, 1791-1854" (Ph D, Carleton University 1981)

Fraser, R.L. "Like Eden in Her Summer Dress: Gentry, Economy and Society: Upper Canada, 1812-1840" (Ph D, University of Toronto 1979)

Guest, H.H. "Baldwin of Spadina: The Life of William Warren Baldwin, Central Figure in the Movement for Responsible Government in Upper Canada" (MA, University of Manitoba 1961)

Hutton, I.C. "The Baldwins become Reformers" (MA, University of Toronto 1970)

Lepine, J.J. "The Irish Press in Upper Canada and the Reform Movement" (MA, University of Toronto 1946)

MacDonald, Donald C. "Honourable Richard Cartwright, 1759-1815" in *Three History Theses* Toronto: Ontario Department of Public Records and Archives 1961, 1-185

MacPherson, G.R.I. "The Code of Brockville's Buells, 1830-1849" (MA, University of Western Ontario)

Mood, W.J.S. "The Orange Order in Canadian Politics, 1841-1867" (MA, University of Toronto 1950)

Patterson, G.H. "Studies in Elections and Public Opinion in Upper Canada" (Ph D, University of Toronto 1969)

Quealey, F.M. "The Administration of Sir Peregrine Maitland, Lieutenant Governor of Upper Canada, 1818-1828" (Ph D, University of Toronto 1968)

Read, Colin F. "The Rising in Western Upper Canada, 1837-38: The Duncombe Revolt and After" (Ph D, University of Toronto 1974)

Romney, Paul, M. "A Man Out of Place: The Life of Charles Fothergill; Naturalist, Businessman, Journalist, Politician, 1782-1840" (Ph D, University of Toronto 1981)

Sanderson, C.R. "Sir George Arthur, last lieutenant governor of Upper Canada, 1838-1841: A Vindication" (MA, University of Toronto 1940)

Saunders, R.E. "John Beverley Robinson: His Political Career, 1812-1840" (MA, University of Toronto 1960)

Slawuta, G. "Marshal [sic] Spring Bidwell: A Reform Leader in Upper Canada" (MA, University of Ottawa 1968)

Smith, Brian P. "The Political Ideas and Attitudes of William Henry Draper" (MA, Queen's University 1978)

Stagg, Ronald John. "The Yonge Street Rebellion of 1837: An Examin-

ation of the Social Background and a Re-assessment of the Events"
(Ph D, University of Toronto 1976)

Stuart, E. Rae. "Jessup's Rangers as a Factor in Loyalist Settlement," in
Ontario Department of Public Records and Archives, *Three History
Theses*. Toronto: Government of Ontario 1961, 1-158

Walton, J.B. "An End to All Order: A Study of the Upper Canadian
Conservative Response to Opposition, 1805-1810" (MA, Queen's University 1977)

Wearing, J. "Elections and Politics in Canada West under Responsible
Government, 1847-1863" (Ph D, Oxford University 1965)

Westfall, W.E. de Villiers. "The Sacred and the Secular: Studies in the
Cultural History of Protestant Ontario in the Victorian Period" (Ph D,
University of Toronto 1976)

Wilson, Bruce G. "The Enterprises of Robert Hamilton: A Study of
Wealth and Influence in Early Upper Canada, 1776-1812" (Ph D,
University of Toronto 1978)

Index